Forging Political Identity

International Studies in Social History
General Editor: Marcel van der Linden,
International Institute of Social History, Amsterdam

FORGING POLITICAL IDENTITY

Silk and Metal Workers in Lyon, France, 1900–1939

Keith Mann

Berghahn Books
NEW YORK • OXFORD

Published in 2010 by
Berghahn Books
www.berghahnbooks.com

Library of Congress Cataloging-in-Publication Data
Mann, Keith.
 Forging political identity : silk and metal workers in Lyon, France, 1900/1939
/ Keith Mann. -- 1st ed.
  p. cm. -- (International studies in social history ; v. 16)
 Includes bibliographical references and index.
 ISBN 978-1-84545-645-0 (alk. paper)
 1. Silk industry--France--Lyon--Employees--History--20th century. 2. Metal-
workers--France--Lyon--History--20th century. 3. Labor movement--France--
Lyon--History--20th century. I. Title.
 HD8039.T42F856 2010
 331.7'6710944582309041--dc22
                        2010006672

British Library Cataloguing in Publication Data

A catalogue record for this book is available from the British Library

Printed in the United States on acid-free paper.

ISBN: 978-1-84545-645-0 Hardback

To the memory of my Mother
Rosalind Cooper Mann
December 6, 1936–February 13, 2006
And
Charles "Chuck" Tilly
May 27, 1929–April 29, 2008
Teacher, mentor, colleague, friend

CONTENTS

LIST OF TABLES AND ILLUSTRATIONS

TABLES

ILLUSTRATIONS

ACKNOWLEDGEMENTS

This book traces its origins to a dissertation defended at the New School for Social Research under the direction of Charles Tilly and Louise Tilly. It is based on research conducted in archives in Lyon, France in the early and mid-1990s for the period 1900–1935, and postdissertation trips to the archives in 2003 and 2004, as I extended the project through the Popular Front years. It also bears the marks—in a positive sense, I hope—of the great debates that have shaken the field of labor studies over the past several decades.

Along the way I was aided by the generosity of scholars, family, and friends on both sides of the Atlantic, many of whom share my passion for both social science history and social justice. In Lyon, labor historians Yves Lequin and Phillipe Videlier helped me navigate local archives during a year spent in France thanks to a French government grant, the Bourse Chateaubriand.

I met Christian Chevandier as he was finishing his dissertation on a similar subject as mine, a social history of the rail workers at the Paris-Lyon-Marseille shops in Oullins, an industrial suburb of Lyon. Our friendship began with the conversations about French workers and local sources we often had at the home he shared with his wife Christine and their children in Lyon, and continued in Paris after Christian was named Maître de conférences at the Sorbonne. A high point of my summer trips to France is the few days I stay with Christian and his family in their charming house in the Impasse Poule in Paris' XIX arrondissement. Inevitably we work our way to his office where he provides me a list of recent works on French labor that help me keep up with labor scholarship produced in France.

My old friend John Barzman, a US-born scholar of French labor who is a professor of contemporary history in Le Havre, France, was particularly generous with his insights—and hospitality—as we discussed the larger questions that the project seeks to answer, as was Larry Portis, another transplanted American student of French labor and society. Marcel van der Linden, the editor of the *International Studies in Social History* series, for which this book is a part provided rigorous editing with keen insights drawn from his vast knowledge of the French and European labor movements.

I met Michel Parraud and Annie Chaleard during the year I spent in Lyon in 1989–1990. We subsequently became close friends. By offering me lodgings and friendship during my numerous trips to Lyon, often for weeks on end, they provided indispensable support. My memories of working in Lyon's archives are indissolubly tied to the meals we enjoyed together in the evenings, seasoned by discussions about cuisine and politics. The neighborhoods of the three different homes they had during the years I worked in Lyon's archives each had a distinct connection to local labor history. When I met them, they shared an apartment in the Croix Rousse, which during the nineteenth century had become the center of the domestic silk industry for which Lyon had been famous for centuries, and which is the backdrop for much of this book. They later moved to Vaux-en-Velin, a typical working-class suburb that had elected Communist municipalities since the early 1920s. Later, my friends hosted me in their house in Vénissieux, an industrial suburb of Lyon, not far from the huge Berliet auto works, which also figures prominently in the present study.

I met Michael Hanagan when I was a master's student in his labor history seminar at Columbia University. It was Mike who put me in touch with Chuck and Louise Tilly, who had recently come to the New School after years at the University of Michigan. The Hanagan-Tilly connection was a most fortuitous one for me. Mike had been a student of Chuck and Louise at Michigan. His book, *The Logic of Solidarity,* also based on a dissertation written under the direction of Chuck Tilly, was the initial inspiration for my own project. Mike is one of the best French labor historians around and he continues to share not only his vast knowledge of French labor with me, but his broad and sophisticated knowledge of the great debates in history and the social sciences. In the preface to *The Logic of Solidarity,* Mike credits working with Chuck Tilly as making his graduate experience a very special one. That sentiment sums up my own feelings about my graduate experience with not only Chuck and Louise, but Mike as well. Mike continues to be an inspired mentor, colleague, and friend. This book owes much to his advice and support.

Louise Tilly not only helped me learn the literature of French and European labor history but offered extensive practical advice about research in France and the craft of the social historian. Her generosity was limitless. She amazed me by not only offering me close and detailed comments about the dissertation but actually proofreading the manuscript. Ron Aminzade, whose book *Ballots and Barricades* was also intellectual inspiration for my own work, offered me particularly insightful comments as I was preparing a portion of the work for publication in the *International Review of Social History*. Uncoincidentally, Ron was a Tilly student, and his book was dedicated to Chuck and Louise.

Under Chuck's influence at the New School I broadened from a French social and labor historian to a social scientist. Although I join legions of scholars who were influenced intellectually from close or afar by Chuck Tilly, Chuck made me feel very special. I will always treasure my memories of our interactions during graduate school and beyond, and the file I have kept of our correspondence. He was remarkably generous with his advice and encouragement. Whether it was during or after a seminar, through written correspondence, or in the Café de Flore after receiving an honorary doctorate at the Haute école de science politique in Paris, (along with then UN secretary, Boutros Boutros-Ghali), that advice was always thoughtful and rigorous. It was with great sadness that I learned of his passing in April 2008 as I was nearing the end of the final revisions for this book. It was Chuck who encouraged me to write this book, and he helped at every stage from choosing a suitable publisher to constructing the argument. Intellectually, it reflects his profound influence on my own thinking.

My family and friends offered steady encouragement for my research. Christine Mann combined support and patience for the project and the work it involved. Our daughter, Chloé Rose Mann, came along on Bastille Day, 14 July 1996, to the great joy of her French historian daddy. My grandfather Rufus Cooper gave me unconditional love and support. He died shortly after I finished my master's degree at Columbia, and therefore before I began this project. I still miss him. My dear uncle Bob Mann, for years a progressive Illinois state legislator, served as a lifelong inspiration to me for social justice. He passed away shortly before this manuscript went to press. I miss him already. Carole Hetzel came into and enriched my life in the final stages of the project. The moral and intellectual support she offered helped me sharpen and clarify my arguments and the manuscript is better as a result.

From my earliest years, my mother—through the example of her voracious reading, her direct encouragement of my intellectual pursuits, and boundless love—has been one of my greatest supporters. The love and support she and my father, Richard, showered on me and my three siblings has been more than anyone could hope for. Her passing in February 2006 was a great blow. I dedicate this book to her memory.

ABBREVIATIONS

ADR   Archives du department du Rhône

CGT   Confédération générale du travail

CGTSR   Confédération générale du travail syndicaliste révolutionnaire

CGTU   Confédération générale du travail unitaire

LWA   Left-wing Alliance

PCF   Parti communiste français

SFIO   Section française de l'Internationale socialiste

SP   Socialist Party

USR   Union syndicale du Rhône

POS   Political Opportunity Structure

ISR   Industrial Social Relations

INTRODUCTION
French Labor History and Political Identity

From the barricades to the ballot box, workers in nineteenth- and twentieth-century France played an active and often central role in local and national politics. Politics affected workers as much as they affected politics. Their everyday experiences were permeated with politics as they encountered the programs, ideologies, and symbols of political and union organizations at work and in their communities. Many French workers joined unions and radical political organizations and many more regularly identified publicly with political currents speaking on their behalf. Male workers voted for, and working-class men and women joined radical labor and political organizations in such large numbers that union and socialist and communist parties could legitimately describe themselves as working-class organizations. These experiences generated, reflected, and reinforced class- and occupational-based social and political identities.

Competing socialist, anarchist, revolutionary syndicalist, and communist organizations vied for working-class support. Although the main labor organizations all presented themselves as classwide organizations and aspired to attract the support of the working class as a whole, no organization or ideology in France ever enjoyed complete hegemony over workers' allegiances and identities. There was therefore more than one political identity available to French workers during the period under question. Entire occupational groups possessed political identities associated with a given radical union and/or political current. For example, early nineteenth-century printers were usually anarchists, textile workers and teachers became associated with the current represented by Jules Guesde's Parti ouvrier socialiste (POS), and metal workers were big supporters of the CGT in its revolutionary syndicalist phase (1895–1907) before joining the PCF in large numbers. These identities have been re-

Notes for this chapter begin on page 14.

markably solid, usually lasting generations in many cases. But occasional rapid identity changes have occurred as well.

While these connections have been long noted by labor historians, they have been largely assumed rather than explained. Explaining the dynamics of the formation and mutations of working-class political identities in France is the central aim of this book. Based on archival research in Lyon and drawing on social science literature on social class and identity, this is at once a work of French labor history and historical sociology. We will focus on two occupational groups, silk and metal workers, in the industrial city of Lyon between 1900 and 1939, a period of large-scale social, economic, and political change. By the turn of the century silk and metal workers had each acquired a distinct political identity. Later each experienced significant identity shifts as historical conditions changed.

This book benefits from decades of social and labor historical research and writing and the rich debates that accompanied them. Aspects of the broad intellectual movements that have shaken the field over the last four decades such as the cultural turn, varieties of postmodernism and post-structuralism, and women's and gender history have served to enrich the present analysis. I part company, however, with the hegemonic claims of some scholars from these traditions that dismiss the power of class analysis, structures, and materialism as intellectual tools and objects of research and reflection. In a recent book, Keith Nield and Geof Eley have pointed to the unfortunate polarizing tone of some of those debates. They suggest—rightly I think—that elements of seemingly contradictory positions that have been staked out in labor history over the last several decades can in fact be integrated into powerful synthetic theoretical tools.[1]

The Cultural Turn, Postmodernism, and the Linguistic Turn

The debates surrounding the cultural turn in history and labor studies are a good example. The cultural turn called attention to broad areas of working-class life that had previously received scant attention. First-rate studies of leisure, family, and other themes cast light on previously ignored areas of working-class life. The political identities under examination here were certainly cultural phenomena, and in this sense the present work benefits from that intellectual tradition. But some saw attention to culture as obviating not only the importance of the arena of production but the whole structural logic upon which those studies had been based. Ultimately, the entire social history project was rejected.[2] I join Eley and

Nield in affirming the continuing usefulness of structural accounts of social life as well as the importance of the cultural.

Postmodern analytical frameworks inspired by the work of thinkers such as Michel Foucault and Jacques Derrida began to find their way into labor history in the early 1980s. By calling attention to multiple sources of power and a proposing a critical view of social categories, postmodern thinking opened up new possibilities for empirical and theoretical research in labor studies. It helped open the way, for example, for the consideration of other identities such as gender and race and how they intersect with class. But here again, some writers used their understanding of postmodern logic as negating structural analysis in general and social class in particular.

One of the central concepts of the social and labor history tradition of the 1970s was that of class. A strand of each intellectual tradition that has appeared in relation to social and labor history has challenged the notion of class and its usefulness as an object of scholarly research. Some postmodern critiques saw class as just another intellectually constructed social category. Joan Scott and Gareth Stedman Jones, both leading proponents of the "linguistic turn," called for an approach to class that would study it solely as a cultural-linguistic phenomenon. Elsewhere, Scott has called for replacing class analysis with gender analysis.[3] Historian William Reddy has also explicitly argued for abandoning class as a concept.[4]

The "linguistic turn" in labor history reflected logics from both the cultural turn and postmodernism. Attention to language has certainly enriched our understanding of class as lived phenomenon. Indeed, the political identities under consideration in this book were often articulated in slogans shouted by demonstrators. Analyzing the content, origin, and dynamics of those slogans enriches our understanding of political identity. But while the importance of language has been widely acknowledged, social historians remain sharply divided over the relationship between language and class. Joan Scott, Gareth Stedman Jones, and Jacques Ranicière were among the leading social historians who came to believe that there is no social reality outside or prior to language.[5] They rejected the notion that material factors play a decisive role in forging social identity and class. In response, social historian Bryan D. Palmer, a leading defender of materialist class analysis, has analyzed the ways that the linguistic turn "tends to reify language, objectifying it as unmediated discourse, placing it beyond social, economic, and political relations, and in the process displacing essential structures and formations to the historical sidelines."[6] The linguistic turn also involves a specific research strategy. Its proponents would shift the focus of labor history away from the investigation of the role of the working class as an actor in social protest and national political events toward the study of language communities.

The most promising investigations of language and class seem to be those that see language streams used (or rejected) by various workers at various times as grounded in class conflict and material social relations. Social historians like Marc Steinberg have integrated forms of linguistic analysis into the study of social protest and collective action, but defend a materialist approach to class against the idealistic logic of the linguistic turn that holds that class does not exist prior to its articulation in language.[7]

A Gendered Labor History

Some of the most promising avenues for further research in labor history in recent years have been suggested by women's historians. They have pointed out that labor history has always been de facto men's labor history. Joan Scott in particular laid the groundwork for a series of fine studies that explored women in a variety of work settings, both within and outside the home, as well as ways that women participated in collective action.[8] Men's studies, an outgrowth of women's and gender studies, have explored the gendered experiences of working men.[9] Some have taken gender and labor history to a higher level by using gender to explore the ways that work-related institutions and structures themselves are gendered, thereby going beyond male and female labor histories towards an approach that promises to lead to a labor history of greater explanatory power. As Ava Baron has explained, "Gender is created not simply outside production but also within it. It is not a set of ideas developed separately from the economic structure but a part of it, built into the organization and social relations of production."[10] The categories used to collect the labor statistics used by labor historians are themselves highly gendered.[11]

It is quite clear that all the elements of the present study were highly structured along gender lines. The occupations in the two industries studied here had built-in gender assumptions relating to gendered notions of work, skill, and family. At the turn of the century where this study begins, silk weavers and dyers were skilled males working in domestic settings aided by women, often family members in allied (but less prestigious and less paid) occupations. Metal working was a quintessential male occupation built on highly gendered assumptions about skill, physical strength, gender, family, and work. As skilled male workers, metal workers often advanced notions of the family wage, thereby marginalizing women's claims to access to skilled jobs. Gender was integral to the changes in both industries that began before the war and were accelerated in the interwar period. Women first found widespread employment in metal working plants during World War I. The postwar period began with many driven out of the factories, but many returned in significant numbers later. The rise of mechanized semiskilled work that occurred in this period was a highly gendered process.

The political opportunity structure was highly gendered as well. The political arena excluded women of all classes from voting and running for office. French women only gained the right to vote in 1945. Shop floor struggles particularly before WWI largely excluded women as well, based as they were on the power of skilled workers exercising a monopoly of knowledge about the labor process. Women nevertheless were present in industrial work, formal labor organizations, political parties, and collective action. It was in these arenas that many of them acquired the same political identities as their male counterparts. The identities whose dynamics this study seeks to explain were themselves highly gendered, based as they were on gendered notions of class and citizen that had shop floor and electoral terrains of public representation. It should be clear how attention to the ways that structures themselves are gendered can greatly enrich social and labor history. But here again, some voices have called for *replacing* class analysis entirely in tones that would seem to banish class and structure in general from scholarly research altogether.[12]

Materialism

Behind all this has been a sometimes implicit, sometimes explicit rejection of the materialism that had underpinned early labor studies. But as Eley and Nield and others have demonstrated, the materialism attacked by some versions of postmodern, cultural, linguistic, and women's scholarship has been a one-dimensional caricature of Marxist and materialist theory, a sort of reductionist straw person. Scott and Jones in particular attacked reductionist base and superstructure logics by which economic bases determine political and cultural superstructures, including consciousness, an approach that they equated with materialism and Marxism in general. An actual reading of those works, however, including perhaps Scott's own book on the miners of Carmaux (which she repudiated in later writings), as well as Marx's own writing, reveals a far more nuanced relationship between economic structures and consciousness than had been charged.[13] Nonetheless, if we accept that base and superstructure arguments did inform some of the labor histories of the period, discussion of the shortcomings of such an approach represents a positive critique. The theory proposed here rejects base and superstructure logics, but adheres to a view of social class rooted in material relations of production. It is the contention here that material conditions of existence, such as the conditions under which people acquire the means to sustain and reproduce life, powerfully shape social existence in general but neither in a direct manner nor independent of other variables. The relational approach employed here underscores both the importance of material social relations and the ways that it helps shape political identities, not in a direct unilateral way but through interaction with political structures.

Politics and Labor History

Politics were often at the center of research and writing on French labor history from the 1930s to the 1960s. But by the 1970s labor historians inspired by the new social history had largely turned away from the study of politics in favor of community studies, collective action, and other themes. But recently, a newly configured labor history has returned to the study of politics combining political and social history.[14] In their book on debates in social and labor history, Eley and Nield call for "recovering a viable relationship between politics and class: a recovery that neither reduces the one to the other nor banishes class from the field of determination altogether. We want neither the kind of reduction that restores the justly discarded economistic forms of causality nor the one that makes class purely an effect of language or politics, as a purely discursive construction rather than being locatable in social structures in some analytically useful nondiscursive or prediscursive way."[15] This is a particularly timely statement at this juncture in labor studies. It is exactly what the present work aims to do.

Social and Political Identity

One of the major themes of social science literature on identity is the multiplication of social identities. The metal workers who are the object of this study were certainly bearers of multiple identities. In addition to being members of an occupation, class, and nation, they were men, women, siblings, parents, etc. They may have had strong regional or even religious and other identities as well. But their identity as workers and citizens differed from these other identities because they became the basis of public collective action. For much of the nineteenth and twentieth centuries, workers' lives were heavily connected to not only their membership in the various trades that made up their industry but to trade organizations like unions and political organizations based on membership in a broader class community. As Bert Klandermans and Marge de Weerd have pointed out, people who share collective identities and come from "identical walks of life," including working-class communities, tend to share group memberships as well. They cite the example of the Netherlands where "it was part of the collective identity of Catholics to vote for the Catholic party, to be a member of a Catholic labor union or a Catholic women's or farmer's organization."[16] Indeed, for much of the nineteenth and twentieth centuries, class membership in France heavily overlapped with political identities. French workers tended to identify with left-wing political parties and unions while members of the liberal professions, small shopkeepers, and—depending on the region—landowning peasants strongly identified with the Radical party throughout the Third Republic.

Political identities are understood here as subjective, self-identified, shared social identities that involve public identification to various degrees with one or more of the following: (1) political groups especially, but not limited to parties; (2) leaders and other figures contemporary and/or historical (e.g., Robespierre, Babeuf, Jaurès, Blum, Marx, Lenin, Trotsky, etc.); (3) political programs like a cooperative workers' republic, parliamentary democracy, welfare state, socialism, and communism in its various forms; (4) specific social issues—for example, reproductive rights, stem cell research, and the death penalty are currently ideological and partisan issues in the United States; and (5) general social outlook and attitudes about human nature. For example, individualism is a widespread ideology in capitalist countries that purports to explain individual and group success in terms of individual effort. It sees its reflection in conservative political programs calling for lower taxes for the wealthy and less government programs (primarily welfare for the poor). In the United States, a liberal political identity would involve identification with the Democratic Party, leaders like FDR and John F. Kennedy, and support for welfare state social policies funded with progressive income taxes. Conservatives tend to identify with the Republican Party, a leader like Ronald Reagan, support less government intervention, especially on behalf of the poor, and believe that inequality reflects personal traits, rather than social policy and structure.

Political identities are often transmitted through family ties. One is from a democratic family or a republican family in the United States, or a communist, socialist, labor, Christian democratic, etc. family in Western Europe. Political identities are often displayed publicly through dress, the wearing of badges, and the display of iconographic material like banners and pictures.

Fashion has been understood by social scientists as markers of social class.[17] It can also be understood as a marker of political identity. The wearing of buttons and the display of campaign posters and bumper stickers at election time is not only part of a political campaign; it is also a public act of political identification. This explains why those same buttons, posters, signs, and bumper stickers often continue to be displayed well after the elections are over. The *sans-culottes*—itself both a political and social designation—of the early years of the French revolution wore a distinct dress: Phrygian bonnets (in homage to the Roman republicans), breechless pants (an economic necessity cum socio-political costume), and blue, white, and red *cockards*. The political climate forced aristocrats and wealthy commoners to adopt that style of dress as well. After the Thermodorian reaction, French elites returned with a vengeance to fancy dress styles. The *incroyables* wore particularly outlandish outfits while the *sans-culottes* toned down their revolutionary dress code.[18] The singing of certain songs and the display of flags and other iconographic images in mass demonstrations in France during the period treated in this book were also public markers of political identity.

Political Identity Formation

This then is what is meant by political identity. But how are these identities formed? How and under what circumstances can they change? Social scientists have tended to view identities as personality traits located in individuals or groups closely connected to individual consciousness. Some recent social science theoretical and empirical work, however, has offered far more dynamic and satisfying accounts of public political identity formation. Building on the work of his late friend and collaborator Stein Rokkan, Charles Tilly argues, "(1) Political identities are relational and collective; they therefore alter as political networks, opportunities, and strategies shift; (2) the validation of political identities depends on contingent performances to which other parties' acceptance or rejection of the asserted relations is crucial; (3) their validation both constrains and facilitates collective action by those who share the identity."[19] Scott Hunt and Robert Benford also argue for a relational approach to the formation of political identity in social movements. Political identities, they write, are "interactionally constituted; that is, they are constructed, reinforced, and transformed by the interactions between and among movement participants and outsiders."[20] Linda Gordon sees "political identities as socially constructed and changeable to be sure, but also rooted in material structures, culture, and experience."[21]

Building on these relational approaches, I argue that the various political identities that emerged among various groups of workers during this period were shaped by the intersection of the prevailing political opportunity structure in France at that time and evolving industrial social relations.[22] Unlike base-superstructure models, this theoretical framework does not see politics or social relations as directly causing one another. Rather, they are seen as *interacting* in ways that shaped metal worker political identity. Culture is not a mere reflection of material social relations either. As Tilly argues, social actors use "the cultural means at their disposal and drawing on collective memory, adopting or adapting available models" as they experience identity construction.[23] This too calls into question "any representation of identity as a straightforward reflection or expression of social position."[24]

Industrial Social Relations

What does *industrial social relations* mean here? These are the relations between workers and the productive process, between workers and employers, and among workers themselves that are shaped primarily by the productive process as well as the structure of labor markets and the balance of forces between workers and employers. The productive process is a high-stakes terrain between workers and employers because it determines a great deal of the bargaining power of capital and labor. Skill is an important factor here because the scarcity of skill resulting from either the complexity of difficult-to-master work tasks or the structure of labor markets (for example, union-controlled apprenticeship programs) puts workers in a relatively strong bargaining position. Employers strive to reduce their reliance on skilled workers while workers struggle to control as much of the production process as possible. The possession of scarce skill helps workers in their struggle with employers over wages, working conditions, benefits, and the very organization of production. A long tradition of social science theory and research going back to Marx's early writings on alienation suggests that intrinsic as well as extrinsic concerns also makes skilled work desirable for workers because it involves imagination and creativity, while semiskilled work in continuous process manufacturing, retail, and service industries is abhorred as repetitive and boring.[25]

During the Second Industrial Revolution in the late nineteenth and early twentieth centuries, industrial capitalists used Taylorist-inspired methods—often, but not always, with mechanization and machinery—to reorganize the productive process in order to seize areas of control held by skilled workers.[26]

Industrial social relations also involve the structure of labor markets. Where are workers recruited? And who controls those channels? Industrial social relations also involve relations between workers. What percentage of a workforce is skilled, semiskilled, and unskilled? Differences in skill, as well as gender, nationality, ethnicity, race, religion, etc. are potential sources of both solidarity that strengthens workers' collective action and division that weakens workers' bargaining power. Ultimately, industrial social relations shape political identities because their tenor makes the various forms of collective action that political groups propose more or less possible and attractive.

These social relations are important here because they powerfully shape forms of collective action. Various forms of collective action often correspond to the particular strategies proposed by political currents that represent working-class political identities. For example, highly capitalized firms in terms of industrial plant and machinery had very different ramifications for workers' collective action than industries with lower levels of capitalization. Highly capitalized firms like medium- and large-scale metal-working plants (auto, etc.) were vulnerable to the shop floor-based forms of worker struggle like strikes and slowdowns that the class independence, antinationalist current favored because operations could not be easily transferred. The sit-down strikes in France, the United States, and other places were so powerful because they not only suspended production but implicitly threatened employers with the expropriation or destruction of their expensive capital investments. The favorable match between the Industrial Social Relations in France's metallurgy sector and revolutionary syndicalist and later communist strategy helped build the class independence, antinationalist current among metal workers.

Industries with lower levels of capital investment like Lyon's silk industry were far less vulnerable to shop floor strength because they could easily relocate to rural areas. Until the rise of mechanized factories in the 1920s, it was the silk workers themselves who owned their own looms. Shop floor forms of struggle in such industries are more difficult to conduct and usually less powerful as a weapon against employers. This alone suggests that the extra–shop floor strategies proposed by the class collaboration, nationalist current including those in the electoral arena might be more efficacious and therefore more appealing as a means of labor struggle. These then are industrial social relations. They interact with political opportunity structure (POS) to shape the formation (and mutation) of political identity.

Political Opportunity Structure

Political opportunity structure refers to the ways the structure of politics in a given social formation renders some courses of collective action more or less possible or efficacious. The concept figures prominently in social movement theory. Sidney Tarrow explains it as the "consistent—but not necessarily formal, permanent or national—dimensions of the political environment which either encourage or discourage people for using collective action."[27] The "most salient changes in opportunity structure result from the opening up of access to power, from shifts in ruling alignments, from the availability of influential allies and from cleavages within and among elites."[28] Doug McAdam has offered a useful synthesis of this and other strands of POS theory in the following way: (1) the relative openness or closure of the institutionalized political system, (2) the stability or instability of that broad set of elite alignments that typically undergird a polity, 3) the presence or absence of elite allies, and (4) the state's capacity and propensity for repression.[29] In addition to these, I would add a fifth element: the availability of political (here including revolutionary syndicalist) programs, as well as a sixth: historical traditions or myths. Political opportunity structure therefore helps structure the terms of political action, favoring some paths over others. Some of the labor historians mentioned above who have recently returned to the study of politics have employed similar approaches. Although he does not refer explicitly to political opportunity structure, Iowerth Prothero has argued in favor of situating worker politics in a broad political framework taking into account the "importance of political circumstances, the extent of toleration or repression, the balance of political forces, the nature of elite politics, the strength and confidence of a movement, the ways in which people read the situation, and responded to it, the possibilities and strategies they canvassed."[30] The political opportunity structure in France at both the national and local Lyonnais levels will be analyzed at several junctures in the following pages. Once again, the central argument of this book is that it is the particular *interaction* of POS with the industrial social relations of a given occupational group that helps shape the political identity of that group.

Design of Study

The silk and metal workers of Lyon are ideal subjects for the study of working-class political identity formation in France. Lyon has been one of France's most important industrial cities since the late Middle Ages. In the sixteenth century urban merchants developed a large and innovative silk industry. The *fabrique,* as it was called locally, was favored by the city's strategic position at the crossroads of some of Europe's most important trading routes and its access to abundant amounts of skilled and unskilled labor. By the turn of the twentieth century the industries emblematic of the Second Industrial Revolution—electrical, chemical, and a variety of metal-working industries—had joined the silk industry as the motors of the local economy. Today, the silk industry plays only a minor role in the city's economic life, but Lyon in general remains a major French industrial center.

For centuries the silk workers were skilled, independent artisans working in domestic settings. During the Second Industrial Revolution, production shifted to mechanized, semiskilled work organized in hierarchical factory settings. By contrast, late nineteenth-century metal workers tended to be skilled wage workers employed in small shops. During the Second Industrial Revolution, workers in many metal-working occupations saw their skills gradually rendered redundant as semiskilled wage labor slowly became the norm.

From the beginning, the men and women who worked in these two industries developed distinct occupationally linked political identities. Silk workers were closely connected to reformist socialist politics while metal workers were mainstays of the city's revolutionary syndicalist organizations. Following World War I metal workers shifted their allegiance to the newly formed Communist Party while silk workers maintained their loyalty to the reformist Socialist Party, the SFIO. In the early 1930s silk workers began to shift their support to the communists as well. The Popular Front, as we shall see, saw longstanding political identities transformed. The silk and metal workers therefore represent contrasting political and industrial trajectories.

The evidence and arguments in this book are presented both chronologically and thematically. A difficulty in presenting a purely chronological presentation of the material here is that industrial and political developments and changes often do not march in harmony. A political watershed may not signal significant industrial change and social change within the world of labor, and big changes in the productive process may occur without corresponding changes in political structures. Nevertheless, the years 1900–1939 constitute a coherent historical period of continuity and change from a number of political and economic angles. Most notably, they were those of most of the Third Republic and Second Industrial Revolution. But in order to see how they actually connected to form, reinforce, and change the political identities of silk and metal workers, I have chosen to break those years into three smaller segments: 1900–1921,

1921–1935, and 1935–1939. The first of these periods opens shortly after economic historians date the beginning of the Second Industrial Revolution. I will describe the industrial change of the period and how it affected industrial social relations, and then review a series of important political developments laden with implications for worker political identity, notably the end of World War I, the Russian Revolution, the 1920 rail strike, and the splits in the Socialist Party and CGT leading to the formation of the French Communist Party and the CGTU—all of which reconfigured the framework in which working-class political identities were expressed. The second period covers the years 1921–1935, a period when employers stepped up the "rationalization" of industrial production begun earlier. It was also a period of state repression of labor radicals. The final period presents a challenging variation to the problem of workers' political identity as it is posed for preceding periods. The heavy patriotic tones of the Popular Front, which were promoted most aggressively by the entire labor movement, were embraced by workers themselves and integrated into their identities. This stood in stark contrast to longstanding political identities based on antipatriotism.

Within each of these periods I will review the industrial social relations of both groups of workers and the prevailing political opportunity structure placing events in Lyon in a broader national context. I will focus on flash points such as strikes, demonstrations, and elections where political identities were displayed and reinforced. As Klandermans and de Weerd point out, "a group's collective identity can be studied in its own right by examining such phenomena as the group's symbols (and) rituals."[31] The symbols and rituals of the French labor movement were important elements in working-class political identity, and will be examined in the following pages. Some of the material discussed here is well known to historians of French society and politics while other material is a new addition to our knowledge of labor and politics in Lyon during the years in question. But in both cases, I have tried to present this material in ways that illustrate the ways that industrial social relations and political opportunity structure interacted to shape political identities.

The heart of this study consists of case studies of silk and metal workers during different periods. While those chapters contain specific information about the industrial social relations and political opportunity structures facing silk and metal workers at various junctures, other chapters take up the overall industrial scene and political opportunity structures more generally for France and Lyon. These chapters are essential for situating the metal workers and silk workers in a broader context.

Chapter 1 takes a long view of industrial development in France and the way it shaped industrial social relations. Chapter 2 provides a full description of the two political identities present in French labor. It situates those identities within the political- and trade-union wings of France's labor movement from the 1870s until the early 1920s. Chapter 3 reviews the national and local political opportunity structure from the beginning of the Third Republic until 1921. Chapter 4 begins our case studies with Lyon's silk workers from 1900–1921. Chapter 5 covers metal workers during the same period. Chapter 6 traces the political opportunity structure for the period 1921–1935. Chapter 7 returns to the silk workers for the period 1921–1935, and Chapter 8 does the same for metal workers. Chapter 9 introduces the popular front as a distinct period in French political history and explores the way the political identities of silk and especially metal workers were transformed.

Notes

1. Geoff Eley and Keith Nield, *The Future of Class in History* (Ann Arbor, MI, 2007).
2. The most ambitious antistructural arguments were advanced by Joan Scott, in her article "Gender: A Useful Category of Social Analysis," *American Historical Review* 91, no. 5 (1986): 1053–75; Gareth Stedman Jones in *Languages of Class; Studies in English Working Class History* (Cambridge, 1983), and Patrick Joyce, *Visions of the People: Industrial England and the Question of Class, 1840–1914* (Cambridge, 1991). William Sewell describes his own migration from social historian to cultural historian in "Whatever Happened to the 'Social' in Social History?" in *Schools of Thought; Twenty five years of Interpretive Social Science*, ed. Joan W. Scott and Debra Keates. (Princeton, NJ, 2001).
3. Joan Scott, *Gender and the Politics of History* (New York, 1988).
4. William Reddy, *Money and Liberty in Europe* (Cambridge, 1987).
5. See Scott, *Gender and the Politics of History,* Jones, *Languages of Class,* and Jacques Rancière, *La nuit des prolétaires* (Paris, 1991).
6. Bryan D. Palmer, *Descent into Discourse* (Philadelphia, 1990), 5.
7. Marc W. Steinberg, "Talkin' Class: Discourse, Ideology, and Their Roles in Class Conflict," in *Bringing Class Back In,* ed. Scott McNall (Boulder, CO, 1991), 265–66.
8. See Joan Scott, *Gender and the Politics of History,* and Ava Baron, "Gender and Labor History: Learning from the Past, Looking to the Future," in *Work Engendered*, ed. Ava Baron (Ithaca, NY, 1991).
9. Ava Baron provides a fine summary of this scholarship in her "Masculinity, the Embodied Male Worker, and the Historian's Gaze," *International Labor and Working-Class History* no. 69 (Spring 2006): 143–60.
10. Baron, "Gender and Labor History," 37.
11. See Adrian Mata Greenwood, "Gender Issues in Labour Statistics" in *Beyond Borders: Thinking Critically About Global Issues,* ed. Paula S. Rothenberg (New York, 2006).
12. In *The Future of Class in History,* Eley and Nield offer a detailed analysis of how Scott, Jones, and Joyce have counterposed their culturalist approaches to analyses employing structural and class analysis.
13. Eley and Nield dissect the ways that Jones in particular has equated Marxism "exclusively with its economistic versions," which "massively simplifies the intellectual history of the

Marxist tradition, not least during the last four decades." *The Future of Class,* 127. They cite Marx's discussion of the work day in chapter 10 of *Capital* as an example of the nuanced, nonreductionist manner in which Marx actually analyzed social reality, 188.

14. Examples of this trend include Ronald Aminzade, *Ballots and Barricades* (Princeton NJ, 993); Iowerth Prothero, *Radical Artisans in England and France, 1830–1870* (Cambridge, 1997); Don Kalb, *Expanding Class: Power and Everyday Politics in Industrial Communities: The Netherlands, 1850–1950* (London, 1997); and Keith Mann, "Political Identity and Worker Politics: Silk and Metalworkers in Lyon, France 1900–1914," *International Labor and Working Class History* 47 (2002): 375–405 and "Political Identity in Transition: Metalworkers in Lyon during the French Popular Front, 1935–39," *Labor History* 48, no. 3 (August 2007) : 301–25. For an overview on this trend in US labor history, see Julie Greene, Bruce Laurie, and Eric Arnesen, eds., *Labor Histories* (Urbana, IL, 1998).
15. Eley and Nield, *The Future of Class,* 55.
16. Bert Klandermans and Marga de Weerd, "Group Identification and Political Protest," in *Self, Identity, and Social Movements,* ed. Sheldon Stryker, Timothy J. Owens, and Robert White (Minneapolis, 2000), 75–76.
17. Georg Simmel, Thorstein Veblen, and Pierre Bourdieu are among the classical and twentieth-century sociologists who have explored this theme.
18. Albert Soboul's *The Parisian Sans-Culottes and the French Revolution, 1793–1794* (Oxford, 1964) remains the classic work on the sans-culottes and their political culture.
19. Charles Tilly, *Stories, Identities, and Political Change* (Oxford, 2002), 66–67.
20. Scott Hunt and Robert Bedford, "Identity Talk in the Peace and Justice Movement," *Journal of Contemporary Ethnography* 22, no. 4 (1994), 489.
21. Linda Gordon, "Moralizing Doesn't Help," *International Labor and Working Class History* 67 (Spring 2005): 31–32.
22. I sketched out this approach to studying political identity formation in my articles on silk and metal workers in Lyon, 1900–1914, and metal workers during the Popular Front cited above.
23. Tilly, *Identities and Political Change,* 49.
24. Ibid.
25. Karl Marx outlined his famous theory of alienation in the *Economic and Philosophic Manuscripts of 1844,* translated by Martin Milligan (Moscow, 1959 [1844]).
26. For a concise summary and analysis of Taylor's scientific management theory, see Harry Braverman, *Labor and Monopoly Capitalism* (New York, 1974).
27. Sidney Tarrow, *Power in Movement: Social Movements, Collective Action and Politics* (Cambridge, 1994), 18.
28. Ibid.
29. Doug McAdam, "Conceptual Origins, Current Problems, Future Directions," in *Comparative Perspectives in Social Movements,* ed. Doug McAdam, John D. McCarthy, and Mayer N. Zald (Cambridge, 1996), 10.
30. Prothero, *Radical Artisans,* 315.
31. Klandermans and de Weerd, "Group Identification and Political Protest," 76.

CHAPTER 1

INDUSTRIAL SOCIAL RELATIONS IN FRANCE'S SECOND INDUSTRIAL REVOLUTION

Industrial social relations differed significantly within and across industries. Chapters 4, 5, 7, and 9 provide detailed descriptions of social relations for Lyons' silk and metal workers at various points over the first four decades of the twentieth century. The aim of this chapter is to situate industrial social relations in general within the context of France's industrial economy. We will see how industrial change involved a general trend toward increased proletarianization of French workers, the decline of craft labor markets, and the rise of capitalist labor markets. The chapter concludes with a brief discussion of how these developments stimulated new forms of industrial protest.

The time span under study here largely corresponds to an economic period historians call the Second Industrial Revolution. The turn of the twentieth century was a time of great change in French economic and social life. The last two decades of the nineteenth century saw the beginnings of a dramatic rupture with the scale and overall character of French industry. New mechanized industries such as steel, electricity, chemicals, and motor construction arose steadily on a large scale, while industrial sectors of the first industrial revolution—iron, coal, and textiles—were transformed to various degrees by mechanization and capital and labor concentration. Running from around 1890 or even from the end of the long depression in 1886, and ending with the beginning of the Second World War, this industrial age therefore corresponds to the entire period under question here.[1]

A few economic statistics give an idea of the scale of the changes for our period. Between 1913 and 1929 the index of industrial growth rose 40 percent, the highest rate of growth in any industrial country including

---

Notes for this chapter begin on page 28.

Germany and the United States.[2] According to Labrousse and Braudel, the rate of annual industrial growth reached the impressive rate of 4.58 percent between the years 1905–1910.[3] This dynamism was mostly the result of the growth of the new industries of the second industrialization. By 1929 France was the world's second largest producer of aluminum and the third largest in steel production. Between 1864 and 1913, the total energy power of French industry expanded by 1,400 percent. The use of electrical power in particular vastly increased. The needs of the war effort were largely met through big advances in developing this source of energy. Through the 1920s electrical power continued to rapidly increase.[4]

The Second Industrial Revolution also involved a slow concentration of capital with a shrinking proportion of small enterprises and an expansion of medium and large ones. In 1906 32.3 percent of workers were employed in small industrial enterprises. By 1931, this had shrunk to 19.7 percent while the proportion of workers employed in medium- and large-size enterprises expanded during this period. Large enterprises employing over fifty-five workers accounted for 18.5 percent of the total in 1906 and 26.6 percent in 1931.[5]

Though the period was one of overall economic expansion, it also involved periods of boom and bust. The effects of World War I on the economy were uneven. Industrial enterprises working for the war efforts had abundant orders to fill and were assured labor supplies. But other industries such as textiles, food, building, and glass suffered as well. Many began a slow recovery after the war. Between 1924 and 1930 the economy as a whole experienced a boom. Industrial production grew by 5 percent a year. The economic crisis provoked by the 1929 stock market crash came to France in the second semester of 1930. Between 1929 and 1935 industrial production dropped by 25 percent.[6]

Industrial change was accompanied by big changes in French society. Between 1866 and 1906 the proportion of the French population living in cities increased from 30.5 percent to 42.1 percent. During the same period, the proportion in agricultural occupations declined from 51 percent to just over 40 percent.[7] It was only in 1931 that there were finally more French men and women living in cities than in the countryside.[8] This was also the period of the rise of industrial suburbs. With the Second Industrial Revolution, factories begin to be located on the periphery of large cities. These industrial suburbs often become both the location of work and residence of the new industrial proletariat.

Accordingly, the number of workers employed by the new and transformed industries expanded dramatically. Between 1906 and 1911 alone the working class grew by 1.3 million.[9] The 600,000 workers employed in the metal industry in 1906 increased to over 1.2 million by 1931. The number of those employed in the steel industry tripled in that period, those in the automobile industry increased five times over those in electrical construction by 7.5 percent, and the number of workers in the chemical industry doubled in that period.[10] Part of this process involved a shift in the percentages of labor devoted to different industries. Throughout the nineteenth century the textile industry employed over half of all those involved in industrial labor. By 1930 this percentage had declined by more than half—to 25 percent of the labor force—while the percentage of metal workers in the industrial labor force had risen to 25 percent.[11]

Female wage labor outside the home greatly expanded during this period. The 1906 census revealed that women accounted for 33.9 percent of France's industrial labor force. This increased during the war, reaching over 40 percent by 1918, and then declined after the armistice. The percentage of female labor varied greatly over time and between industries. By 1929, half of all workers in French textile factories were women, but they were a much smaller proportion of the labor force in metal-working plants.[12] This question will be explored in greater detail in the chapters dealing with silk and metal workers. Significant numbers of women also found employment in the service sector. Many worked as stenographers and secretaries in banks and industrial establishments. Their numbers grew steadily throughout the period under question here.[13]

Immigrants became an important component of the French labor force during this period. Foreigners accounted for 2.8 percent of the population in 1911 and 7.1 percent by 1931. In certain working-class suburbs like Vénissieux just outside of Lyon, they accounted for 40 percent of the population, the great majority of whom worked in industry. After the First World War, the overwhelming number of miners in France were Polish immigrants. In Lyon the Berliet automobile company had a large immigrant workforce.[14]

The changes associated with the Second Industrial Revolution appeared so dramatic to an earlier generation of scholars largely because the forms of industrial production of the First Industrial Revolution in France persisted longer than they did in other countries, particularly England, long considered the model of industrial development. At the time of the French Revolution, fully 55 percent of the active population was involved in agricultural pursuits and only 15 percent were "industrial" workers. By 1881, the percentage of the active population involved in agriculture had only fallen to 47.5 percent while those in industry had only risen to 26.7 percent. During the First Empire fully 60 percent of these workers were part of the textile industry. Throughout the nineteenth century the scale of industrial production as measured in the numbers employed per shop was exceedingly low. The 1866 census revealed that there were just over two workers for every *patron* (employer).[15] The vast majority of these industrial workers were artisans. Only in the spinning parts of the textile trade was there any mechanization at this time. Even when steam power was used, the size of industrial plant remained quite small.

Earlier generations of social and economic historians considered the low level of capital concentration, small percentage of mechanized industry, the small number of workers per shop, the small percentage of the population engaged in urban industrial pursuits, and other such indices as evidence of the "slow" or "backward" nature of French industrial development because it failed "to turn over earlier and more completely to large scale production or to mass production methods."[16] In the 1970s however, many historians began to revise both the premises and reasoning behind this assessment. The premise was that French industry was retarded in relation to the world's first industrialized nation—Great Britain. Yet, it has become increasingly clear that the British case was just one possible model among many. Furthermore, the notion that "small-scale artisanal forms of industry should have been superseded as early as possible in the nineteenth century by larger-scale factories in all forms of industrial enterprise" has been sharply challenged.[17] Accordingly, more and more economic historians have now begun to consider the character of nineteenth-century French economic development as taking a *different* route. Industrialization in France "simply took place in a different legal, political and cultural tradition and it does not seem to be illuminating to single out elements of that process as symptoms of relative backwardness, particularly when there seems to be a normative assumption in the typology that the 'English way' constitutes not merely initial but best or normal practice."[18]

Protoindustrialization

Studies of protoindustrialization were generated by the need to understand and explain the large amount of commodities produced in rural domestic settings for a mass regional, national, and international market before the first industrial revolution. This type of production was not only a ubiquitous feature of European economic life from the end of the Middle Ages through the old regime, but persisted well into the nineteenth century, even after urban factory manufacture had made its appearance.[19]

Like other "putting out" systems, protoindustrialization involved a relationship between merchant capitalists who provided raw material to domestic workers who spun or wove cloth, silk, and so on in exchange for an agreed-upon price or tariff. Unlike other forms of domestic production, however, finished goods under this system were produced for and sold in distant markets.[20] Many French writers employ an expanded notion of protoindustrialization that is not limited to rural domestic commodity production but includes some forms of urban handicraft production as well. As we will see below, the structure of Lyon's silk industry corresponds to this expanded view.

Protoindustrialization involved subcontracting—a social relationship that had extremely important implications for France's class structure. Subcontracting was at the center of both rural protoindustrialization and a great deal of urban industrial production including the Lyonnais silk industry. Subcontracting was also quite widespread in urban craft industries, especially in carriage building and the building trades.[21] In the case of the domestic sweating system and in most other cases, subcontracting meant that wages were reduced as subcontractors took their share from the sum paid by merchant capitalists for a given order. As we will see, subcontracting arrangements were greatly resented.

In France, as elsewhere, most protoindustrialization began in textiles. Until the end of the Middle Ages, textile production for the market had been an exclusively urban affair. The considerable amount of rurally produced textiles were produced and consumed by the family unit. This began to change in the sixteenth century. Growing demand could not be accommodated within the confines of urban textile production, as it then existed. Productivity could not be markedly increased with existing methods, and substantial technical innovation did not occur before the second half of the eighteenth century. Demand could only be met by turning to rural labor supplies. The supplementary income that came from domestic weaving was vital to the precarious budgets of many poor peasant households. Spinning also became a forceful presence in the French countryside in the late seventeenth and early eighteenth century. Both spinning and weaving, then, came to be largely rural occupations. There were other factors besides the search for labor that led urban merchants to transfer textile production to the countryside. The regulations of Colbert and his successors and the power of highly organized urban guilds capable of imposing wage and production standards also fueled the movement towards rural industrial production. Rural labor was 20 to 50 percent cheaper than in the cities.[22]

The move toward mechanized, urban industrial production did not signal the end of protoindustrialization. In fact, certain aspects of concentrated, mechanized industrial production actually helped preserve and extend rural protoindustrialization. For example, the hydraulic and steam-driven mechanization of cotton spinning in the 1820s sharply increased production at the spinning stage. This created bottlenecks at the following stage of the productive process, weaving, in which mechanization was perfected later. In the early nineteenth century, merchants solved this problem by resorting to hand-powered rural weaving on a large scale. In doing so, they reaped the advantages of protoindustrialization: flexible hiring tied to the rhythm of orders, a labor supply superior to that needed, and lessened risks of confrontation with a dispersed labor force.[23] Protoindustrial work was increasingly important to a peasantry fighting to stay on the land. While weaving was a source of supplementary income in the first third of the nineteenth century, it became the principal economic activity of a growing number of peasants as the century progressed. This phenomenon was central to Lyon's silk industry. As we shall see in greater detail, this industry was urban from its beginnings, and saw a full third of its looms move to the countryside between 1830 and 1850.

The reasons for the high proportion of industrial production carried out in the countryside were not only a function of the low level of urbanization and the small scale of industrial production in general. It was also a by-product of the class struggle between capital and labor. The lack of control that merchants could exert over rural textile workers concerning production schedules, theft of raw materials, quality standards, etc., has often been viewed (usually in the British case) as an incentive for developing centralized mills and factories where workers could be more easily forced to submit to capitalist work discipline. However, the opposite movement, from urban to rural settings, was often also desired by capitalists anxious to bypass highly organized and militant urban craftsmen. After the furious uprisings of the tightly organized silk workers of Lyon in 1831 and 1834, merchant capitalists sought to bypass the power of the *canuts,* as the silk workers were called, and relocate as much of the weaving operations as possible in the surrounding countryside. In the Lyonnais region, far from all workers engaged in the silk trade lived in the city of Lyon. In the 1860s over 300,000 silk workers lived in small towns and rural areas throughout a two-hundred-kilometer radius of Lyon.[24]

Protoindustrialization and Class Structure

Widespread protoindustrialization and craft production meant then that the class structure of nineteenth-century France was quite complex. In many cases the boundaries separating artisans and small shopkeepers and other owners of small capital were quite porous. The vague lines of division between master craftsmen and journeymen underscored the complex class structure of the country. As in the old regime, master craftsmen might, depending on the trade, be formally the owners of tools and "capital," employing one or more journeymen workers, but he (or occasionally she) was often a highly skilled craftsman who worked and lived alongside the journeymen. The role of the master as employer of wage labor was often overshadowed, as in the case of the silk trade in Lyon, by merchant capitalists who provided orders and raw materials. But even the distinction between master and journeymen was blurred as a result of the fluctuating fortunes of various industries. Furthermore, many of those belonging to the popular classes worked in industrial pursuits only as a means of sustaining themselves between harvests, as was the case for many peasants and agricultural workers, before marriage for young women, or before military service in the case of young men.

Industrial Change and Labor

The changes from artisanal to mass production that characterized the Second Industrial Revolution involved a wholesale onslaught on the independence that craftsmen had previously enjoyed, as well as the multioccupational lifestyles of the large number of workers who had hitherto had an ambiguous relationship to industrial activity. In fact, the "archaism" of French industry was often blamed on the large degree of control over the work process exercised by craftsmen and skilled workers and was explicitly cited by employers as the reason why mechanization, the factory system, and the end of the independence of the craftsmen were necessary if French industry was to survive.

The goal of the employers was to seize control over the labor process by rendering the skills possessed by craftsmen and skilled workers redundant through the use of machinery, which would simplify the labor process and increase productivity. The underlying end goal was to strip workers of the control over the labor process that their skills gave them. The Second Industrial Revolution is largely about how employers turned to mechanization and other forms of reorganizing the labor process with existing technology, all in the quest for "rationalization."

Even before the Second Industrial Revolution French employers had sought to wrest control over the labor process from craftsmen and skilled workers or otherwise attempt to bypass the control over entry into the trade, monopoly of skills, and other factors, which placed workers in a relatively strong bargaining position in the labor market. At several junctures in various industries throughout the nineteenth century, employers attempted to reorganize the labor process to their advantage—usually with mixed results. But the Second Industrial Revolution as it affected older industries involved such processes on a far greater scale than it had before. The big difference, of course, was the use of mechanization previously unavailable due to technological limitations.

The objectives of employers could not however, be realized merely through the implementation of machinery. Employers aimed at a far more global transformation of production. The ideas of Frederick Winslow Taylor represented a "scientific" approach to this problem.[25] At the beginning of the twentieth century, Taylor's industrial theories found support in France in the person of Henry Le Chatelier, who as a government engineer and professor at the state mining school embodied the links between applied science, industry, and state power.[26] However, French industrialists initially met Taylor's ideas with indifference and even hostility. The theoretical and scientific, rather than technical, focus of the education of French engineers made it difficult to adapt Taylor's ideas in France, and French industrial culture, with its obsession of secrecy, led industrialists to distrust outsiders. By 1910, however, these attitudes had begun to change. French automakers like Louis Renault and André Citroën personally visited Ford's Detroit auto works. In Lyon, Marius Berliet, whose large auto works will figure prominently in the following pages, sent his lieutenants to Detroit in order to gather first-hand knowledge of Ford's assembly lines. These early French auto pioneers became enthusiastic converts to Taylor's scientific management methods, including the use of the chronometer. By the 1920s assembly lines were installed not only in automobile factories, but in the clothing and shoe industries as well.[27] Scientific management involved specific forms of wage systems, usually some sort of piece rate system. As we will see, struggles against piecework and rationalization in general figured prominently in the industrial strife of the period.

Labor Markets

Thinking in terms of labor markets helps to illustrate many features of industrial social relations and their relationship to industrial change. Labor markets consist of workers, employers, jobs, hiring arrangements, and networks linking employers with job seekers and therefore involve several components of what is called *industrial social relations* here. The distinction between craft and capitalist labor markets provides a particularly handy intellectual tool with which to study the evolution of labor in the transitional period that was the Second Industrial Revolution. Broadly speaking, craft labor markets can be thought of as a system in which workers exert a great deal of control over the various features of the labor market just mentioned. Workers laboring under craft labor markets tend to enjoy a large amount of shop-floor autonomy as a result of this as well as their possession of scarce skills. When capitalists seize control of labor markets through measures including the establishment of central hiring practices and time-disciplined labor on their own premises, a capitalist labor market effaces the craft labor market. The latter describes the situation in many industries for much of the nineteenth century. It was only around the First World War that full-fledged capitalist labor markets emerged in advanced industrial countries, though craft labor markets continued to exist in some sectors.

Skill

Skill is an important element of industrial social relations because it affects and reflects the balance of forces between labor and capital. With skill comes control over the labor process, exactly the domain of production that capitalists believed essential to control in order to maximize production and profit in an expanding economy. Industrial capital turned to scientific management in its struggle to wrest shop floor control from skilled workers. Skill is a slippery concept in which imprecision, impressionism, and confusion reign. If skill is commonly understood as the possession of the technical knowledge or other physical capacities necessary to carry out a given task, the determination of who is skilled and the titles and prerogatives including (but not limited to) wages that accompany it often bear only a tangential relationship to labor in the literal sense. Skill reflects a social relation far broader than a narrow technical description of human labor.

The ways in which gender and skill have been associated underscores in a dramatic way the social dimension of skill. Skill is full of gender assumptions about work, gender, and family that are full of inequalities. It intersects with gender at a number of points, from the extended apprenticeships nearly always reserved for young males to the higher wages skilled male workers received. Women were not only excluded from the pathways leading to skilled status but usually restricted to jobs that came to be considered unskilled or semiskilled *because* they were exercised by women.

As Charles Tilly has explained, "Although knowledge, experience, and cleverness all contribute to skill, ultimately skill lies not in characteristics of individual workers but in relations between workers and employers; a skilled worker is one who is hard to replace or do without; an unskilled worker is one who is easily substitutable or dispensable."[28] More precisely, skilled workers are "those who 1) perform essential steps in production and 2) exercise monopolies over both a) required knowledge and b) the supply of labor to jobs requiring that knowledge."[29] The existence of this situation on a wide scale signals the presence of a craft labor market. Employers during the Second Industrial Revolution sought to replace these craft labor markets with capitalist ones.

Measuring skill and its evolution over time is a difficult task. This is partly because information about the workings of the actual labor process in many industries, including some under study here, is often surprisingly incomplete. Examining wage rates between different workers and available information about the evolution of actual labor processes helps shed light on the ways in which skill as a social category arises from the intersection of technical know-how and the wider balance of forces between capital and labor that are labor markets. Broader labor market concerns aside, there is a great deal of controversy over the degree to which industrial development in France affected workers on the shop floor. Surprisingly little is known about the actual pace of this process in many industries and occupations. The actual timing of some of them is highly contested by labor historians, while little is known about many others. Scholars agree, however, in refuting the traditional view of an across-the-board homogenization of labor through deskilling and loss of job autonomy. Sylvie Schweitzer concludes that "at least during the period of the institution of scientific management, it is erroneous to speak of a systematic and accelerated deskilling of labor: although it is undeniable that continuous process production involved the hiring of unskilled workers and the appearance of machine tenders, the breakdown favored skilled workers for many years."[30] But, whatever the actual pace and rhythm within and across specific industries, the composition of the industrial labor force in many industries *was* considerably altered in this period.

Generally, in some cases semiskilled workers were drawn from the ranks of "deskilled" skilled workers unable to prevent their skills and control over the labor process from being degraded by employers armed with rationalizing methods and labor-saving and labor-simplifying technology. For the many unskilled workers whose jobs had previously been as carriers of tools and small parts around the shop, however, mechanization often meant the acquisition of new skills—relatively modest, to be sure—necessary to work in automated industry. In sum, then some former craftsmen and skilled workers on one hand, and some unskilled workers on the other, became semiskilled factory operatives or *ouvriers specializes*—"OS's" in French. The process was not, of course, a strictly linear one. Craftsmen in some trades merely moved into the factory, in which they carried out the same type of labor as they had in smaller, unmechanized shops, sometimes owned by them. And, while some skilled trades virtually disappeared in the face of new technology, new trades, particularly at the beginning of the process, were created.

The traditional view of skilled workers and craftsmen as generally conservative and hostile to less skilled workers, immigrants, minorities, and women has been challenged by work such as Victoria Bonnell's study of Russian workers, Michael Hanagan's work on three industrial towns in the French *département* of the Loire not far from Lyon, Michael J. Neufeld's study of metal workers in Nuremberg, and Kim Voss's book on the American Knights of Labor, all of which show how under certain circumstances craft and skilled workers united with the unskilled and semiskilled and led powerful industrial actions and radical political movements.[31]

Collective Resistance

The attacks on skilled worker control represented by Fordism and Taylorism stimulated much of the industrial strife of the first period of the Second Industrial Revolution. French economic historians believe that worker resistance retarded the widespread institution of assembly line manufacturing in France by twenty years.[32] Michael Hanagan describes the situation in French industry between 1890 and 1914 in the following way: "In shops and factories throughout the country a tremendous struggle raged over the control of the production process. Everywhere employers strove to seize control on the shop floor and acquire a monopoly of expertise over the manufacturing process; everywhere skilled workers resisted these attempts. The growing power of the machine gave the employers an inestimable advantage in the conflict, but they faced a determined and resolute opponent."[33] This struggle was reflected in the character of many of the demands raised in strikes during this period. Disputes relating to the perceived brutality and capriciousness of foremen and other supervisory personnel were typical of this period. In 1907, struggles around regulations and fines were key issues in seventy-eight strikes involving 20,000 workers in 277 factories throughout France.[34] They reflect resistance to rationalization. We shall see in later chapters how struggles against "rationalization" were at the center of worker protest in the 1920s as well.

The demands of factory life were greatly resented and resisted. Many industrial disputes involved the defense of traditional peasant and village practices. In 1888 for example, nine hundred miners in the *département* of the Gard struck over regulations requiring them to bring their lunch and eat it on the premises, rather than take their midday meal at home as was their custom.[35] The permanent move into the factory or mine, and the work rules and regulations—along with the fines levied to enforce them—were strongly resented by workers. The factory was often compared to a prison in which workers labored like convicts. This attitude was reflected in many ways, such as in the names of worker's newspapers such as the *Le Forçat* (The Convict), *Le cri du Forçat* (The Cry of the Convict), and *La Révanche du Forçat* (The Revenge of the Convict), all of which appeared in the textile-producing regions of the north between 1883 and 1890. These skirmishes continued for a long time and compromises were made in a number of cases, but over time, permanent workforces were assembled. For the most part, the agricultural crisis of the 1880s and 1890s forcibly signaled the end of the industrial part-time agricultural worker.

The beginnings of this period saw the rise of the strike as the classic form of industrial working-class protest. Though strikes had been legal in France since 1864, this form of protest only began to be used with great frequency towards the end of the century. Around 1880 the annual number of strikes was around 100 per year. After 1906 there were always over 1,000 per year.[36] 1906 was an important year for labor conflict; there were 1,400 strikes involving 400,000 workers—one striker for every sixteen industrial workers.[37] The ensuing years saw "a continuation of the patterns laid down in 1906."[38] In the universal postwar strike wave, France experienced 2,000 strikes involving 1,300,000 workers in 1919 and 1,800 strikes also with 1,300,000 strikers in 1920. In the euphoric strike wave of 1936, 2,400,000 workers were involved in 16,000 strikes! The length of strikes also increased steadily as well, from an average of seven days in 1875 to twenty-one in 1902.[39]

Political practices associated with the modern workers' movement and modern forms of collective action such as demonstrations and political strikes like May Day also arose during this period. The new class-based "Internationale" takes its place alongside traditional popular songs such as the "Marseillaise" and the "Carmignole."

Conclusion

As we have seen, French industrial development in the nineteenth and twentieth centuries departed considerably from the view associated with Great Britain, in which large factories, machinery, and semiskilled labor rapidly replaced a world of small-scale, unmechanized artisanal production with little division of labor. Although while capital concentrated industry, mechanization and deskilling did occur, the process in France was slower than in other industrial countries. Forms of industrial production and labor associated with what some have labeled the *Artisanal phase* continued to exist side by side in the mass-production phase.

Industrial development strongly shaped France's social structure. Although it was extremely uneven, the Second Industrial Revolution involved a net proletarianization of French workers as capitalist labor markets replaced craft labor markets and skilled workers found their skills and the control it gave them over the productive process determinedly challenged. Independent artisanal production disappeared in favor of hierarchical factory relationships in which the conflictual relationship between workers and capitalists became increasingly clear, but subcontracting relationships, widespread in the nineteenth century, only gradually declined. The move to the factory continued to provoke worker resistance well into the twentieth century. The beginning of the period covered in this book was therefore a period of great change in French economic and social history with great ramifications for the formation of France's working class and industrial social relations in general.

The Second Industrial Revolution slowly altered the composition of the working class in terms of skill and gender. Semiskilled labor steadily grew at the expense of unskilled and particularly skilled labor. By changing the balance of power between capital and labor, proletarianization, the rise of capitalist labor markets, and widespread deskilling had profound implications for various forms of collective action that were themselves attached to political identities.

The aim of this chapter has been to describe how industrial change involved the gradual proletarianization of many French workers. Workers' material interests are largely conditioned by their level of proletarianization, which structures a field of possible choices. The actual form of worker politics emerges out of the prevailing political opportunity structure. The next chapter examines POS in the French Third Republic until the First World War.

Notes

1. Various scholars have described industrial change in broadly similar ways. In *Evolution du travail aux usines Renault* (Paris, 1955), French industrial sociologists Serge Mallet and Alain Touraine break down industrial development into three phases: (1) the Artisanal phase, (2) the Mass-production phase, and (3) the Science-sector phase. Although Touraine balked at assigning time frames to these periods, others have offered general time frames for each. In *Strikes in France, 1830–1968* (Cambridge, 1974), Edward Shorter and Charles Tilly considered the Artisanal phase as running roughly from 1800 to 1880, the Mass-production phase from 1880 to World War II, and the Science-sector phase from

World War II on. They consider the period from the 1820s to the 1890s as one of "initial proletarianization," the period from the 1870s to World War II as the "homogenization of labor," and the period from the 1920s as the "segmentation of labor."

2. Gérard Noiriel, *Les ouvriers dans la société française, XIXe–XXe siècle* (Paris, 1986), 120.

3. Cited in Michelle Perrot, "On the Formation of the French Working Class," in *Working Class Formation: Nineteenth Century Patterns in Western Europe and the United States*," ed. Ira Katznelson and Aristide Zolberg (Princeton, NJ, 1986), 101.

4. Denis Woronoff, *Histoire de l'industrie en France du XVIe siècle à nos jours* (Paris, 1994), 381.

5. Ibid., 418.

6. Ibid., 464–69

7. Noiriel, *Les ouvriers*, 87.

8. Ibid., 124.

9. Perrot, "Formation," 101.

10. Noiriel, *Les ouvriers*, 123.

11. Ibid., 121.

12. Woronoff, *Histoire de l'industrie*, 432.

13. For a recent treatment of this subject see Delphine Gardey, *La dactylographe et l'expedionnaire: Histoire des employees de bureau, 1890–1930* (Paris, 2001).

14. Woronoff, *Histoire de l'industrie*, 434.

15. Noiriel, *Les ouvriers*, 13.

16. Tom Kemp, *Economic Forces in French History* (London, 1971), 287.

17. Patrick O'Brien and Caglar Keyder, *Economic Growth in Britain and France, 1780–1914* (London, 1978), 18.

18. Ibid., 21. The nagging persistence of pockets of skilled labor and, indeed, entire industrial subsectors that should have died out long before, according to an older vision of industrial development, has led some historians to rethink traditional ideas about industrialization. Some writers have employed the concept of "dualism" to explain this phenomenon. According to this notion, large-scale, capital-concentrated industrial production developed along with, rather than at the expense of, small-scale production with little division of labor. Jonathan Zeitlin and Charles Sabel go further. They argue that if governments and industrialists often favored mass production for a variety of factors, not the least of which were psychological, there was nothing inevitable about mass production, which was in any event not inherently superior to small batch artisanal production. Jonathan Zeitlin and Charles Sabel, "Historic Alternatives to Mass Production: Politics, Markets and Technology in Nineteenth-Century Industrialization." *Past and Present* 108 (1985): 133–76.

19. See Peter Kriedte, Hans Medick, and Jürgen Schlumbohm, *Industrialization before Industrialization: Rural Industry in the Genesis of Capitalism* (Liverpool, 1976), 34. Economic and social historians disagree about the place of protoindustrialization in the development of industrial capitalism. Franklin Mendels considers it as "a first phase in the industrialization process," while the authors of *Industrialization before Industrialization* characterize it as "one of the central elements which mark the second phase in the disintegration of the feudal system and the transition to capitalist society." French social historian Alain Dewerpe also disagrees with Mendels. He considers protoindustrialization as "a set of relationships between a domestic mode of production and an expanding capitalist market." Alain Dewerpe, *Industrie et travail en France, 1800–1968* (Paris, 1993), 41.

20. The *verleger* system for example, involved direct relationships between producers and usually local consumers. See Alan Dewerpe, *Le monde du travail en France, 1800–1950* (Paris, 1989), 30.

21. See Bernard Mottez, *Systèmes de salaire et politiques patronales. Essai sur l'évolution des pratiques et des idéologies patronales* (Paris, 1966).

22. Woronoff, *Histoire de l'industrie*, 81.

23. Woronoff, *Histoire de l'industrie,* 217; Dewerpe, *Le Monde du Travail,* 25.

24. Noiriel, *Les ouvriers,* 34.

25. Harry Braverman succinctly summed up the three main principles of scientific management in the following manner: (1) "the dissociation of the labor process from the skills of the worker." Here management gathers all the knowledge concerning the labor process that had been previously the preserve of the worker; (2) the "separation of conception from execution" in which all "brainwork" and decision making becomes the preserve of management rather than of the workers; 3) management uses "this monopoly over knowledge to control each step of the labor process and its mode of execution." *Labor and Monopoly Capitalism: The Degradation of Work in the 21st Century* (New York, 1974), 113–19.

26. See Aimée Moutet, "Les origines du système de Taylor en France: Le point de vue patronal, (1907–1914),"*Le mouvement social* 58 (1965): 15–49.

27. Woronoff, *Histoire de l'industrie,* 415.

28. Charle Tilly and Chris Tilly, "Capitalist Work and Labor Markets," working paper no. 139, New School for Social Research, Center for Study of Social Change (New York, 1992), 71.

29. Ibid., 88.

30. Sylvie Schweitzer, "Les hiérarchies dans les usines de la deuxième industrialization " (Masters thesis, University of Paris, 1994), 27.

31. Victoria Bonnell, *Roots of Rebellion: Workers' Politics and Organizations in St. Petersburg and Moscow, 1900–1914* (Berkeley, CA, 1983); Michael P. Hanagan, *The Logic of Solidarity: Artisans and Industrial Workers in Three French Towns, 1871–1914* (Urbana, IL, 1980); Michael J. Neufeld, *The Skilled Metalworkers of Nuremberg: Craft and Class in the Industrial Revolution* (New Brunswick, NJ, 1989); and Kim Voss, *The Making of American Exceptionalism: The Knights of Labor and Class Formation in the Nineteenth Century* (Ithaca, NY, 1993).

32. Aimée Moutet, "Les origines," 19.

33. Hanagan, *Logic of Solidarity,* 3.

34. Michelle Perrot, "The Three Ages of Industrial Discipline in Nineteenth-Century France," in *Consciousness and Class Experience in Nineteenth-Century Europe,* ed. John Merriman (New York, 1979), 161.

35. Perrot, "Formation," 86–87.

36. Ibid., 104.

37. Noiriel, *Les ouvriers,* 98.

38. Shorter and Tilly, *Strikes in France,* 122.

39. Noiriel, *Les ouvriers.* 100.

CHAPTER 2

THE FRENCH LABOR MOVEMENT AND WORKER POLITICAL IDENTITY

By 1900, sharply defined working-class political currents represented by organizations that promoted their ideologies and programs through newspapers and pamphlets, electoral campaigns, and in workshops and factories had established deep roots in the French working class. The ideologies and practices of these currents constituted political identities for many French workers. This chapter describes in greater detail the two sets of working-class political identities under consideration here and the organizations that represented them nationally and locally.

From the beginning of the Third Republic, great debates shook the labor movement. Reformists and revolutionaries; advocates of trade union federalism versus union centralization; and proponents of close ties between trade unions, socialists, and political parties versus those demanding strict union independence from political parties and politicians all competed for the allegiance of French workers at the workplace, in working-class communities, and in labor organizations.

The French labor movement up until the Paris commune had been divided between cooperativists and collectivists. The former were best exemplified by the followers of Jean Pierre Proudhon, widely credited as the father of anarchism, who saw worker liberation coming in the form of cooperatives organized by each trade, while the latter called for the outright abolition of private property. All significant elements of the postcommune French labor movement, including most anarchists, had become collectivists. The main fault line in the workers' movement after the amnesty of the Communards in 1879 turned around the proper terrain of struggle. French followers of Russian anarchist theorist and leader Michael Bakunin believed that the sole area of anticapitalist labor struggle should be economic struggles at the point of production. Electoral activity, the struggle for reforms, and especially the cross-class alliances they might entail were

Notes for this chapter begin on page 53.

worse than useless in their view because they led to implication in bourgeois society at the expense of proletarian identity. The revolutionary syndicalist leadership of the union federation, the Confédération générale du travail (CGT) founded in 1895, inherited, extended, and modified these ideas and practices.

Revolutionary syndicalism played an important role in the French labor movement from 1895 to 1914 and even into the postwar period. It challenged the socialists for the loyalty of French workers during this period. Though never a clearly defined doctrine, syndicalism "stressed three points: complete hostility to the existing system; a belief that the only way to attack this system was by economic rather than political means, notably a great general strike; and a vague indication that the future society would be organized without a central political structure, on the basis of local economic units directed by producers themselves."[1] It also sought to nourish a working-class culture distinct from and in opposition to reigning bourgeois culture. Revolutionary syndicalist propaganda pointed out that while universal manhood suffrage integrated male workers into the nation as citizens, it ignored them as producers. Their integration into the institutionalized political system only masked their social marginalization. Revolutionary syndicalists sought to use this contradiction to help workers think of themselves as producers rather than as citizens.[2] Their condemnation of institutional politics and politicians went beyond bourgeois parties and leaders to include socialists as well. The latter, they argued, drew workers into useless cross-class alliances and parliamentary activity at the expense of the proper terrain of working-class struggle, the point of production. This strategy segregated workers from other class groups in the nation. By shunning elections and political groups of all stripes, the workers associated with this strategy did not experience political alliances and rub shoulders with middle-class politicians during parliamentary elections. The struggles at the point of production that they favored required worker unity and underscored the deep differences between them and their employers.

Together these ideas crystallized into a distinct political identity featuring an autonomous working-class culture and a focus on class independence in social and political struggles. The emphasis on proletarian solidarity across trades and borders, coupled as it was to a rejection of the Jacobin tradition of a centralized state governed by a republic resting on a multiclass alliance, had as a corollary a hostile stance towards patriotic nationalism. Workers' only true allies were the workers of the world. It was not only ideologically that the CGT counterposed class to nation. The confederation led antimilitarist activity sponsoring the *Sou au Soldat* program, by which money was collected for young workers serving obligatory military service, and organized revolutionary propaganda campaigns among the draftees. It also claimed to be revolutionary rather than reformist. In its recognition of the class struggle and the affirmation that the capitalist system was fundamentally exploitive of labor, syndicalism resembled Marxism. But the absolute rejection of all forms of politics, political parties, and governments made syndicalism on one side, and Marxism and other brands of socialism on the other, intense *"frères ennemis."*

This identity was shared by distinct occupational groups, including the metal workers examined in the present study. It took various organizational and theoretical forms that emphasized one or another of these points. Anarchists, revolutionary syndicalists, and a minority of socialist groups embodied this identity before the First World War. Elements of this current were modified by the war and the Russian Revolution. Anarchists and revolutionary syndicalists had opposed electoral activity, parliamentarianism, and political parties in general on the principle that they were inherently corrupt and reformist. But the Russian Revolution showed in practice that a political party—the Russian Bolsheviks, a member of the Second International (before leaving to found the Third International in 1919)—could be indeed revolutionary. In France leading revolutionary syndicalist leaders like Pierre Monatte and Alfred Rosmer joined the new communist movement on this basis. We can call this current and its attendant political identity the *class independence, antinationalist current.*

The other main current and identity in the French labor movement was represented by most socialist parties. We can call this current the *class collaboration, nationalist current.* It viewed economic and political struggles as two sides of the same coin. Workplace struggles were therefore only part of the terrain on which workers should defend their interests. This current had a heavy electoral dimension. It looked to elections and parliamentary reform to defend the short- and long-term interests of the working class. Significantly, these campaigns involved alliances with middle-class forces. This reflected the minority position of workers in French society at this time as well as the Jacobin republican tradition that emphasized the multiclass identity of citizenship as opposed to the class exclusivity of the rival current. The Jacobin current was a patriotic one that viewed state and republican institutions as expressing the will and interests of the "people," understood as constituting peasants, workers, and small and medium owners of land and capital. This current was reflected by several of France's socialist parties and the SFIO following its foundation in 1905. It found its most eloquent spokesperson in Jean Jaurès, the socialist parliamentarian, party leader, and intellectual. By 1900 this political identity had been firmly rooted among a number of occupational groups including Lyon's silk workers. These identities and the programs and ideologies upon which they were based assumed distinct organizational forms. These organized currents often competed with each other in the same unions. In the next section we will review the main features of the French and Lyonnais labor movement.

The Lyonnais labor movement of the closing decades of the nineteenth century developed largely along the lines of the Third Republic labor movement as a whole. Even before the advent of the Republic, the local workers' movement was part of national and even international working-class formations. A delegation of workers from Lyon participated in the London exposition of 1862 that led to the formation of the International Workingmen's Association, later referred to as the First International. In 1864 labor militants in Lyon founded one of the first sections of the International in France. By 1867 there were about five hundred members divided into eighteen local neighborhood groups. According to local authorities they were as influential as other political groupings.[3] The organization suffered a split in 1867 and by the next year seemed to have practically disappeared. But in 1869 the First International in Lyon began to grow again as the result of the contacts established between Albert Richard, the son of a silk dyer, and the Russian anarchist leader Mikhail Bakunin. The influence of the International increased, thanks to the ability of members of the International to participate in, and lead, an important strike wave that took place at that time.[4] The Paris Commune found a brief echo in Lyon in an insurrection on 22 March 1871, which proclaimed a commune in the working-class quarters of the Croix-Rousse and La Guillotière but was suppressed almost immediately.[5] The repressive climate following the defeat of the Paris Commune had loosened somewhat by 1875 to permit the revival of radical working-class political agitation.

Trade Unions

The first *chambres syndicales,* forerunners of modern labor unions, were established in 1867, the same year that strikes became legal. By 1875 there were 135 of these craft organizations throughout the country. These organizations lived a precarious, semilegal existence until trade unions were officially legalized in 1884. The following years saw a sharp expansion of trade unions throughout France.

Over twenty unions were established in Lyon between 1884 and 1886 alone. By 1891, sixty-nine unions were organized into a central unit called the Conseil local Lyonnais (CLL). By 1893, Lyon counted 123 different unions with 13,053 members. As was common in France at this time, most of these unions were quite small. The majority had less than sixty members, and some had as few as ten. Even the largest were of modest size: the glass workers union had 400 members, as did the velvet weavers; there were 300 typesetters, 340 unionized shoe workers, and 280 dyers.[6]

The Bourses du travail or labor exchanges all arose in the 1880s. The bourses were one of the most original features of the French labor movement. They were run by the trade unions and provided workers with meeting space, helped workers find employment, and offered courses designed to improve their professional knowledge. They also provided support to strikers. By 1895 there were over forty bourses operating throughout the country. Their initiator, Fernand Pelloutier, was the driving force behind the foundation of the national trade union federation, the CGT. At the beginning, the CGT was led by revolutionary unionists who shunned electoral politics and collaboration with politicians of all sorts. They placed greater value on organizing revolutionary unions than mass, all-inclusive ones. They considered strikes as training grounds for the powerful general strike that would end the wage system, rather than as a means to improve the material living standards of their members. This made the CGT an important component of the politics of the class independence, antinationalist current. After 1880, increasing numbers of local unions united in national trade federations. Local trade unions were linked through membership in the bourses as well as through national trade federations. In 1886 the trade federations united in a nationwide umbrella structure. In 1897, the Fédération des syndicats du Sud-Est was founded.

In 1908, 44 unions were part of the Union des syndicats du Rhône (USR) of the CGT. The fifty unions it organized in 1909 made it the third largest in the country; only the Departmental Unions of the Seine (the Paris region) and that of the Bouches du Rhône represented more unions. In following year, the Lyonnais CGT grouped 75 unions, making it second only to the *département* of the Seine. The progression continued in 1911 with 88 unions and 103 in 1912.[7] Throughout the period 1895–1914, then, the number of unionists in the region steadily increased. By 1914 about 10 percent of Lyon's workers were unionized.

After the turn of the century, union militants in Lyon had to contend with the appearance of a number of company or "yellow" unions. Active members of these unions tended to be jaded former anarchists who had been marginalized in the workers' movement. An initial attempt by the tramway authorities to create a yellow union in August 1901 failed. In 1902, however, local employers succeeded in establishing an independent Bourse du Lyon, which grouped together twenty unions and six hundred

members by 1904.[8] Among the affiliated unions was a union of men
and women mechanical weavers.[9] Although always rather marginal to the
workers' movement as a whole, the yellow unions increased their membership in 1906 as part of a concerted effort by the employers to coun-
teract the influence of revolutionaries. The independent bourse attained
a membership of 1,900 that year.[10] This fit a pattern that continued until
the war: the yellow unions tended to reappear during periods of industrial
strife and decline afterward.

The opening years of the century also saw the rise of Christian unionism. These organizations were particularly active among women textile
workers throughout the southeast in sectors where the CGT lacked influence.[11] Like the yellow unions, these unions aimed to undermine the
spirit of class struggle in favor of class collaboration. Nevertheless, in
some cases they actually put forward authentic worker demands around
wage issues and established unemployment funds.[12]

From 1893 on, in spite of their hostility to all organization, whether
political or trade union, anarchists began to join unions. The appeal that
anarchists saw in the unions at this time was summed up by the legendary
syndicalist leader Emile Pouget, who wrote in his publication the *Père
Peinard:*

> When we say that all political groupings are traps, that the only reality is on the
> economic plane, there is no better base than the craft group... The problem is
> the following: I'm an anarchist, I want to sow my ideas; in what soil will they best
> grow? I've already got the factory, the bistro. ... I want something better; a place
> where the *proles* get together to consider the exploitation that we suffer from and
> who put their heads together to do something about it. Does this place exist? Yes
> by God, and its unique: It's the craft organization.[13]

By 1880 the southeast in general, and Lyon in particular, was one of
the most important—if not *the* most important center—of French anarchism.[14] With their intransigent opposition to electoral alliances, (indeed
of electoralism of any kind) and their fierce mistrust of parliamentary
reform and middle-class politicians, the anarchists were the quintessential
representatives of the class independence, antinationalist current before
the advent of revolutionary syndicalism. Anarchism tended to appeal to
French artisans in small-scale industries. In Lyon, anarchists enjoyed particular success in recruiting shoemakers and *canuts*.[15] Like the Guesdists,
the anarchists were also influential among the silk workers in the Croix-
Rousse.[16] Although initially well implanted in Lyon, the Guesdists saw
their influence decline in the closing years of the nineteenth century. This
was largely due to state repression following the January 1883 trial of
several anarchist leaders accused of bombing a restaurant at the Place Bellecour in October 1882, and the assassination of French president Sadi

Carnot in Lyon by the anarchist Ceaserio on 24 June 1894.[17] Whenever possible, however, anarchists continued to organize public lectures on anarchism and antimilitarism, often featuring nationally known anarchist figures like the Communard Louise Michel.[18]

Propaganda for the general strike began in Lyon following the establishment of the Fédération des syndicats du Sud-Est in 1897. But it was only really around 1904 that "the idea of the general strike as the supreme means of making the social revolution penetrates more and more within Lyonnaise union circles."[19] Revolutionary syndicalists were later behind the effort of the USR to launch the syndicalist newspaper, *Le Syndiqué*. The paper agitated consistently around the theme of the "conscious minority, herald of the social revolution," which was the "driving idea of the USR."[20] It was revolutionary syndicalist activists who participated in various CGT campaigns like the committee for the eight-hour day, the committee for the general strike, and the antimilitarist association.[21]

Political Parties

Socialist parties seeking to recruit workers to their programs and organizations sprang up in France shortly after the amnesty for the Communards was voted in 1879. While most belonged to the class collaboration, nationalist current, a minority shared the class independence and antipatriotism of the anarchists and revolutionary syndicalists. Throughout the pre–World War I period, these groups enjoyed substantial electoral success and influence in trade unions but only modest success in recruiting workers to their organizations. In 1904, the Parti ouvrier français (POF) had only seventeen thousand members and the estimated combined membership of the other socialist groups was only ten thousand.[22]

Jules Guesde, the "Grandfather of French Marxism," was the driving force behind the Parti ouvrier (PO) founded in 1879 at a convention in Marseilles. At a convention held in Le Havre in July 1880, the PO changed its name to the Parti ouvrier français (POF). The "Guesdists" were particularly influential in the French trade union movement between the years 1877–1890. They believed that union struggles were only worthwhile if they were connected to the struggles of political parties for control of the state. A national trade union conference held in Lyon in 1886 that founded the Fédération nationale des syndicats ouvriers passed a resolution of obvious Guesdist influence which read in part that the Fédération "declares itself the sister of all existing socialist worker federations, and considers them as an army in another wing of the battle; these two armies will in the near future come together at the same point to crush the common enemy."[23] But "the Guesdists—especially after 1887—accorded no particular value to union action; they were only interested in it because of the possibilities it afforded for agitation, and because it could lead to the awakening of political consciousness."[24] Indeed, the Guesdists were known for holding party conventions and trade union conventions consecutively in the same town. Their conception of unions as mere springboards for political action no doubt brought about the dissatisfaction or the hostility of numerous workers towards them, and perhaps drove them to neglect somewhat union organization where their forces dominated.[25]

Classifying the POF in terms of the two currents of the French labor movement requires disassociating the party's programmatic claims from its actual practice. The Guesdists claimed to be revolutionary followers of Karl Marx. They also appeared to support an autonomous working-class identity against a nationalistic one. For example, POF members were prohibited on pain of expulsion from participating in Bastille Day celebrations or singing the *Marseillaise*. But the Guesdists were considered reformists by revolutionary syndicalists and others in the labor movement due to the emphasis they placed on parliamentary reforms and their efforts aimed at capturing the state through electoral means. Although the Guesdists opposed the entry of Alexander Millerand, a leading promoter of class collaboration and reformism, into a "bourgeois" government in 1899, their orientation on capturing the state through elections made it easier for socialist groups to support the Millerand ministry. POF political practice had involved electoral alliances with the Radicals much earlier. Guesde himself later became an enthusiastic supporter of World War I, going so far as to accept a ministerial portfolio in the Sacred Union government based on a multiclass alliance. As such, Guesdists can be considered as belonging to the class collaboration, nationalist current.

Nationally, the majority of Guesdist militants in the early 1890s belonged mainly to the following three socioprofessional categories: industrial workers (30 percent of the POF membership); café owners and other small businessmen (23.3 percent), and artisans including the canuts (22 percent). The rest were made up of peasants (11.6 percent), full-time party workers (2.3 percent), and professionals (3.5 percent).[26] In Lyon, many of the recruits to the POF in the 1890s were proletarianized silk weavers.[27] As we will see in chapter 4, these workers were an intermediate category between artisans and industrial workers: they received wages inferior to master weavers and bore the brunt of the periodic crises of the silk industry of these years.

The Guesdists were well implanted in Lyon from an early date. At a meeting on 29 February 1880, a number of small local socialist organizations in Lyon joined together to found the Lyonnais section of the PO.

A convention on 7 July 1880 of the organization's Fédération de L'Est, which included Lyon, approved a revolutionary socialist program drawn up by Guesde and Marx.[28] The socialists of the POF organized a series of educational conferences during this period where Guesde himself gave lectures on socialist theory.[29] In the early 1880s five local Guesdists were members of the party's National Council.[30]

By 1881, they had established themselves firmly in the city's fourth arrondissement, the Croix-Rousse—the center of the silk trade, which was both the work and residential quarter of the *canuts*. Electoral results, particularly those of 1889, 1893, and 1898, underscored the hegemony of the POF in this part of the city. As early as 1884, the POF had established local groups in the principal working-class districts of Lyon and its suburbs: two in La Guillotière, two in Brotteaux, and one in Villeurbanne in addition to the two in the Croix-Rousse.[31] In those years, voters elected POF members as deputies to parliament, garnering nearly 30 percent of the votes cast in the 1893 and 1898 elections.[32] The POF was also active in extraparliamentary political action. The success of the first May Day demonstration in Lyon in 1890 was largely due to the organizing activity of the Guesdists.[33]

By 1891, the original Parti ouvrier had given birth to three socialist parties. The Guesdist-controlled POF faced competition from the Parti ouvrier socialiste révolutionnaire (POSR) led by Jean Allemane and the Fédération des travailleurs socialistes de France (FTSF) led by Paul Brousse. The main political differences separating the POSR and the POF involved the relationship between party and trade unions in socialist politics. As we have seen, the Guesdist stress on political action over economic struggles led them to subordinate trade unions to their party. The POSR, on the other hand, accorded primacy to struggles on the economic plane, leading them to prioritize trade unions over parties even though they did participate in elections. Their support for the General Strike put them close to the anarchists. Brousse's FTSF members were also known as the "Possibilists" for their belief in the possibility, as they saw it, of progressively transforming private industry into worker-controlled public services with the aid of the state, itself transformed through incremental change effected through the ballot box. This was one of the few nationwide socialist groups to fail to develop an organization in Lyon.

Another significant socialist group of the day was the Comité révolutionnaire central (CRC). The CRC, a group of Blanquist inspiration, was led by former Communard Edouard Vaillant. They worked on both the trade union and political planes, and were partisans of the general strike advocated by the anarchists. Some socialists refused to belong to any of these groups. These were the "independents." Benôit Malon, a former

Communard, Guesdist, and Broussist, was the recognized leader of this tendency.

The followers of the legendary revolutionist Auguste Blanqui played only a minor role in the Lyon Commune in 1871, but they became more important in Lyon from 1880 on. Most of the Blanquist committees were made up of activists who were not native to Lyon, or were too young to have participated in the Paris Commune or its provincial echoes. The Blanquists had little success among the *canuts* of the Croix-Rousse, but they found a real echo in the new industrial neighborhoods of the left bank, like La Guillotière where many metal workers lived and worked. The Blanquists, defined by French labor historian Edward Dolléans as representing more "a temperament than a political doctrine," called on workers to struggle solely in the economic arena, a position they shared with anarchists and revolutionary syndicalists.[34]

Opposed to the reformism of the Guesdists, the Blanquists nevertheless took part in elections. But unlike the Guesdists, they adopted an intransigent position of class independence, refusing alliances with the radicals and denouncing the "parliamentary illusions" of the POF. In 1895, they managed to elect a deputy, and in 1896, two of them were among the five socialists elected to parliament. Up to that time, the Blanquists had represented the socialist version of the class independence, antipatriotic current. By the turn of the century, however, the question of reform or revolution had split their ranks. One wing joined the Guesdists as practitioners of reformist socialist politics and organized themselves into local sections corresponding to the cities' electoral districts. They became staunch defenders of the Republic, going so far as to defend alliances with bourgeois parties when the latter seemed to be threatened by conservative antirepublican parties. Other Blanquists, however, maintained the class independence, antipatriotic orientation. Many of them joined with the anarchists in founding revolutionary syndicalism, the antielectoral, anti-Republic version of the class independence, antipatriotic current in Lyon. The electoralist, reformist Blanquists adopted a political program close to the Guesdist POF, and the two groups attempted to unite and create a revolutionary socialist party in January 1902. Nine local Blanquist groups and sixteen POF sections briefly entered a common organization, but dissension over electoral questions drove them apart.[35]

The 1905 unification of France's several socialist parties into the French Section of the Workers' International, SFIO, initially encountered difficulties in Lyon. At a meeting held to unite the major socialist forces in Lyon on 5 May 1905, the followers of radical-socialist mayor Augagneur succeeded in blocking unity by a small majority. Nevertheless, by the next month, the Guesdists and independent socialists succeeded in establishing the Fédération of the Rhône of the Socialist Party, SFIO. A meeting of five thousand acclaimed speeches by Jean Jaurès and Paul Constans with the cries "Vive l'unité" and "Vive la sociale." The Fédération rapidly gained two thousand members and opened a cooperative as well.[36] That convention also condemned socialist participation in bourgeois governments. Earlier, two deputies from Lyon, H. Palix and P. Kraus, had been expelled. Both had voted in favor of socialist participation at the SFIO convention of Japy.

The founding of the SFIO did not fundamentally change the political orientation of local socialism, which was anchored solidly in class collaboration, nationalist politics, and on electoral alliances with the radical parties. Although participating in a bourgeois government was going too far for the Guesdists, reformist Blanquists, and other reformist socialists, they continued to practice a strategy of republican electoral alliance with the radicals. SFIO leader Jean Jaurès had long used his considerable erudition and intellectual gifts to popularize a particular vision of the French nation that had workers cast as the best element of the "people." Jaurès and others drew on the popular revolutionary tradition of 1789 that saw the Republic as a force for social change and equality.

In spite of the heterogeneity of its social composition and the various traditions of its members, the new party acquired an important working-class audience in prewar Lyon. In addition to its influence in the reformist unions, it had an impressive electoral record; in 1906 it held two seats in the Chamber of Deputies and four out of ten by 1914.

However, not all socialists in Lyon joined the newly unified organization. Prominent members of the Fédération autonome (FA) remained profoundly attached to the Republican Bloc. Among them were Augagneur, parliamentary representatives Colliard and Fort, and several municipal councilors. In general, members of the liberal professions dominated the Fédération autonome while those coming to the SFIO from the Guesdist POF were usually of working-class origin.[37] The Fédération autonome held two seats by 1914.[38]

The FA represented the organizational expression of the radical-socialist alliance pushed to its extreme. While the Guesdists would never have dreamed of actually fusing their organization with the radicals and always sought the most advantageous balance of forces in each electoral district with an eye for victories, the right wing of local socialism joined the FA under the leadership of the left-wing radicals who led the middle class–working class coalition in Lyon.

Throughout the 1880s these tendencies had varied success in extending their influence over different sectors of the Lyonnais working class. As we saw, the Guesdists were largely dominant in the silk industry. They drew their main body of militants from the *canuts* of the Croix-Rousse.[39] The anarchists were quite influential among the locksmiths and wood workers, while the Blanquists were the chief political tendency among glass workers.[40] The Blanquists also found strong support in the new industrial quarters of the left bank of the Rhône, especially among the metal workers of La Guillotière. Struggles between the various currents were carried out within working-class institutions. The Fédération nationale des syndicats, which was formed in 1886 by a nationwide convention held in Lyon, became the arena of "a bitter struggle between Guesdists, Blanquists, anarchists and other socialists for influence over the Lyonnais unions."[41] From 1884–1895, the Guesdists of the POF in Lyon were the dominant force in the local trade union movement. Leading members of the CLL like the former weaver Gabriel Farjat and the shoe cutter B. Peronin were also POF militants.[42] The POF actively organized workers in the city's new industrial sectors including mechanical weaving, dyeing, and finishing. The influence of the POF grew in 1891 when the anarchists were expelled from the CLL and the Blanquists turned their attention to the conquest of the Bourse du travail, inaugurated in Lyon on 8 February of that year.[43] POF leader Gabriel Farjat became general secretary of the bourse in 1894. But by 1903, "the revolutionary syndicalist partisans of the general strike and proponents of struggle exclusively on the economic plane who led the CGT had edged out the Guesdists for influence."[44]

An analysis of voting patterns in the electoral districts where the presence of certain working-class occupational groups was particularly marked also reveals much about the relative strength of these currents. The third arrondissement, which corresponded to the La Guillotière neighborhood where many metal workers lived and worked, reflected a distinct political profile. This quarter voted to the left of all others in all of the prewar elections for which information is available. It was the district in which the bloc in 1900 and 1904 registered some of its greatest successes, and where socialists outside the bloc also presented candidates. In the same period, the third arrondissement was where voter abstention was the highest in the city in the 1900, 1904, and 1908 elections, a reflection of the strength of revolutionary syndicalist propaganda in this quarter of metal workers, the classic occupation of the revolutionary syndicalist worker. In the fourth arrondissement, which corresponded to the Croix-Rousse, the old stronghold of the *canuts,* the bloc enjoyed great success. The 52.8 percent of the vote that the fourth gave to the radicals and independent socialists in 1908 was the highest in the city. With 22.2 percent of the vote, the SFIO in that year only did better than average in the third arrondissement, where it polled 24.2 percent.

By 1900, therefore, many of Lyon's silk workers were largely identified with Guesdist socialism and the political identity associated with it. After 1905, the SFIO inherited silk worker support. Metal workers as we have seen were associated with revolutionary syndicalism and the political identity associated with that current. This situation persisted throughout the prewar period. The war had a huge effect on the French labor movement, both solidifying and modifying this political sociology.

World War I

The effects of the war on the labor movement were as great, if not greater, than those on French industry. The debates surrounding the war provoked substantial realignments within the French labor movement, which were the source of the profound changes of the early 1920s. As was the case nationally, these developments affected the question of class alliances and independent worker politics in Lyon.

For years preceding the outbreak of hostilities in August 1914, the international labor movement had repeatedly affirmed its opposition to the coming war, promising energetic measures to prevent it.[45] A resolution passed by the VII Congress of the Socialist International held in Stuttgart in August 1907 and reaffirmed by the VIII Congress held in Copenhagen in 1910 promised that if war threatened, the international proletariat would "do everything to prevent the war." The Basel conference of 1912 called on workers from all countries to oppose "capitalist imperialism" with the "international solidarity of the proletariat." In France, the class impendence, antinationalist wing of the workers' movement placed antimilitarism and antipatriotism towards the top of its priorities. In the years before the war, the frequent use of the military against strikers assured support in the working class for these positions. In 1900, the CGT (which was under revolutionary syndicalist leadership at that time), launched the "Sou du Soldat" program discussed above. Antiwar pamphlets and articles directed at conscripts and workers were published. The 1913, antiwar demonstration that brought out 200,000 to the Parisian suburb of Pré-Saint-Gervais was typical of the rich antiwar tradition in the French labor movement.

The highly charged atmosphere that characterized international relations in those years had a tonic effect on relations between the CGT and the SFIO. In 1912, the French general staff demanded legislation increasing the term of obligatory military service from two to three years, a change that was widely interpreted as direct preparation for war. On this occasion, the CGT agreed for the first time to make an exception to the Charter of Amiens, which had prohibited union participation in political campaigns, and joined forces with the SFIO in a vast campaign against the bill.

The almost immediate support given to the war effort by the labor movement in all of the belligerent countries was the first great surprise of the war, as trade unions and socialist parties throughout Europe rapidly became active collaborators of their respective governments. In France, the funeral of Jean Jaurès, killed literally on the eve of the war by a deranged nationalist outraged by Jaurès' tireless efforts to prevent the war, was turned into the first demonstration of labor support for the war by the right wing of the CGT around Léon Jouhaux and the reformists around Pierre Renaudel who seized control of the SFIO apparatus.

The question of labor's stance vis-à-vis the war is of prime importance here because it was around these themes that the question of class collaboration and independent worker politics was posed. Labor support for the war was a key pillar of the Union Sacrée (Sacred Union), which held that the war presented such a threat to France that all sectors of the nation had to set aside their differences and unite against the common enemy. Working-class support for the Sacred Union amounted to a form of class collaboration far greater than at any time under the Third Republic. Likewise, opposition to the war and the Sacred Union in a context of fervent nationalism and mobilization for the war represented a continuation and deepening of working-class political independence vis-à-vis the middle-class radicals with whom much of the labor movement had allied in the early decades of the Third Republic.

The French authorities breathed a sigh of relief as it rapidly became clear that opposition to official policy in the CGT and the SP was extremely weak and isolated. As a result, the plan to arrest a large number of left-wing militants, those listed on the so-called Carnet B, was abandoned. Labor support for the war was solidified with the entry into the government of socialist leader Jules Guesde and the syndicalist Marcel Sembat on 26 August. In May 1915, the socialist Albert Thomas was given the important ministerial portfolio of artillery and military equipment. Labor participation in the Sacred Union took other forms than ministerial portfolios as well. Léon Jouhaux accepted appointment to the Secours national (an institution created to distribute relief to those made destitute by the war), where he sat with eminent conservative leaders of the nation such as high-ranking bankers, the archbishop of Paris, and Charles Maurras, the far right-wing nationalist leader and author of articles calling for the lynching of Jaurès.

In the initial stages of the war, the energetic participation of CGT and SFIO leaders in the Sacred Union met with little effective opposition.

The official CGT publication, *La Bataille syndicaliste,* allowed itself to be so swept up in anti-German hysteria that it went so far as publishing a chauvinist, racist article favorably comparing the French "spirit of independence" to the Germans, who with their "heavier blood" had a "more submissive and resigned" spirit. Léon Jouhaux himself signed a bellicose article proposing that since the German merchant fleet was blockaded, France should cooperate with England in taking over German markets.[46] In these first few days and weeks of the war, proletarian internationalism seemed to be a distant memory indeed.

Nevertheless, the abandonment of the antimilitarist and internationalist principles of the French labor movement was not unanimously accepted. In both the Socialist Party and the CGT, a small number of leaders and rank and file activists throughout the country avoided being swept up in pro-war, anti-German hysteria. Furthermore, they sought to establish contact with one another and coordinate their activity. In the CGT Alphonse Merrheim, secretary of the Federation of Metal Workers, opposed the chauvinist line of the leadership, rapidly becoming a bitter opponent of Léon Jouhaux and the majority of the CGT leadership. The militants around the revolutionary syndicalist magazine *La Vie ouvrière* founded by Pierre Monatte conducted an energetic if isolated opposition to the war and those in the labor movement who supported it. Opposition to the Sacred Union in the Socialist Party initially came from a few provincial party federations and isolated militants. Over the long run, however, the results of the Sacred Union for French workers eventually brought mass support to these previously isolated CGT and SP militants.

The syndicalist and socialist opposition faced major obstacles. Governmental censorship of the press was seconded and enforced by the Jouhaux leadership in the CGT and the Renaudel leadership in the Socialist party. Bitter confrontations occurred between pro- and antiwar forces over a number of issues relating to labor's stance vis-à-vis the war and the Sacred Union. One of the first concerned an international conference called by Swedish syndicalists and others from nonbelligerent countries. The majority of the CGT Comité confédéral supported Jouhaux's proposal to simply ignore the invitation on the grounds that those behind it could only be German agents. Merrheim found little support for his proposal to participate in the conference.

Opponents of the official line of the CGT and SFIO resorted to audacious tactics to make their views known. Merrheim organized a militant antiwar issue of the trade newspaper of the Fédération des Métaux, the *Union des métaux,* to commemorate the first May Day of the war in 1915. In order to avoid the censor's scissors, an anodyne counterfeit issue was inserted on top of each bundle. The militants around *La Vie ouvrière,* especially Alfred Rosmer, sent out a "letter to subscribers" making their views known. But the first significant breach in the wall of labor support for the war on a national and international level was the meeting of antiwar unionists and socialists in Zimmerwald, Switzerland, in September 1915. Merrheim, representing the Fédération des Métaux and Albert Bourderon of the coopers' union (also a member of the Socialist Party), were the only participants from France. A similar meeting was held in Kienthal in April 1916. These meetings laid the groundwork for the formation in France of the Committee for the Resumption of International Relations (CRRI) in January 1916 and later the Comité de défense syndicale. By the end of the war, the CGT and SFIO minority had become the majority.

Against the backdrop of this brief overview of the labor movement on a national scale, we can examine how syndicalists and trade unionists in Lyon responded to the challenges posed by the war and what that meant for working-class formation and the evolution of autonomous worker politics. No account of the major themes of the war can ignore developments in the French provinces; this is particularly true of opposition to the pro-war line of the CGT and SFIO leadership. One of the first stirrings in this direction within the SFIO came from the Fédération of the Haute-Vienne, the *département* whose capital was the porcelain manufacturing center of Limoges.

Lyon as a manufacturing center also occupied an important position in the war and the developments in society and politics that surrounded it. The links between the local labor movement and the national minority leadership were underscored by the fact that Merrheim, in addition to being secretary general of the metal worker's federation, was also delegate to the Comité confédéral from the Union des syndicats of the Rhône and the Loire. Pierre Monatte was a delegate from the Union départementale de syndicats from the Rhône and the Gard before he resigned from the Comité confédéral to protest that body's support for the war. And Raoul Lenoir, whom we will meet in chapter 5 on prewar metal workers in Lyon, cosigned the minority declaration with Merrheim discussed above.

On 25 July 1914, Jean Jaurès came to Lyon to support the candidacy of Marius Moutet, the local SFIO candidate for parliament. The speech he gave in the industrial suburb of Vaise was to be his last. It was a powerful antiwar speech that was later published by the militants around *La Vie ouvrière* as part of an antiwar pamphlet. On 30 July, a modest demonstration called by the SFIO estimated at two thousand to three thousand persons was held at the Place Bellecour. But this protest was not followed by other public displays of opposition to the war for some time. "Worker and socialist Lyon therefore, only very partially mobilized against the war." Industrial strife was also virtually eliminated with the outbreak of hostilities.[47]

But after an initial period of lassitude, the Lyonnais trade union movement distinguished itself as an important component of the CGT national minority. In January 1915, the Union des syndicats du Rhône adopted a resolution affirming the principles of internationalism and declaring itself ready to join any sincere effort for peace. As was the case nationally, union opposition to the war was centered in the metallurgy unions seconded by the teachers' union. C. Calzan, a local high school teacher, member of the teachers' union, and president of the Rhône Federation of the Socialist Party, became an ardent antiwar activist. The local Socialist Party was also part of Lyon's antiwar movement. "By the end of 1915 Socialist opposition to the 'majority' policy of the SP on the national level was particularly well established in Lyon."[48] Calzan and another teacher activist took the initiative in drafting a manifesto aimed at building support throughout the SP for antiwar demonstrations on May Day.[49] On 20 December 1915, the Rhône departmental convention of the SP approved the position laid out by Calzan.[50] In adding its voice to the minority, the Rhône federation of the SP joined those of the Haute-Vienne, Bouches du Rhône, Vaucluse, and Haute Garonne.[51] A delegation from Lyon planned to participate in the Zimmerwald conference in 5 September 1915 but was refused passports.[52]

The Committee for the Resumption of International Relations (CRRI) found support in Lyon. One of its leading activists, Branche, a vocal oppositionist in the Socialist Party, promoted the campaigns of the CRRI in strike committees and union meetings. The fiery feminist anarchist and trade unionist Jeannne Chevenard was also a member of the CRRI. The Union départementale, the metal workers' union, and the clothing workers' union were all affiliated to the CRRI.

Mobilization itself played an important role in altering the composition of the labor movement. Militants of all tendencies and sensibilities were drafted. In Lyon, UD leader Francis Million was called up and stationed with the French garrison in Morocco in the first few months of 1915. His place was taken by the anarchist Henri Bécirard, ineligible for military service due to a paralyzed leg.[53] The prominence of Bécirard and the secretary of the clothing workers' union, Jeanne Chevenard, in the wartime left-wing labor movement were emblematic of a general trend during the period: the return of anarchist influence after its marginalization in the years before the war.

The war linked labor protest and left-wing politics far more than was the case in peacetime. In the context of the war and Sacred Union, labor protest, even when limited to questions of wages, hours, and working conditions, often assumed radical, even revolutionary proportions. The connections between opposition to the war and opposition to the Sacred

Union implicit in the labor struggles that appeared late in the first half of the war became explicit from the spring of 1917 on.

Strike activity began to reappear in early 1915, but at an extremely modest level. Between January and April 1915, there were only nineteen strikes in France involving only 1,180 strikers.[54] Strike action was discouraged by the mobilization for the war that scattered labor activists, the high unemployment of the initial period of the war, and the pro–Sacred Union stance of the CGT and SP leaders that made them hostile to any rank-and-file action that might appear to call into question working-class support for the war. When strike activity became common later in the war, workers faced both company and government repression. Minister of War Alexander Millerand told a delegation of metal workers in July 1915 that "there are no more workers' rights, no more social laws: there is only the war." Public marches were banned by the prefect during the June 1917 strikes in Lyon, and the police did not hesitate to employ violence against strikers. Unionists complained that strikers arrested in June 1918 were poorly fed and subjected to rough treatment at the hands of their guards.[55]

The radicalization of labor struggles in this period was accompanied by changes within the labor movement, particularly among the minority. The most notable of these was the passage of Alphonse Merrheim from a position of intransigent opposition to the pro-war and Sacred Union policy of the CGT majority to one of accommodation with the Jouhaux leadership. At the CGT conference held in Clermont-Ferrand in late December 1917, Merrheim joined Jouhaux in supporting a resolution that called for military victory in the framework of national defense, while the minority continued to fight for an internationalist, class-struggle line. The rapprochement with Jouhaux was made possible by the latter's slight move to the left, dissociating himself from the chauvinist right wing of the CGT under growing pressure from the rank and file. The prefect of the Loire reported that Merrheim's speeches during his tour of that *département* in January 1918 had "no revolutionary or pacifist character whatsoever."[56] Several months later, his slide to the right manifested itself in his hostility to the CDS conference organized by the minority in Saint Etienne in May 1918. He also joined the right in proposing to hold the CGT convention on 1 May, as opposed to the minority proposal to call the conference for 21 April in order to give militants time to return home early enough to prepare energetic May Day demonstrations. By the time of the CDS meeting in July 1918, Merrheim had lost his position as secretary general of that bastion of left-wing opposition. A good number of the trade unionists throughout France who had been part of the Zimmerwald minority with Merrheim joined him in his move toward the center. In Lyon, however, the minority leadership resisted the pressures that led others to abandon their intransigence against the war, the Sacred Union, and those in the labor movement who gave them support in one way or another. In February 1918, Jeanne Chevenard noted that Merrheim's attitude had become questionable.[57] On the eve of May Day, Antoine Garin of the metal workers, who had previously collaborated closely with Merrheim, told a union meeting that the latter had become as bad as Jouhaux.[58] He continued his attacks on Jouhaux and Merrheim throughout the following period. The Lyonnais labor movement in both its trade union and political wings was, therefore, firmly anchored in the revolutionary wing of the French labor movement.

It was in this context of worker mobilization and victories followed by defeats and repression that several important CGT and SFIO conventions took place. The positions expressed at these conventions crystallized into the two organizations that dominated the French labor movement in the interwar period. The two tendencies that had formed and developed during the war and whose positions had been clarified during the events of the spring and summer of 1919 squared off at the first postwar CGT convention held in Lyon in September 1919. The minority led by Pierre Monatte based its sharp criticism of the Jouhaux majority on the record of the majority during the war and its attitude toward the events of 1919. Speaking of the war, Monatte told the majority that "for us this war is the great crime for which we must blame the bourgeoisie. You are no longer worthy, comrades, to interpret the thought of the French workers' movement."[59] For the minority, the tasks of the labor movement consisted of defending and extending the Russian Revolution. The line expressed by the majority reflected the degree to which its wartime experiences had altered its attitude to the traditional program of the CGT and French revolutionary syndicalism. While the minority hailed the Russian Revolution and the Soviets as consistent with its own vision of workers' power, the Jouhaux leadership viewed the Bolshevik-led Revolution with thinly disguised horror and hostility. Against the idea of a cataclysmic, violent revolution, Jouhaux counterpoised the idea of a gradual, "economic" revolution that would develop from within the system. The revolutionary syndicalist insistence on the primacy of the general strike was also cast aside. Parliamentary democracy, no longer considered as a bourgeois trick, was now viewed as the terrain where workers' interests could be defended.

The votes expressed at the Lyon convention reflected the still solid position of the majority. The minority only gathered 588 votes against the report approving the record of the CGT leadership during the war (which received 1,393 votes) and 324 against another key resolution for which the majority received 1,633. The voting pattern of the Lyon delegation, however, reflected the strength of the minority in Lyon. The sixty-four-member delegation, led by the wartime USR leadership including Jeanne Chevenard of the clothing workers' union and Antoine Garin of the metal workers' union and other leading members of the militant antiwar opposition in the CGT, voted for the minority resolutions in greater proportions than seen on the national level. Thus twenty-eight voted against the balance sheet of the CGT leadership during the war—only slightly behind the thirty-five whom approved it (there was one abstention). Forty approved the main report against sixteen oppositions and eight nonvoting.[60]

The next CGT convention held in Orléans between 27 September and 2 October 1920 took place against the backdrop of the defeated strikes and repression earlier that year, as well as the defeat of the Red Army in Poland in the summer of 1920. The deliberations of the Second Congress of the Third International (CI) held in July in Moscow of that year also weighed heavily on developments in the French workers' movement. All these developments served to widen the differences between the minority and the majority. A decision taken at the CI congress, which called upon trade unions to affiliate to the CI but at the same time did not call for a revolutionary trade union international organized in opposition to the existing reformist-dominated Amsterdam international, became a bone of contention within the CGT. Both the majority and the minority sought to use its understanding of the Charter of Amiens to bolster its position. The majority used the provision calling for trade union independence from political parties to attack the minority's ties with the Bolsheviks. The minority in turn brandished the revolutionary aspects of the charter against the reformist practices of the majority. The vote totals once again confirmed the hegemony of the majority. The two main reports saw a majority victory of 1,482 to 691 and 1,515 against 596. It was at this time that the minority organized itself in the Revolutionary Union Committees (CSRs).

While the Orléans conference confirmed the hegemony of the majority, it also registered the advance of the revolutionary minority in the Rhône. In a close vote, the Rhône CGT delegation became a majority in the Lyon region. The minority received 29 votes from delegates against 28 for the majority and 2 abstentions for the first of the main reports, and 31 to 28 with 1 abstention voted against the other main report.[61] The majority of the region's unions were now part of the national minority. This convention also registered important changes in the local composition of the two camps. While Antoine Garin of the metal workers, Nicolas Berthet for the construction workers, Robert Fourcade for the mechanical sawyers, and others remained part of the national minority, ex-minority leaders Francis Million, Henri Bécirard, and Jeanne Chevenard joined Merrheim in the majority. In line with these changes, Robert Fourcade replaced Henri Bécirard as secretary of the USR.[62]

The CGT split at its Lille convention in July 1921. Movement in this direction had been considerably accelerated by the split in the Socialist Party that led to the formation of the French Communist Party in December 1920. Shortly before the Lille convention, leading members of the minority had participated in the founding convention of the Red International Union in Moscow. The Lille convention was a bitter one. The minority reproached the majority for abandoning the traditional revolutionary mission of the CGT in favor of becoming a "governmental cog." The Jouhaux leadership was also blamed for failing to defend the eight-hour day, which had at that point had become a dead letter in most industries. For its part, the majority centered its attacks against the minority around its connections with the Russian Revolution and subordination to the Communist Party, which it claimed was a party that aimed at conquering "political power for itself and not for the working class." The pace quickened with a majority-led condemnation of the CSRs. On 26 December 1921, the CGT administrative commission condemned the minority convention that had been held earlier that month. This led directly to the split and the founding of the CGTU, which held its first convention in June 1922 and formally joined the pro-Moscow international trade union confederation, the Internationale syndicale rouge (ISR), in November 1923. Until its unification with the CGT in 1934, the CGTU was the trade union expression of the class independence, antipatriotic current in France.[63]

Founding of the French Communist Party

The immediate postwar period was also thick with changes in the political wing of the workers' movement. The small but vocal antiwar, anti–Sacred Union minority in the Socialist Party grew at a somewhat faster rate than in the CGT, and that minority was well entrenched in Lyon from an early date. On the national level the minority scored its first victory in July 1918 when a motion moved by Jean Longuet won 1,544 votes against 1,172 for a motion by Renaudel at a meeting of the party's national council. This new balance of forces was confirmed at the party convention in November at which the minority officially became the majority and Ludovic Frossard, future first general secretary of the Communist Party, became secretary of the Socialist Party.[64]

The Communist International was officially founded in Moscow on 4 March 1919. The partisans of affiliation with the CI were quite active in Lyon from an early date. Shortly thereafter, a Lyon Committee for the Third International was founded. By July, heated discussions were held over the possibilities for founding a Communist Party.[65] During the months preceding the SP convention in Tours, organizing efforts in favor of the Third International increased. In May 1920, a group described by the police as a "revolutionary communist group" calling itself the "Group of 40" was created in Lyon. It was led by Heyer, organizer of a food cooperative and secretary of the veteran's organization the ARAC for the sixth arrondissement.[66] In the midst of the May 1920 strikes, the Lyon group for the Third International reorganized and expanded itself in order to intensify its propaganda efforts and establish itself in neighborhoods throughout the city as well as in neighboring Villeurbanne. The group involved rank-and-file activists as well as left-wing municipal councilors including Calzan and Cuminal and members of the Young Socialists. On 8 May, the committee held a meeting that drew four hundred people.[67]

One of the most salient features of the early period of the Parti communiste français (PCF) was the sympathy that the Russian Revolution and the Third International gained in anarchist and revolutionary syndicalist quarters, though this often proved to be of short duration. Nationally, Pierre Monatte and Alfred Rosmer joined the PCF. In Lyon, long-time anarchist militant Henri Bécirard proclaimed his support for the Third International in September 1920. Although the Rhône SP voted overwhelmingly for the Third International (80 of the 101 delegates of the Rhône delegation voted for the resolution accepting Lenin's twenty-one conditions), only three of the city's twenty-five socialist city councilors voted for the Third International.[68] All three—Cuminal, Calzan, and Legouhy—had distinguished themselves during the war as vocal leaders of the antiwar SP minority. In neighboring Villeurbanne however, eighteen of twenty-nine city councilors as well as SP mayor Jules Grandclément joined the Third International.[69]

As we have seen, these left-wing socialists were joined by some revolutionary syndicalists like Pierre Monatte and Alfred Rosmer in signing onto the Third International and the PCF on the basis of its revolutionary orientation. With its emphasis on international proletarian solidarity, opposition to nationalist rhetoric and cross-class alliances, and promotion of militant shop floor struggles, the PCF continued the tradition of class independence, antinationalist politics in France's postwar labor movement. With its electoralist orientation built on cross-class alliances, the postwar Socialist Party continued to represent the class collaboration, patriotic current.

Notes

1. Peter Stearns, *Revolutionary Syndicalism and French Labor: A Cause without Rebels* (New Brunswick, NJ, 1971), 9.
2. Jacques Julliard, *Autonomie ouvrière* (Paris, 1988), 23.
3. Yves Lequin, *Les ouvriers de la région lyonnaise, 1848–1914* (Lyon, 1971), 2:207–8.
4. Ibid., 209.
5. Ibid., 212–13.
6. Jacques Leschiera, "Les débuts de la CGT à Lyon, 1890–1914" (Master's thesis, University of Lyon, 1972), 14.
7. Ibid., 63.
8. Marie-Françoise Roux, "L'ouvrière du textile à Lyon, 1880–1914" (Master's thesis, University of Lyon, 1981), 131.
9. Lequin, *Les ouvriers,* 2:343.
10. Ibid.
11. Ibid., 346.
12. Ibid.
13. Quoted in George Lefranc, *Le mouvement syndical sous la Troisième République* (Paris, 1967), 91.
14. Michelle Marigot, "L'anarcho-syndicalisme à Lyon, 1880–1914" (Master's thesis, University of Lyon, 1966), 1.
15. Ibid., 24.
16. Ibid., 10.
17. Lequin, *Les ouvriers,* 2:228.
18. Ibid., 230.
19. Leschiera, "Les débuts," 58.
20. Ibid., 97.
21. Ibid., 71.
22. George Lefranc, *Le mouvement socialiste sous la Troisième République* (Paris, 1963), 118.
23. See Claude Willard, *Les Guesdists* (Paris, 1965), 34, for an extensive discussion of this question.
24. Lefranc, *Le mouvement syndical,* 34.
25. Ibid.
26. Willard, *Les Guesdists,* 277.
27. Madeleine Thévenet, "Le Guesdisme à Lyon, 1882–1905" (Master's thesis, University of Lyon, 1971), 50.
28. R. Chevailler, B. Girardon, V. T. Nguyen, and B. Rochaix, *Lyon: Les traboules du mouvement ouvrier* (Paris, 1980), 100.
29. Ibid., 101.
30. Lequin, *Les ouvriers,* 2:231.
31. Ibid.
32. Ibid., 36.
33. Ibid., 2:234.
34. Ibid., 2:235.
35. Ibid., 302.
36. Chevailler et al., *Les traboules,* 103.
37. Ibid., 38
38. Ibid.
39. Robert Chagny, "La presse socialiste à Lyon, 1896–1914" (Master's thesis, University of Lyon, 1960), 33.
40. Leschiera, "Les débuts,"16.
41. Ibid., 22.

42. Ibid., 9.
43. Ibid., 12.
44. Ibid.
45. The following discussion on the war and labor movement is largely drawn from Alfred Rosmer, *Le mouvement ouvrier pendant la première guerre mondiale,* 2 vols. (Paris, 1993).
46. Ibid., 118 and 122.
47. Edmond Pèle, "Le mouvement ouvrier lyonnais pendant la première guerre mondiale, 1914–1918" (Master's thesis, University of Lyon), 99.
48. Ibid., 111.
49. Ibid., 109.
50. Chevailler et al., *Les traboules,* 114.
51. Pèle, *Le mouvement ouvrier lyonnais,* 111.
52. Rosmer, *Le mouvement ouvrier,* 373.
53. Claire Auzias, *Mémoires libertaires, Lyon, 1919–1939* (Paris, 1993), 58.
54. Edouard Dolléans, *Histoire du mouvement ouvrier* (Paris, 1967), 230.
55. ADR 10/Mp/C/59.
56. Rene Mouriaux, *La CGT, crise et alternatives* (Paris, 1982), 76.
57. ADR 10/Mp/C/59.
58. Ibid.
59. Dolléans, *Histoire,* 319.
60. Jean-Luc Pinol, "Les origines du communisme à Lyon" (Master's thesis, University of Lyon, 1972), 281.
61. Auzias, *Mémoires,* 66.
62. Ibid., 67.
63. See Dolléans, *Histoire.*
64. For recent treatments of the founding of the French Communist Party, see, Jean-Louis Robert, "1914–1920," in *La France ouvrière,* ed. Claude Willard, vol. 1 (Paris, 1995); and Stéphane Courtois and Marc Lazar, *Histoire du Parti communiste français.* (Paris, 1995).
65. Annie Kriegel, *Aux origines du communisme français.* (Paris, 1969), 233.
66. ADR 10/Mp/C65.
67. Ibid.
68. Chevailler et al., *Les traboules,* 111.
69. These percentages approximate the national norm. See Robert, "1914–1920," 449.

CHAPTER 3

POLITICAL OPPORTUNITY STRUCTURE FROM 1875 TO 1921

France's political opportunity structure created a terrain of possible choices of collective action whose public representations were important elements of political identity. POS helped shape worker political identity by interacting with the industrial social relations analyzed in the last chapter. This chapter reviews and analyzes the main features of France's national and local political opportunity structure from the beginning of the Third Republic up until 1921. We begin with a chronological narrative that highlights the significant features of France's political system in this era. We conclude by analyzing and characterizing them in terms of POS theory.

The Third Republic was officially born in 1875, well before France had recovered from the trauma of the Paris Commune of 1871. Its early years were characterized by a struggle between republicans of all stripes on the one hand, and monarchist opponents of the Republic on the other, the latter harboring hopes that a form of monarchy might still prevail. When the Republic later became a firmly established fact somewhere around the turn of the century, an opposition between republicans and nationalists replaced the opposition between republicans and monarchists. The great political battles of the day were fought along these lines. Two fin-de-siècle political issues—the Dreyfus affair and the struggle to separate church and state—were particularly emblematic of both the intensity of the debates between republicans and opponents of the republic, and the manner in which the political issues of the day allied workers and the middle class, socialists and Radical Party politicians.

The Dreyfus affair split France almost exactly along the lines of the republican and antirepublican camps. Supporters of the archconservative army officer corps, monarchists, anti-Semites, and the church were all aligned against Dreyfus even after his innocence was clear to anyone willing to review the evidence dispassionately. Supporters of Dreyfus tended to come

Notes for this chapter begin on page 78.

from the republican ranks, although some radical republicans like Maurice Barras, Paul Déroulède, and Henri Rochefort were anti-Dreyfusards. By the end of the affair, all had moved well to the right. Though socialists like Jules Guesde and Jean Jaurès initially called on workers to refrain from taking sides in what they viewed as a struggle within the bourgeoisie, many socialists and workers became committed Dreyfusards at the time of the revision in 1898. The link between the republic and the affair, though always present, became unmistakable in 1899. In June of that year, the anti-Dreyfusard campaign against representatives of the republic reached its climax when the president of the republic, Emile Loubet, was physically assaulted at a racetrack.

The struggle for a lay republic saw virtually the same forces pitted against each other. Republicans of every sensibility joined together to support separation of church and state, an issue that was as popular in working-class circles as it was in middle-class ones. Separation of church and state had figured in republican programs ever since Gambetta's Belleville program in 1869 and was formally inscribed in the program of the Parti socialiste français in 1902.

These struggles gave birth to organizations that both reflected and reinforced the working class–middle class alliance. The Ligue des droits de l'homme was founded during the Zola trial in 1898 to defend Dreyfus on the basis of the principles of 1789. An overwhelmingly middle-class organization led by members of the Radical Party, the ligue developed close ties with the organized labor movement; the CGT often lent its meeting halls to the ligue.[1]

Middle-class republicans sought to win workers to the Republic through the enactment of progressive social measures. They fought for institutional measures to provide a legal basis for worker collective action. A majority of France's lower parliamentary chamber, the Chamber of Deputies, passed legislation that would impose heavy fines and jail penalties on employers who violated the workers' right to organize, but the conservative senate blocked passage of this bill.[2] Later, laws limiting child labor, fixing maximum hours, and guaranteeing weekly rest days were also passed.[3]

The Republic in Lyon

Republican forces enjoyed hegemony in Lyon from the 1880s on. In fact, local republican circles considered their city as the true capital of the Republic and lost no opportunity to compare Lyon favorably on this score with Paris. While the capital flirted with Boulangism, Lyon reveled in its solid republicanism. Thus, one of the city's leading indicators of public opinion, the daily newspaper *Le Progrès,* vaunted the city's solid attachment to the Republic while editorializing on 29 January 1889 that "Paris must not be taken more seriously than a capricious child." At the time of the 1900 municipal elections, when a nationalist backlash swept Paris, *Le Progrès* returned to the same theme, editorializing, "While Paris returns to its first love, Boulangism, which is today called nationalism, Lyon still remains the old republican city, a beacon of French democracy."[4] Throughout the belle époque impressive statutes to the glory of the Republic were erected in conspicuous public places around the city. Squares and streets bearing the names of royalist and religious figures and institutions were replaced by names consistent with the republican and humanist sensibilities of the dominant social and political forces of the city.[5]

Parties and organizations representing conservative, antirepublican opinion were a distinct minority in Lyon. Reactionary, clerical, anti-Semitic parties and royalist forces had only a relatively ephemeral existence in the city. Their only real bastion of electoral strength was in the second arrondissement, which has remained a conservative stronghold to the present day.

The considerable breadth of Lyonnais republicanism was underscored by the fact that even local Catholic groups were prorepublican.[6] Perhaps more so than in other places, politics in Lyon were exemplary of the broad republican alliance. Behind the facade of cordial relations, however, centrifugal forces undermined the republican alliance and worker support for it. As we will see below, around 1906, the alliance began to pull apart in several places, reaching a climax around 1908.

The Radicals

Throughout most of its existence, the core of the Third Republic was the Radical Party, the political organization of broad layers of France's middle classes. It was through electoral collaboration between the Radical Party and the Guesdists and other socialist forces that the multiclass republican alliance was realized.

Perhaps even more than in most French cities, the radicals were the dominant political force in republican politics in Lyon. There as elsewhere they were far from being a homogenous political bloc. Numerous currents, ranging from a right wing barely distinguishable from the liberals, to a left wing close to the socialists, were all part of the loose political formation known as the Radical Party. Leo Loubère offered a useful breakdown of the various currents on the left of the party, which helps identify the fault lines and dynamics of the radical-socialist alliance.

Loubère identified a group of "left-wing radicals" (LWRs) who, during the first three decades of the Third Republic, "generally voted for legislation designed to improve the living standards of workers and all strongly championed labor's right to organize and strike." The LWRs were strongest in the legislature of 1885–1889 and weakest in those of 1877–1881 and 1889–1893.[7] Loubère identified three subcurrents among the left-wing radicals. "The hard core radical socialists" (HCRS) were those radical members of parliament "whose voting record attained a total of about 90 percent on bills and orders of the day of an advanced social nature." On many issues they were virtually indistinguishable from the socialists. They were never numerically strong. In the chamber of 1885–1889 they numbered sixty; in the legislature of 1889–1893, only thirty.[8]

Slightly to their right were the radical socialists (RS), whose voting record on progressive issues was 75 percent. "Among them were deputies whose stand for reform was about as consistent as the average socialist." Georges Clemenceau was part of this group. The right wing of the left-wing radicals, about twenty-five deputies, was known as social radicals or *radicaux de gauche* (SRs). Their voting record on progressive issues was 60 percent. The moderate or orthodox radicals were not LWRs. Loubère viewed them as left-wing liberals. The divisions among the LWRs often fluctuated. For example a given deputy might vote along with the HCRSs in one legislature, but produce a voting record closer to the radical-socialists in the next.[9]

The Alliance in Lyon

In the 1880s radical republicans in Lyon successfully recruited many workers and artisans to their cause. The various Third Republic Bloc des gauches radicals and reformist socialists always found a strong echo there. Victor Augagneur embodied this spirit even before the fifty-year reign of Edouard Herriot, the radical who became mayor in 1905. Augagneur had distinguished himself in 1898 as the only prominent local nonsocialist supporter of the revision of Dreyfus's trial. He was instrumental in putting together an electoral alliance of radicals, members of the Fédération autonome socialiste, and Guesdists that won 51 of 54 seats in the 1904 municipal elections.[10] Incidents like his support for Dreyfus and his refusal to attend a banquet in honor of President Loubet in November 1900 because it was hosted by the conservative, antirepublican Chamber of Commerce, and his hard line against the revolutionaries on his left in the Bourse du travail affair discussed below, underscore his radical-socialist convictions.

As was the case everywhere throughout France, the Dreyfus affair also had a large impact on the socialist movement in Lyon. A certain number of radicals like Colliard, the deputy of the sixth arrondissement, turned to socialism after becoming convinced of the innocence of Dreyfus. This moderate actively collaborated with the POF in the late 1890s, though he and other socialist office holders complained about what they saw as the sectarianism and overly strict organization of the POF; in 1900, they left to found the Fédération autonome du Rhône, local affiliate of the Parti socialiste français, founded by Jaurès in November of that year.[11]

The city's leading newspaper *Le Progrès* served as the public organ of republican sentiment. Its political coloration was summed up in the motto, "Neither reaction nor revolution." It was one of the rare newspapers in France to take a position in favor of Dreyfus, and more generally, partisan to progressive social reforms. The daily enthusiastically hailed the passage of the Millerand-Colliard law fixing the workday at eleven hours (a notable reform of the day). Though the "collectivist" charge hurled against the paper by clerical forces was far from accurate, *Le Progrès* was sufficiently left wing that it occasionally opposed radical republican electoral lists to its right and on occasion endorsed socialist electoral lists when the socialists where the sole republican force facing off against right-wing liberal forces. Such was the case in the 1900 municipal elections. In the industrial working-class district of La Guillotière, *Le Progrès* supported a republican list including socialists against another republican list, so moderate in the eyes of the daily, that it "played the game of reaction."[12]

Many socialist forces appreciated the *Progrès'* progressive stance. In the first issue published after resuming publication in 1929, the socialist weekly *L'Avenir Socialiste,* which had ceased publication on the eve of the war in 1914, explained that publication in the intervening years was not necessary as *Le Progrès* had reflected socialist political sensibilities.[13]

The organized political force behind this solid early Third Republic republicanism was a series of "central committees"—political clubs organized by arrondissement. Their primary task was to organize Radical Party activists and designate electoral lists for elections, especially for the municipal council. At the apex of Lyonnais politics and government was the mayoralty. Between 1881 and 1900 Antoine Gailleton occupied the mayor's office. A solid republican, Gailleton never presented himself as a socialist. In terms of the currents within the radical camp sketched out by Leo Loubère, Gailleton can perhaps be considered a Radical de gauche (SR), that is, a right-wing LWR. It was under the administration of Victor Augagneur, who unseated him in the 1900 municipal elections, that the grand alliance uniting the socialists of the POF and later SFIO with the radicals was forged.

Augagneur's association with socialists and the left of his own party dated from 1898 when he became the sole Lyonnais political figure apart from the socialists to endorse the statement of support for Emile Zola's campaign on behalf of Dreyfus that appeared in the *Progrès.* It was out of the Ligue des droits de l'homme and the Ligue de la défense républicaine of which Augagneur was one of the more prominent members, that the personnel of the Bloc républicain that brought Augagneur to power was formed. Augagneur successfully ran on a platform that included support for the government of Waldeck-Rousseau; suppression of the *octroi,* the local customs toll; and a pledge to raise the salaries of municipal employees as well as promises to improve substandard housing—a platform that closely resembled the POF program of 1891.[14]

At the end of his inauguration speech, he proclaimed "Vive la République démocratique et sociale," earning him the accolades of the socialist newspaper *Le Peuple,* which wrote that "he is one of ours even if he doesn't belong to one of our specialized schools."[15] The right-wing organ of clerical reaction, the *Salut Public,* responded to Augagneur's declaration by doubting that the new mayor could govern with "Jacobin principles."[16] A telegram sent by Augagneur's staff to President Emile Combes upon the reelection of the former in 1905 reflected the multiclass social and political tenor of his republicanism. It expressed the desire of the municipal council to see Combes "continue policies of a democratic nature and assuring the intellectual emancipation of the country by a struggle against the church and for the economic emancipation of the proletariat by the enactment of the necessary social laws."[17]

Once in office, Augagneur pursued an agenda of progressive reforms. Foremost among these was a progressive household tax, which the mayor considered as a precursor to a progressive income tax. Although the city council failed to approve the progressive tax and succeeded in watering it down to a proportional one, the measure—approved in June 1901—placed Lyon for many years in the vanguard in France in the domain of municipal fiscal policy.[18] Augagneur's suppression of the *octroi* was another notable reform appreciated by the socialists. During the campaign for the 1904 municipal elections, *Le Progrès* hailed the suppression of the *octroi,* which eliminated a direct tax that "struck above all, small consumers," as a great act of "social justice."[19] At the same time, his tough stand against the revolutionaries in the Bourse du travail underscored the limits of his left-wing leanings—an example of his adherence to the local republican notion of "neither reaction nor revolution."

The 1904 program of the Bloc républicain epitomizes the type of reformist politics that united radicals and socialists and appealed to the middle and working classes. Alongside proposals for the construction of a canal linking the Rhône in Lyon to the sea, tax relief for small businesses squeezed by the large department stores, and traditional public works of a charitable nature, was an explicit promise to "improve the condition of the working class," the organization of a bureau of labor statistics, elimination of placement bureaus, the construction of worker housing, and the suppression of the housing tax for rents under two hundred francs.[20]

In 1905, Lyon's political landscape was disrupted by the sudden departure of Mayor Augagneur, who accepted the post of governor of Madagascar for motives that remain unclear to this day.[21] Although some considered the reformist socialist Colliard as Augagneur's natural successor, the mayor assured that the city's top political office would remain in radical hands.[22]

His hand-picked choice was the young Edouard Herriot. He remained mayor of Lyon for the next fifty years, combining his local duties with those of deputy, minister, and later president of the council. As Herriot remained mayor throughout the period covered by this book, a careful assessment of his place along the republican spectrum is important.

In response to a conservative city councilor who reminded him that he had come to power partly as the result of liberal support, Herriot responded, "Elected out of the Republican Party, I will always defend the policies of the republican bloc and of the union of the left."[23] Herriot's speech at a major public meeting during the campaign for the 1908 municipal elections, published in its entirety in the *Progrès,* helps establish with more precision the tenor of his republicanism. The speech was a balance sheet of the accomplishments of his administration since assuming power in 1905. Most of the speech concerned the technical and administrative aspects of city government—sanitation, water management, the construction of bridges, and so on. A small portion of the speech was devoted to the political and social questions of which the politics of the Herriot administration in these years can be evaluated. Herriot reported plans for the establishment of a primary school for boys and girls where manual and occupational courses were to be offered. This involved a combination of primary and secondary instruction, which "all left republicans" favor. Along the same the lines, he spoke of plans to continue the secularization of all schools, especially in the clerical stronghold of the second arrondissement where progress in this area was slow. Herriot also announced the creation of fifty-two new teaching posts. In matters of a more direct social nature, Herriot was proud to report that the work day of city employees was eight hours; that of city manual workers, nine hours; and all enjoyed a full day off weekly. This was noteworthy at a time when most workers worked eleven hours a day. In the Croix-Rousse where unemployment had reached alarming proportions (this was the district where the traditional domestic labor of the *canuts* was being re-placed by the factory system), the municipality organized soup kitchens. He also announced plans for the construction of low-cost lodging for workers, reported that the Bourse du travail affair had been resolved, and spoke of the establishment of a municipal labor office.[24] Such a balance sheet placed the Herriot administration solidly in the camp of the LWRs, but it was considerably less left wing than the program upon which Victor Augagneur successfully ran on in 1904.

The political alliances established in Lyon between the Guesdists of the POF and the radicals in the 1900 municipal elections prefigured the for-mation of the nationwide Bloc des gauches that emerged during the 1902 legislative elections and lasted through the 1904 municipal elections. An examination of these elections reveals the dynamics of this alliance as well as the fortunes of the working-class forces that remained outside of it.

The 1900 municipal elections took place in a context of increasing tension within the radical-socialist alliance, although the cement holding it together was still solid. In the first round of the 1900 municipal elec-tions, the POF ran candidates on the same slates as the radicals in several of the city's arrondissements. For example, in the sixth arrondissement where Augagneur himself headed the Comité pour la défense républicain, Victor Darme, the president of the union of tramway employees and a prominent socialist, occupied the fourth slot, while Fagot, a worker and *conseiller prud'homme,* and Voillot, a cabinetmaker, were placed in the fifth and sixth positions. The considerable social breadth of the alliance was underscored by the presence of these working-class socialist activists alongside Roux, owner of a small mechanical construction shop, in the third position on the list.

The negotiations for the composition of the candidates' list for the third arrondissement were a bone of contention between the radicals and the POF. In this arrondissement, which was that of the working-class district of La Guillotière, the POF demanded three slots, which the radi-cals refused to grant. Feeling that they were on their own turf in this ar-rondissement, the Guesdists refused to desist in favor of the radicals in the second round in the tradition of republican discipline as they usually did, and presented their own slate.

Class independence, antipatriotic electoral politics had only an ephem-eral presence in the 1900 elections. The Blanquists presented their own slate in the third and fifth arrondissements. In the third they received 7.9 percent of the vote against 8.8 percent for the POF who, as we have seen, exceptionally refused an alliance with the radicals, who won 41.9 percent. In the fifth, the Blanquists received only 3.8 percent against the 39.8 percent registered by the radical-POF slate.

In the 1904 municipal elections, the local republican coalition led by Augagneur was even more solid than in 1900. From the first round, radicals and representatives of the Parti socialiste de France ran on the same lists in the third, fifth, and sixth arrondissements. Apart from the right, only the Vailliantistes of the Parti socialiste révolutionnaire and a small group of disaffected radicals ran separate lists. The results were a major political victory for Augagneur. In the third, fourth, and sixth arrondissements, the entire slate of the Bloc républicain et socialiste was elected. In the third, the bloc took 63.4 percent—the highest percentage in the city. In the second round, the bloc conquered the sole bastion of right-wing political strength—the second arrondissement. Socialists presented separate lists from those of the bloc in only one arrondissement, the second, where they received 16.7 percent of the vote. All told, the Bloc républicain et socialiste won fifty-one out of fifty-four seats in the city council that year, results that "surpassed the hopes" of the LWRs of *Le Progrès*.[25] The foundation of this coalition was the left-leaning program discussed above. A program of reforms that was truly in the Lyonnais spirit of "neither reaction nor revolution," the platform appeared to appeal to the needs and interests of the city's middle and working classes. On the national level this was the period when the Bloc des gauches used its parliamentary weight to carry out most of its program. Around the turn-of-the-century, worker pensions, the separation of church and state (1905), and factory legislation was passed.

Opposition to Alliance in Labor Movement

At the same time that the radical-socialist alliance became a reality, centrifugal forces worked to undermine it. As we shall see below, developments began to pull it apart around the period running from 1906 to 1908. Even before that the contradictions of the alliance had been exploited by the forces representing the class independence, antipatriotic current, which, although a minority current in the French workers' movement at this time, had a solid presence in France in general and Lyon in particular. The social and political basis for support for the class collaboration, patriotic current in working-class circles and the ways in which local factors favored the alliance have already been briefly outlined. Before examining how changes in the local political situation in Lyon led to the decline of the working class–middle class collaboration between the radicals, Guesdist and other socialist forces, and their trade union allies, it is worth pausing here to examine some of the national-level political factors that created political space for the class independence, antipatriotic current.

This was the period in the French labor movement when distrust of political parties and politicians by anarchists and revolutionary syndicalists was at its height. The relationship between unions and political parties was spelled out clearly at the first national congress of the CGT held in Limoges in 1895, in an amendment calling for the rejection of politics not only by the confederation but by its member organizations as well. The amendment passed by a vote of 124 to 14. The famous 1906 CGT Charter of Amiens, which reiterated this position, was the countermotion to a defeated resolution favorable to political action that had been introduced by veteran Guesdist textile union leader, Victor Renard.[26]

Anarchist and syndicalist railings against the inevitably corrupt nature of political parties and parliamentarianism and their pernicious effects on the workers' movement seemed to be vindicated by the scandals that shook fin-de-siècle France. In 1892 it was revealed that over one hundred members of parliament had been implicated in a bribery scandal concerning loans to construct the Panama Canal. The year before, the reputation of the Republic had been greatly tarnished by the massacre by government troops of an unarmed working-class crowd on May Day at Fourmies.

Perhaps the development that was most damaging to socialist efforts to win workers to their movement and overcome syndicalist suspicion of political parties was the entry of the socialist Alexander Millerand into a bourgeois cabinet in the Waldeck-Rousseau government in 1899. Participation in elections had been justified by the socialists as a way of bringing about pro–working-class legislation and eventually winning control of the state. However, joining a bourgeois-dominated cabinet was another matter. Anger and opposition over Millerand's action was heightened when it was learned that General Gallifet, one of the leaders of the repression of the Paris Commune, was also to be part of this cabinet. The socialists themselves were divided over this issue, with Jaurès defending Millerand's actions and Guesde strongly opposed. Although the French socialists, including Jaurès, later accepted the decision of the 1904 Amsterdam congress of the Socialist International to reaffirm socialist opposition to joining bourgeois governments, the incident reinforced revolutionary syndicalist claims as to the inherently corrupt nature of parliamentary participation. And as we have seen, incidents of this sort undermined the revolutionary pretensions of French socialists in general.

Once in office, Millerand attempted to bring about progressive legislation concerning workers' issues. Revolutionary syndicalists responded with a campaign to discredit the strategy of securing pro-worker legislation, opposing any laws that claimed to do so. George Yvetot had argued, "All laws are made by the bourgeois" and that laws, "even the best, are worthless." For example, he cited the law legalizing unions, which was "nothing other than the permission given to workers to unionize when they already are." With a bitter and ironic tone he reviewed the 1889 law on accidents, which, after eighteen years of discussion and debate, was useless, and the law prohibiting night work for women and children, "universally applied ... except by the bosses who demand and are granted exceptions to the law when it suits them, or who easily defy it thanks to the corruption of labor inspectors." The same could be said, he continued, for the ten-hour law, and "the law on worker retirement was a swindle."[27] The meager record of Third Republic social legislation helped to fill the sails of syndicalist propaganda. The law abolishing the worker passport, the *livret ouvrier,* was passed only after nine years of debate, and thirteen years were needed to pass the poorly enforced law limiting work hours for women and children.[28]

All of this worked to the advantage of revolutionary syndicalists and the socialists who remained outside of the radical-socialist alliance. In Lyon the contradictions of the local alliances linking middle-class politicians with labor activists also gave rise to sharp battles and realignments within Lyon's labor movement. One of the most noteworthy of these was a conflict over the local Bourse du travail. From 1886 on, municipal governments throughout France began to subsidize Bourses du travail for unions. By 1910, 103 bourses were receiving 355,000 francs of municipal subventions and 52,000 francs from the departments, plus free rent and maintenance in local public buildings.[29] But the national government used its power of the purse against the more militant bourses. In 1905 Clemenceau cancelled subsidies for bourses in Lyon, Lille, La Rochelle, and other places.

In Lyon, municipal subsidies to the bourses became a bone of contention between revolutionaries and reformists. In 1891, the future mayor, Victor Augagneur, led a struggle in the city council against revolutionary worker militants. He accused bourse leaders of wasting money by paying the travel expenses of certain union leaders. In 1892, the city government suspended the salaries of bourse personnel and closed its offices for six months.[30] This "municipal interference was driven by the Gailleton and Augagneur administration's fear of anarchist and revolutionary socialist ideas."[31]

In 1905, a conflict broke out between radical-socialist Mayor Augagneur, and revolutionary syndicalists. The immediate cause of the conflict involved the use of the bourse for benefit concerts for strikers and infirm union militants. Augagneur claimed that the modest entrance fee of 30 centimes contravened city regulations. He cancelled the 10,000-franc municipal subsidy to the bourse, which effectively prevented it from functioning. According to union militants this was only a pretext. A long struggle had begun earlier when unionists refused to turn over lists of bourse members as demanded by the Augagneur administration.[32] The conflict later led to the expulsion of the Fédération des syndicats du Sud-Est and the offending unions.[33] The police at Augagneur's request carried out the expulsion on 4 October 1905. The unionists left the bourse singing the "Internationale."[34] The majority of the unions left at that time, but about a quarter of them took the side of Augagneur and maintained their affiliation with the bourse. Nationally known syndicalist leaders like Victor Griffuelhes and Georges Yvetot publicly supported the position of the Union locale.[35]

The ninth congress of the CGT decided to expel from its ranks those who remained with the Bourse du travail and recognized only the Union locale as representatives of the Fédération des syndicats du Sud-Est.[36] While the "clash in Lyon between reformist and revolutionary syndicalists occurred often within each union," it is notable that among those who immediately signaled their fidelity to the CGT were the silk dyers and mechanical weavers.[37] In the following period, however, some unions that had become discouraged by the results of the unsuccessful strikes for the eight-hour day and were attracted by the prospect of municipal subsidies returned to the Bourse du travail, which grouped together fifty unions by 1 June 1905.[38] The success of the 1906 May Day demonstration initially benefited the revolutionary unions of the Union locale. However, the defeats suffered by these unions in the period immediately following May Day checked this trend to the advantage of the reformist unions affiliated to the Bourse du travail.[39]

From 1907 on, the increasing influence that reformists enjoyed within the Bourse du travail reflected a larger trend involving a sharp decline of revolutionary syndicalist influence throughout France. The 1906 May Day demonstrations, designed to win the eight-hour day through either a cataclysmic general strike or a mass refusal of workers to continue work after eight hours, succeeded in frightening the bourgeois public and launching the largest strike wave in France ever up until that point. Class tension in Lyon was particularly sharp around May Day 1906. Following a meeting where six thousand workers listened to revolutionary speeches, angry crowds broke the windows of tramways and factories in La Guillotière. Ten thousand workers were still on strike on the fourth of May.[40] However, the poor coordination of the strike and its failure to win the eight-hour day for most workers, coupled with an increasingly hostile and repressive climate afterwards, signaled both the apogee and the end of revolutionary syndicalism's' *age d'or*. The mobilizations of May 1906 amounted to an authentic meeting of revolutionary militants and a large fraction of the working class. From then on, the influence of revolutionary syndicalism among workers declined as the movement became quite marginalized. Subsequent May Day mobilizations afterwards fell considerably short of that of 1906.

The bourse split did not last long. By 1907, Lyonnais unionists "drew the lesson of worker division" and worked for a "tacit accord with the Bourse du travail for the realization of a minimum of unity in action."[41] Shortly afterwards, a fusion took place between the Bourse du travail and the Union locale. The revolutionaries apparently were too isolated to remain outside. The new organization was named the Union des Chambres Syndicals du Départment du Rhône (USDR), a member of the CGT.[42] At this point the "situation of Lyonnais syndicalism appears therefore to be clarified. The Bourse du travail would administer union services (placement bureaus, courses, libraries, etc.) and participate in local actions. The Union départmentale could implement CGT decisions and coordinate union propaganda among all the unions of the Rhône. The unions of Lyon would belong to two organizations, membership in the UDSR implying membership in the CGT."[43] The Bourse du travail remained firmly in reformist hands. During the years 1907–1911, no antimilitarist or revolutionary propaganda emanated from the Lyon Bourse du travail.[44] The Bourse du travail affair, while initially shaking the radical-socialist alliance, did not, however, end it. Likewise, the reformist/class collaborationist current in the local labor movement remained hegemonic.

Decline of Alliance

The political and social unity that underpinned the radical-socialist alliance at the end of the nineteenth and beginning of the twentieth centuries soon gave way to mutual suspicion and fear, which in turn translated into a loosening of the electoral alliance. By the time of the 1908 municipal elections, the Bloc des gauches was virtually finished. In January 1904, the center of gravity within the bloc nationally shifted to the right as an influential number of radicals looked to consolidate their ties with the business community and reduce their ties with the socialists.[45] In January 1905, a large group of socialist and LWR deputies refused to cast a vote of confidence for the new prime minister, Maurice Rouvier, a conservative radical who was hostile to an income tax. Half of the 373 votes he did receive came from the right and from right-wing radicals, a development that has led historian Madeleine Rébérioux to conclude that from that moment, "the bloc was dead in parliament."[46]

The backdrop to these parliamentary developments was a climate of increasing class tension throughout the country and the contradictions of the alliance noted above. Strikes became increasingly frequent. One out of every sixteen industrial workers struck in 1906. Conservative public opinion was especially alarmed by the novelty of strikes among public sector workers from 1905 on. The connections between class and politics were brought out in bold relief in 1906 when the largest strike wave that France had ever experienced up to that point coincided with the CGT May Day campaign for the general strike and the eight-hour day in a year of important legislative elections. The vicious repression meted out to striking workers by the government of ex-LWR Georges Clemenceau in these years served to associate the radicals with bourgeois repression, rather than the policies of social reform, in the eyes of French workers.

Developments within French socialism also contributed to the gradual decline of the radical-socialist alliance. In 1905 the main factions of French socialism including those led by Jules Guesde and Jean Jaurès united into the SFIO on the basis of the resolutions of the Amsterdam congress of 1904. That congress took a firm stand against socialist participation in bourgeois governments and as we have seen, the new Guesdists had earlier held the line against the most extreme expression of class collaborationism.

Local developments also contributed to the decline of the radical-socialist alliance in Lyon. We have already reviewed the conflict between the Augagneur administration and the militants of the Bourse du travail. Augagneur and radical municipal councilors joined with reformist trade unions in a *bras de fer* with the revolutionaries in the city's labor movement. This underscored the alliance between reformist trade unions and the mayor, as well as the isolation of the unions led by revolutionaries.

At the same time, however, the radicals were betraying their socialist allies in Lyon. The local SFIO weekly, *L'Avenir socialiste,* featured an article to this effect in its first issue of 23 February 1907, entitled "The failure of radicalism." Here the newspaper railed against radical politicians who, faced with the choice of supporting a reactionary or a candidate of the SFIO, would not hesitate to support the reactionary. In April, the socialists publicly protested against the alliance of radicals and "independent" socialists (those who stayed out of the SFIO at the time of the unification) against the city employees' union.[47] For the socialists the radical government of Georges Clemenceau carried out the dirty work of the reactionaries to the point that it was no longer possible to distinguish between radicals and nationalists.[48] The alliance was showing signs of strain.

This was the context in which the 1908 municipal elections were held. From the first round socialists and radicals presented separate lists. In an article entitled "Autre Temps," SFIO leader J. Marietton recalled that four years earlier the political situation had allowed an alliance from the first round between the radicals and the socialists. At that time, the government seemed to be "vigorously engaged" on the road of reform. In addition, "the still threatening reaction imposed unity on the most varied elements of the republican army." In 1908, however, the Socialist Party was the only force sincerely fighting for reforms.[49] In Lyon this split in republican ranks revealed the electoral weakness of the SFIO while only slightly weakening the electoral strength of the radicals. In the first round, the SFIO failed to receive more than 25 percent of the vote in any arrondissement, including the third arrondissement, in spite of a vigorous campaign involving ten public meetings (as usual, it was here where the socialists polled their best score). In the second round the SFIO only managed to elect socialist leader Etienne Rognon as municipal councilor in La Guillotière. The SFIO complained about the influence of revolutionary syndicalist propaganda, which it held responsible for the high rate of abstentions in the quarter (41.3 percent abstained—the highest in the city). The old bloc, now reduced to the radicals and the "independent" socialists, won forty seats. This split in republican forces allowed the right-wing liberals to regain lost ground in their fief of the second arrondissement. In the aftermath of the elections, *L'Avenir Socialiste* placed the blame for the split squarely on the shoulders of the "stupidly reactionary policies of Monsieur Clemenceau."[50] As always, *Le Progrès* lamented the intrarepublican divisions that allowed the right to make progress. The daily regretted that the socialists didn't make common cause with the radicals from the first round. It had sharper words for the radicals for having refused to grant the SFIO the places it requested on what would have been the lists of the old bloc. After all, wrote the *Progrès,* the danger was from the right, not the left. On the other hand, the more conservative republican daily, the *Lyon Républicain,* congratulated the radicals for being "definitively cured of their alliance with the revolutionaries."[51]

Throughout the remaining years of the prewar period, the gap between the radicals and the socialists widened. During the 1910 legislative elections, distrust was high as the socialists complained that the radicals betrayed them after having accepted SFIO support during the previous senatorial elections. In 1913, the SFIO campaign against the law raising military service from two to three years served as a further point of conflict between the SFIO and other republican forces. Local party militants vocally took up this national SFIO campaign. In general, the tone of the Lyon socialists against Herriot became harder throughout the prewar period.[52] Although the SFIO position on the radicals did not prevent it from calling for a vote for them in the second round as in 1914 when they applied this policy to their old ally turned nemesis, Victor Augagneur, the alliance was clearly over.

World War I

World War I signaled a very broad social and political alliance in the name of national defense. The collaboration of labor organizations and socialist politicians with middle-class and bourgeois political forces reached unprecedented heights while the class independence political current was marginalized as never before. But towards the end of the war their fortunes began to reverse as political developments once again pulled the wartime coalition apart, creating new space for the class independence, antinationalist current.

With the passing of the initial phase of chaos and disorganization, the manpower needs of the general staff in the trenches and the need to find workers for the war industries created a labor shortage. By "the end of 1916, union activity—half asleep since the beginning of the war—sharply resumed."[53] There were 315 strikes in France in 1916.[54] The pace picked up considerably in the spring of 1917. The first mutinies of soldiers at the front took place between 4 May and 20 June of that year.

Demands for peace began to appear as part of labor protest in the spring of 1917. The highly charged nature of the period has been often evoked by novelists and historians. Enflamed passions and incendiary articles found a reflection in the repression meted out to opponents of the war. In Lyon, police searched the headquarters of the anarchist-led group the Nid rouge in March 1917.[55] Local antiwar activists Calzan, Cuminal, and Henri Michon were jailed in 1918. In February 1918, Jeanne Chevenard announced at a union meeting that the unionist Marion had been arrested for distributing antiwar leaflets. In the high-tension month of June 1918, unionists suspected that the searches of union leaders and union premises were part of a plot by Clemenceau to implicate Bécirard and Jeanne Chevenard in the sedition trial of Raymond Pericat.[56] While Branche's June 1917 allusion to the peace movement in a union meeting created a certain anxiety in labor ranks fearful of repression, such references became increasingly frequent. A meeting on 11 December 1917 of the intertrade commission (Comité intercorporatif) made up of industries working for the war ended with the cry, "Down with the war!"[57] During union meetings in May 1918, Jeanne Chevenard and Garin told strikers that the goal was peace.[58]

Jean-Jacques Becker and Serge Bernstein point to the November 1917 strikes in arms factories in Saint-Etienne as the first in the country that combined demands for peace with union demands.[59] Evidence shows that shortly thereafter, open antiwar demands in Lyon became integrated with labor struggles whose origins were centered on questions of wages, hours, and working conditions. At a union meeting on 8 June 1918, the socialist antiwar activist Branche took the floor to explain that the strikers must not only demand wage hikes but also call for support to the pacifist conference organized in Stockholm.[60] By May 1918 the large strikes that took place in Saint-Etienne, Lyon, Paris, and other centers of arms production were dominated solely by demands for peace; wage demands had dropped out of sight and support for the Russian revolution was common.[61]

The conditions created by the war, especially the challenges faced by labor militants confronted by employers working with a government enjoying the support of the CGT and socialist leadership, led to novel forms of organization. In the trade union movement, the Lyon-based Union départmentale syndicaux, one of the first UDSs established in France, became a bastion of opposition to the pro–Sacred Union policies of the CGT leadership. In order to coordinate activity between workers in the various plants producing for the war effort, a Comité intersyndical (CI) was founded on 26 July 1917 on the initiative of leading metal worker unionists Garin and Bécirard. Its activity attracted the ire of the employers. In December 1917 local industrialist Tobie Robatel wrote to the prefect of the Rhône on behalf of a group of fifty industrialists throughout the region producing for the war effort that the CI "appeared clearly revolutionary" and would likely serve as a future strike committee.[62]

One of the most original and controversial forms of labor organization created during the war was the délégués d'ateliers, or shop stewards, instituted on 5 February 1917 by undersecretary for munitions Albert Thomas to assure an orderly transmission of labor demands that the government hoped would reduce labor strife to a minimum. French labor historians Jean Bron and Max Gallo have written that workers mistrusted the shop steward system and often refused to participate in the elections held to choose the delegates.[63] Whatever the situation in the rest of the country or the original intentions of the government, the shop steward system in Lyon was unmistakably an apparatus for mobilizing workers. In fact, they organized far more workers in the war industries than the unions themselves. The shop stewards turned out to be effective tools for labor in the struggle around wages and working conditions in the war industries. As such, they were bitterly opposed by the largest arms producers; Rochet-Schneider, Robatel, and especially Berliet all resisted recognition of the shop delegates. Police reports of the meetings of the delegates repeatedly recorded the resentment of workers at Berliet's refusal in particular to recognize them and the determination of militant metal workers to force the company to come to terms with them.[64] In January 1918 it was the employers who complained that the delegates were surpassing their intended role, and demanded that they be abolished.[65]

The period of intense strikes and social agitation that marked the last period of the war continued well past the signing of the armistice in November 1918. In fact, far from calming social tensions, the postwar situation was cause for bitter protests. "Though the French aspired, after the miseries of the war, to return to the joys of life in a society of abundance, they had to confront high wages and shortages. The return of peace did not function as a magic wand instantly returning production to its prewar levels."[66] For example, industrial production at the beginning of 1919 was only 55 percent of what it had been in 1913. This declined to 50 percent by July 1921. Rising prices were fueled by the low rate of production as well as the large amount of money in circulation.[67] Coal for heating dwellings, butter, and eggs were difficult to come by, and prices for sugar and meat were so high that they became a luxury for working-class households.[68] Tensions were further increased by the reluctance of the government to demobilize French soldiers and sailors. Part of the reason for government foot dragging on this issue was the Allied plans to crush the Bolshevik-led government in Russia. Committed revolutionaries and many workers opposed allied intervention, while many other workers and peasants in uniform and their anxious families simply wanted the conscripts to come home. Other government measures like the 5 April acquittal of Raoul Villain, Jaurès' assassin, further heightened class antagonisms.

This was the background to the wave of strikes, demonstrations, and mutinies that shook France through May 1920. The period can be divided into an initial phase of offensive worker-mobilization strike success. In this period (from the spring of 1919 to roughly the fall of that year), revolutionaries exerted much influence in the local national and international arenas. A second round of struggles began with the two-phase railroad strike in winter 1919–spring of 1920, which ended in defeat.

The social climate was particularly heated in the spring of 1919. On 19 April, sailors of the French fleet in the Black Sea mutinied. André Marty and Charles Tillon, two leaders of the mutinies, later became leaders of the Communist Party. At the same time, CGT membership expanded dramatically, reaching 1 million in 1919 including 200,000 metal workers organized in the Federation of Metals. By the beginning of 1920 the confederation claimed 1,600,000 members.[69]

On 23 April 1919, Clemenceau's bill guaranteeing the old worker demand for the eight-hour day was passed. This was both a result of pressure from below and an attempt to demobilize workers on the eve of May Day.[70] Sharp struggles around this issue continued when it became clear that the law was largely ignored by French employers. The social climate and the clashes that occurred on May Day, 1919, have been compared to the acute social polarization of 1906.[71] In Paris, police and mounted soldiers attacked demonstrating workers. One of the most impressive May Day worker mobilizations was in Lyon where, according to the *Progrès,* it was the "first time that all worker corporations" deserted their workplaces to peacefully march in spite of a torrential rain.[72] 70,000 workers struck and 18,000 took part in the demonstration that demanded the eight-hour day, a general amnesty, and a halt to intervention in Russia. The eight-hour day was the central demand that united Lyon's workers. A statement signed by the Union des syndicats du Rhône and the Bourse du travail that appeared in the 24 April 1919 edition of *Le Prolétaire lyonnais* solemnly proclaimed that the "proletariat of our great industrial city will powerfully demonstrate with dignity its will to bring about the eight-hour day."

The May Day demonstration itself was only one component of worker agitation around this question. In Lyon, a series of strikes centered on the metal trades demanding the implementation of the eight-hour day as well as wage increases began at this time. Between 29 April and 28 June, metal workers in eleven shops and factories employing from 20 to 310 workers including semiskilled machine operatives and skilled workers, men and women, struck to demand wage increases and the eight-hour day. In at least seven of these strikes, workers actually won the eight-hour day and in three others they succeeded in winning the forty-eight-hour "English week" consisting of time off from Saturday afternoon to Monday morning. A general strike of the city's 1,300 male and female textile workers working for 247 different employers successfully struck between 12 May and 16 June for the eight-hour day.[73]

The large-scale mobilizations of May and June led revolutionaries in the CGT, especially metal workers, to envision the possibility of an insurrectionary general strike. The date of 21 July was fixed for an international strike following a complicated series of interfederal discussions and correspondence with English and Italian trade unions. The official demands of the poorly planned strike included the end of French intervention in Russia and Hungary. Its organizers hoped that if successful, the one-day strike would continue on to the taking of power. In Lyon, meetings of the Union des syndicats du Rhône (USR) and the committee for the Third International were held on the days leading up to the 21 July. A meeting of the members of the union bureaus on 12 July reflected both lack of confidence in the English workers' revolutionary capacity and local enthusiasm for the action; some meeting participants wished to extend the official scope of the strike to two or three days rather than the planned twenty-four hours. The militants of the Committee for the Third International seemed to have less confidence in the mass character of the strike. A meeting of the committee on 16 July rejected a proposition to print posters aimed at the broad masses in favor of a more modest effort of printing and distributing five thousand leaflets of "Bolshevik propaganda" aimed at advanced workers. As it turned out the strike was canceled at the last minute by the CGT, although certain sectors struck regardless.[74] As we will see the mutual recriminations between revolutionaries and reformists around this strike was part of the background to the split in the trade union movement in late 1921.

The next round of labor struggle began the following February with the beginning of the first of the two railroad strikes of the winter-spring of 1920. The strike was sparked by disciplinary action taken against a rail worker unionist at Villeneuve-Saint-Georges. At the origin of the conflict were job issues as well as political reasons. The railroad workers demanded recognition of union status involving delegate rights with the companies. The rail workers who suffered from the incessant raising of the cost of living demanded a minimum wage and the cost of living bonuses that the government had granted to all other functionaries.[75] By 25 February, rail service was greatly reduced and the companies were threatening to fire strikers. The ministry of public works denounced the strike as a revolutionary undertaking with no workplace ramifications. On 1 March, however, an agreement was hammered out including the institution of a sliding scale of wages and recognition of union delegates. In Lyon, the strike was the first in the railroads since 1910. Daily meetings brought out large numbers of strikers, including the four thousand workers who rallied on 2 March.[76] The next day workers returned to work after having been assured that strike days would be paid and that they would not be subject to disciplinary action. While the revolutionaries of *La Vie ouvrière* considered the outcome as a "shameful victory," the PLM strikers at Oullins were pleased with the outcome.[77]

The first railroad strike overlapped with a long strike of Lyonnais metal workers and textile workers. The metal strike lasted from 9 February to 29 March. The strike involved 10,000 metal workers out of a total of 12,500 in the city from 540 of the city's 550 metal working establishments (only workers from Berliet and several small shops did not participate). Leading metal union activist Antoine Garin called it a "partial victory" when workers voted to resume work on 28 March.[78]

The recriminations between reformists and revolutionaries in the railroad unions and the CGT were an important component of the overall situation leading up to the second railroad strike that spring. More generally, very different motives lay behind the second strike: the regret of railroad workers at not having pushed the February strike further and the desire of the CGT majority to flex its muscles and impose nationalization.[79] The federation of railroad workers and the CGT agreed on a plan that would involve successive waves of strikes by miners, sailors, and dockers to paralyze the economy. The strike was planned to coincide with May Day. In Lyon, the leaders of the Rhône Socialist Federation, who were members of the party's revolutionary wing, gave full support to the May Day events organized by the unions.[80] Throughout France "May Day demonstrations were exceptionally large."[81] Nationwide, 220,000 rail workers walked off the job. By 10 May, the strike reached its height. Four hundred thousand metal workers, miners, and dockers joined the railroad workers. In Lyon, the PLM shops came out in force on the morning of 1 May. The tramways were completely idled from 11 to 16 May. The city's striking printers prevented newspapers from appearing from 17 to 23 May. Metal workers in 400 of the city's 550 metal working establishments struck as well. In meetings like the one reported in a 13 May police report, Garin told one thousand striking metal workers that workers must take over the reins of power like their counterparts in Russia.[82]

There were weaknesses in these strikes as well, however. While nationally 220,000 railroad workers participated, another 230,000 did not. The government skillfully manipulated public opinion against the strikers and raised the specter of foreign influence behind the strikes. Pierre Monatte, Gaston Monmousseau, and others were arrested. On 11 May, Alexandre Millerand took steps to dissolve the CGT.

Matters were no easier for the strikers in Lyon. In spite of its impressive beginnings, the Oullins strike faced difficulties. Devoted militants expressed doubts as to the success of the strike, and its organization was inferior to that of the earlier work stoppage. At the height of the strike on 10 May, the police commissioner telegraphed the prefect of the Rhône requesting troops to guard against an insurrection that revolutionaries were supposedly planning in the event that the second wave of strikes called by the CGT failed. The next day, violent clashes occurred between strikers and nonstrikers. On 12 May the company closed down the shops, which were converted into barracks to house soldiers. Defections from the ranks of the strikers became increasingly numerous. By the time the strike ended at the end of the month, eleven strikers had been jailed; seven subsequently received prison terms. Two hundred and fifty workers were fired by the company including all the members of the union committee; nationally, 18,000 rail workers lost their jobs. The local union was decimated. Only 150 members remained out of nearly 3,000 from before the strike. The local sympathy strikes were not without their problems either.[83] The metal strikes led by the revolutionary leaders of the city's metal unions were far from general. Only 800 out of 12,500 skilled workers, 1,900 of 15,000 unskilled, as well as 300 of the city's 2,500 foundry workers joined the strike.[84]

Indeed, the government and the employers had carefully prepared for these strikes. For months the government had conducted extensive opinion polls in order to measure the balance of forces by sector and region and dispatched troops in accordance with its findings. The employers deliberately provoked these strikes by ostentatiously refusing to apply the accords agreed upon during the February–March strikes.[85] In the aftermath, CGT membership dramatically declined. "In several weeks in the second semester of 1920 membership dropped from 1,600,000 to 900,000 and then to 700,000 in 1921," although CGT membership still remained higher than in 1914.[86]

Conclusion

We conclude this chapter by analyzing this review of the Third Republic's POS until 1921 in terms of POS theory. Following Doug Adam, we can view this in terms of (1) the relative openness or closure of the institutionalized political system, (2) the stability or instability of that broad set of elite alignments that typically under grid a polity, (3) the presence or absence of elite allies, and (4) the state's capacity and propensity for repression.[87]

We have seen that a broad republican political alliance united radicals and socialists for the first several decades of the Third Republic, as well as the dynamics that eventually led to the decline of that alliance. We have seen how politics in Lyon paralleled the national political scene as a whole. At the same time, however, Lyon diverged somewhat from the national model. Throughout much of the prewar period, a progressive, militant republican sentiment dominated the city to a greater extent than was the case in Paris, for example. As elsewhere, the radical-socialist alliance was founded on the key political questions of fin-de-siècle France: secularism and the Dreyfus affair. Both of these issues were important in Lyon. The left-leaning radical Victor Augagneur first made contact with socialist forces through his engagement in the Dreyfus affair. This placed him at the head of the left republican movement in a city where clerical reaction was a vocal, but isolated opposition to the city's dominant republicanism. The radical-socialist alliance was built on the basis of a solid left-wing republicanism that was free of any "collectivist" tinge that would have frightened middle-class public opinion, but sufficiently progressive to appeal to working-class voters. Friendly, mildly reformist radical-led national governments that brought about real, if limited, reforms and the willingness of local radicals to include socialists on their electoral lists also facilitated the alliance. This suggests, at least until 1905, both a great stability of elite alignments as well as the presence of elite allies in control of the government who enacted modest but real reforms in exchange for working-class votes. Universal male suffrage, limited restrictions on the press, and limited judicial and police repression made the Third Republic a relatively open institutionalized political system, at least for those who confined their social and political opposition to the electoral and propaganda realms.

But, after 1905, the alliance began to crack. On the national level, the increasingly repressive policies towards strikers of the radical government of the former left-wing republican George Clemenceau repelled working-class voters who began to associate the radicals with capitalist repression rather than with benevolent reforms. Behind the shift of many radical deputies toward the right was a political climate in which the Republic, although still not supported by reactionary groups in France, was solidly established, thus removing a major raison d'être for the alliance. In Lyon, local and national developments combined to undermine the alliance after 1905. The radicals became less generous in granting slots to the socialists on their electoral slates, and began to look to their right for allies. The Bourse du travail affair and the constitution of an SFIO minus the right wing of the local socialist movement that remained outside of the new party served to both isolate left-wing socialists and allow them to set the tone of local socialist politics.

From 1908 on, the rightward drift of the Radical Party seen through its increasingly repressive actions and its search for allies on its right made the alliance untenable and forced the SFIO to rely on its own electoral weight at election time. The results were quite modest. The party was routinely beaten by the radicals and other republican forces. It also believed itself to be handicapped by the large number of abstentions, which it attributed to the strength of revolutionary syndicalist propaganda although the latter was a minority current. In any event, the days when working-class organizations were able to present themselves as a powerful political force independent of the middle-class parties were still to come.

These last years of the prewar Republic therefore signaled a change in POS. The decline of the socialist-radical alliance signaled a lessening presence of elite allies, and the repression of strikes and demonstrations revealed a more repressive republican regime. These trends were vastly accelerated during the war and immediate postwar period when the government enforced the repression of antiwar activity and instituted harsh labor discipline in the factories.

This political opportunity structure affected the ability of various currents to implement their programs, strategies, and tactics as well as their success in attracting different occupational groups to their banners. But it did so through interaction with the industrial social relations discussed in chapter 2 because ISR affected the attractiveness of each of the two currents for various occupational groups experiencing different patterns of ISR. In the next two chapters we will view how the specific ISR and POS of silk and metal workers actually shaped their political identities during the period 1900–1921.

Notes

1. Madeleine Réberioux, *La République radicale? 1898–1914* (Paris, 1975), 44.
2. George Lefranc, *Le mouvement syndical sous la Troisième République* (Paris, 1967), 50.
3. Alain Dewerpe, *Le monde du travail en France.* (Paris, 1989), 129.
4. *Le Progrès,* 15 May 1900.
5. Françoise Bayard and Pierre Cayez, eds., *Histoire de Lyon des origines à nos jours* (Lyon, 1991), 351–53.
6. George Lefranc, *Le mouvement socialiste sous la Troisième République* (Paris, 1963), 177–79.
7. Leo Loubère, "The Left-Wing Radicals and the Military, 1880–1907," *French Historical Studies* 2 (1966): 93.
8. Leo Loubère, "The French Left-Wing Radicals: Their Views on Trade Unions, 1870–1898." *International Review of Social History* 7, no. 2 (1962): 203–4.
9. Ibid.
10. Bayard and Cayez, *Histoire de Lyon,* 355.
11. Robert Chagny, "La presse socialiste à Lyon, 1896–1914," (Master's thesis, University of Lyon, 1960), 37.
12. *Le Progrès,* 4 May 1900.
13. *L'Avenir socialiste,* 9 August 1929.
14. Bayard and Cayez, *Histoire de Lyon,* 362; Jacques Prévosto, "Les élections municipales à Lyon de 1900 à 1908," *Revue historique du sud-est* 14, no. 3 (1979): 52.
15. *Le Peuple,* 21 May 1900.
16. *Le Salut Public,* 1 June 1900.
17. Guy Lapperière, *La séparation à Lyon, 1904–1908.* (Lyon, 1973), 80.
18. Bayard and Cayez, *Histoire de Lyon,* 362.
19. *Le Progrès,* 24 April 1904.
20. *Le Progrès,* 25 April 1905.
21. Bayard and Cayez, *Histoire de Lyon,* 363.
22. Lefranc, *Le mouvement socialiste,* 178.
23. Bayard and Cayez, *Histoire de Lyon,* 364.
24. *Le Progrès,* 18 April 1908.
25. *Le Progrès,* 2 May 1904.
26. Lefranc, *Le mouvement socialiste,* 138.
27. Quoted in Lefranc, *Le mouvement socialiste,* 98.
28. Jean Bron, *Histoire du mouvement ouvrier français* (Paris, 1970), 93.
29. Val Lorwin, *The French Labor Movement* (Cambridge, MA, 1954), 39–40.
30. David Rappe, *La Bourse du travail de Lyon* (Lyon, 2004), 27–29.
31. R. Chevailler, B. Girardon, V. T. Nguyen, and B. Rochaix, *Lyon: Les traboules du mouvement ouvrièr* (Paris, 1980), 105.
32. *La Depèche,* January 1905.

33. Jacques Leschiera, "Les débuts de la CGT à Lyon, 1890–1914," (Master's thesis, University of Lyon, 1972), 63.
34. Chevailler et al., *Les traboules,* 106.
35. Leschiera, "Les débuts," 66.
36. Ibid., 67.
37. Ibid., 67 and 75.
38. Ibid., 65.
39. Ibid., 76.
40. Ibid., 72.
41. Ibid., 88.
42. Ibid., 89.
43. Ibid., 90.
44. Ibid., 100.
45. Réberioux, *La République radicale?* 107.
46. Ibid., 108.
47. *L'Avenir socialiste,* 16 November 1907.
48. *L'Avenir socialiste,* 8 December 1907.
49. *L'Avenir socialiste,*16 May 1908.
50. *L'Avenir socialiste,* 16 April 1908.
51. Quoted in Prévosto, "Les élections municipales," 62.
52. *L'Avenir socialiste,* 6–9 July 1910.
53. Jean-Jacques Becker and Serge Bernstein, *Histoire de la France du vingtième siècle* (Paris, 1994), 109.
54. René Mouriaux, *La CGT, crises et alternatives* (Paris, 1982), 53.
55. Claire Auzias, *Mémoires libertaires: Lyon 1919–1939* (Paris, 1993), 62.
56. ADR 10Mp/C/59.
57. ADR 10Mp/C/57.
58. ADR 10Mp/C/59.
59. Becker and Bernstein, *Histoire de la France,* 121.
60. ADR 10Mp/C/59.
61. Becker and Bernstein, *Histoire de la France,* 128.
62. ADR 10Mp/C/58.
63. Bron, *Histoire,* 22–23; Max Gallo, "Quelques aspects de la mentalité et du comportement ouvrier dans les usines de guerre, 1914–1918." *Le mouvement sociale,* no. 56. (1966): 3–33.
64. I found half a dozen complaints of this nature expressed in meetings recorded in police reports in December 1917 and January 1918. ADR 10/Mp/C59.
65. ADR 10/Mp/C59.
66. Becker and Bernstein, *Histoire de la France,* 181.
67. Ibid., 181–82.
68. Ibid.
69. See Jean-Louis Robert, "1914–1920," in *La France ouvrière,* ed. Claude Willard (Paris, 1995) 1:442, and Edouard Dolléans, *Histoire du mouvement ouvrier* (Paris, 1967), 298.
70. Dolléans, *Histoire,* 298–99; Becker and Bernstein, *Histoire de la France,* 183–84; Robert, "1914–1920," 441.
71. Dolléans, *Histoire,* 300.
72. *Le Progrès,* 2 May 1919.
73. ADR 10/Mp/C65.
74. Ibid.
75. Dolléans, *Histoire,* 159.
76. Christian Chevandier, *Cheminots en usine, les ouvriers des ateliers d'Oullins au temps de la vapeur* (Lyon, 1993), 226.

77. Chevandier, *Cheminots en usine*, 228.
78. ADR 10Mp/C/65.
79. Dolléans, *Histoire,* 332.
80. ADR 10Mp/C/65.
81. Dolléans, *Histoire,* 333.
82. ADR 10/Mp/C65.
83. Ibid.
84. Jean-Luc Pinol, "Les origines du communisme à Lyon," (Master's thesis, University of Lyon, 1972), 311.
85. Robert, "1914–1920," 447.
86. Ibid., 448.
87. Doug McAdam, "Conceptual Origins, Current Problems, Future Directions," in *Comparative Perspectives on Social Movements,* ed. Doug McAdam, John D. McCarthy, and Meyer Zald (Cambridge, 1996), 10.

CHAPTER 4

SILK WORKERS IN LYON, 1900–1921

Like many other French workers, silk workers entered the twentieth century with a distinct political identity. Guesdist socialism and its implications for questions of class and national identity were firmly rooted among the workers of the silk trade. The aim of this chapter is to explore the ways that the industrial social relations of Lyon's silk industry and local political opportunity structures shaped that political identity during the years 1900–1921. We will also look at flash points of social conflict like strikes and demonstrations where ISR and POS came together to reinforce silk worker political identity.

For centuries after it was founded in the sixteenth century, Lyon's silk industry, the *fabrique* as it was called locally, was central to the city's economy. Silk workers, especially the silk weavers—the famous *canuts*—constituted the bulk of the city's labor force. By the beginning of the period treated here, the dominance of the *fabrique* in the local economy had considerably declined in relation to other industries, particularly metallurgy. French labor historian Yves Lequin estimates that there were no more than 15,000–16,000 workers in the city's silk industry in the years directly preceding the war. This represented a decline of two-thirds to three-quarters since the middle of the nineteenth century when nearly one worker out of every two local workers was employed in the *fabrique*.[1] Nevertheless, the silk industry remained important and silk workers continued to play a key role in local working-class political and associational life and social protest in this period. We begin with an overview of the structure of the silk industry and a discussion of how it evolved from the beginning of the nineteenth century through the immediate postwar period.

Notes for this chapter begin on page 108.

Structure of the Silk Industry

The transformation of raw silk into an article of clothing involved a long succession of processes carried out in different places by different workers employing different techniques. The focus here is on workers involved in the latter stages of silk production: weavers (*canuts*), dyers (*teinturiers*), and finishers (*apprêteurs*), although we will occasionally encounter workers in closely allied specialties.

The *fabrique* involved a specific set of commercial, industrial, and social relationships that have remained constant in some sectors from the old regime to the present and that had important ramifications for the questions this book seeks to answer. At the center of this system stood a merchant capitalist called the *fabricant* or *fabricant-marchand* and the *façonnier.* In spite of the name, the *fabricant* was a merchant who often did not even own looms or other equipment. Rather, the *fabricant* was a merchant capitalist who gave orders and provided raw materials to the *façonnier* (the weaver/*canut*) who wove the silk for an agreed upon sum, the *tariff.* One of the peculiarities of the system was that *fabricants* that did own several looms often used them to fill orders for other *fabricants* while their own orders were completed by the *façonniers.* The *façonniers,* who were in fact master artisans, owned their own looms and often employed other weavers who were journeymen (or *compagnons* as they were called under the old regime and well into the nineteenth century). Master artisans (who were also called *chefs d'ateliers*) and their journeymen worked and occasionally lived together under the same roof. This amounted to an ambiguous social position for the master artisans. On the one hand they were manual laborers engaged in an unequal and conflictual relationship with the merchants who provided work by furnishing raw materials to be worked on for payment (the amount of which was always disputed); on the other hand, they resembled independent craftsmen who owned their own tools and employed small numbers of journeymen for wages. For a time this system remained in place side by side with the large, mechanized, hierarchically organized weaving factories that began to appear in Lyon at the end of the nineteenth century.

These were the features of the silk industry in its urban setting. However, silk weaving abandoned Lyon for the countryside during the nineteenth and twentieth centuries. When orders were distributed to rural weavers, a third party was often introduced. The *fabricants* gave orders and raw material to subcontractors called *contremaîtres* (not to be confused with factory foremen who are also called *contremaîtres* in French) who in turn parceled the work out to rural weavers, taking of course a percentage for themselves.

Economic and social historians have divided the history of the modern Lyonnais silk industry into the following three periods: (1) 1825–1875, (2) 1876–1929, and (3) 1930 and after. As we will see, economic cycles, changing women's fashions, and technological advances all played an important role in the evolution of the silk industry. Urban weaving production sharply rose at the beginning of this period. The 13,000 silk looms in Lyon and its immediate suburbs in 1810 increased to 27,000 by 1824.[2] Throughout the first period this growth continued, reaching 60,000 in 1853 and 120,000 in 1875. In 1866 half of Lyon's working population worked in the silk industry.[3]

Technological advances did not accompany the increased number of looms. Looms continued to be the hand-powered Jacquard model invented at the beginning of the century. However, the dyeing and finishing processes were greatly transformed. Changing women's fashions placed a higher value on colors than intricate designs. This in turn stimulated research into artificial dyes, which netted impressive results. This initially presented problems for the weaving stage as the prevailing dyeing process involved dyeing silk sheets before weaving. With multicolored cloth the looms had to be dismantled and set up anew after each application of color—a complicated affair that involved long idle periods in which work was interrupted. Further technological developments solved this problem by permitting dyeing in pieces after weaving. These developments also signaled a precocious industrial development of dyeing and finishing in which small-scale artisanal dyeing began to give way at the end of this period to urban, mechanized, capital-concentrated dyeing in large factories while weaving continued to be carried out in domestic settings.

This period of expansion came to an end with the economic crisis of 1876. It was only in 1914 that the value of silk production reached the level attained before 1877.[4] In the fall of 1876 sales and orders ground to a halt. Half of the looms were idled; by the next year, this had increased to two-thirds. Dyeing decreased by 30 to 40 percent. After a brief recovery, the *fabrique* was again hard hit by the financial crisis of the early 1880s. In 1884 its activity declined 40 percent from what if had been at the beginning of the decade. Two thirds of the looms were once again idled and dyeing had decreased again by 30–40 percent.[5] Lyon's silk industry was also shaken by changes in women's fashions. The elaborate dresses of pure silk that were so fashionable under the Second Empire gave way to simpler styles. These new fashions, along with smaller budgets, favored cloth mixed with cheaper material over pure silk. Though this initially was a problem for Lyon's silk industry, we will see how developments occurring in the following period allowed the *fabrique* to adapt to these new fashions.

The period beginning with the economic recovery of 1885 and running until the worldwide economic crisis of 1929 was one of transformation and expansion punctuated by several short crises. The introduction of cotton and low-quality silk into the production of silk cloth, apart from its commercial advantages, necessitated and signaled important changes in the organization of silk production. The most important of these was the decline of small-scale shop production carried out with handlooms in favor of factory production with mechanized looms. One result of this was a 25 percent decline in the number of merchant-producers, which helped assure the continuing prosperity of the remaining three-quarters. Nevertheless, the *fabrique* continued to suffer from German and Swiss competition. The value of Lyonnais silk production grew substantially during 1900–1928, but this was irregular. The period 1900–1914 was essentially one of stagnation in this sector—a situation that, as we shall see, increased the insecurity of silk workers and aggravated industrial relations.[6]

In addition to the salutary effects of the economic recovery, the transformation of Lyon's silk industry benefited from new technological and commercial developments. One of the obstacles to the mechanization of handlooms had been the fragility of the silk threads that had been in use until then. The stress placed on the threads from the shaking of mechanical looms broke French silk threads too often to make mechanization a practical option. However, by the end of the nineteenth century, sturdier and cheaper Asian silk became available. These threads, reinforced through mixture with other materials such as wool and cotton, were strong enough to permit the use of mechanical looms. Artificial silk (rayon), invented by the Count de Chardonnet at the end of the century, began to make its appearance around 1905. Artificial silk expanded dramatically at the end of the 1920s.

During this period, weaving progressively moved out of Lyon. As had been the case since the uprisings of 1831 and 1834, many capitalists sought to undercut the strength of the local labor movement by locating production in the countryside and adjoining suburbs—developments made easier by the spread of rural electrification. Between 1830 and 1850, one-third of Lyon's looms moved to the countryside. In 1882 there were only 25,000 to 27,000 looms in 8,000 shops remaining within the city. By 1889, this had fallen to 16,000. In 1905 only 6,000 or 7,000 remained.[7] The period 1885–1929 also saw the decline of the handloom and the rise of the mechanical loom in the weaving sector of the silk industry. According to figures provided by Yves Lequin, 114,000–115,000 of the 120,000 silk looms weaving throughout the region in 1873 were hand-powered while only 5,000–6,000 were mechanized. By 1889 the number of mechanized looms had nearly quadrupled to 19,319 while the number of handlooms had declined by nearly half to 66,000–72,000. After 1905, the number of handlooms diminished dramatically—by more than two-thirds in the following ten years. By 1914 "the metamorphosis was total" with 40,623 mechanical looms to 17,270 handlooms, which continued their rapid decline. By 1924 only 5,400 handlooms remained.[8]

Figure 4.1 *Woof winders* (canetteuses) *sometimes worked under the supervision of weavers, though in most cases at home alone on a piece work system. Used with permission of the Lyons Municipal Library, SA18.4.*

By 1933 there were 47,000 mechanical looms and virtually no hand-looms left.[9]

The transformation of the silk industry also involved the concentration of workers and machines under one roof. By the early twentieth century the factory worker was clearly replacing the classic *canut* who worked on his loom in his high-ceilinged apartment. By 1904, 80 percent of Lyon's mechanical weavers worked in factories of over one hundred persons.[10] Some of them were considerably larger—like the Gindre weaving factory established in 1893 in the rue Henon, located in the historic silk-weaving neighborhood of the Croix Rousse, and employing over five hundred mostly female workers.[11] In 1903 there were approximately 2,500–3,000 mechanical loom weavers in the Lyonnais agglomeration, 80 percent of whom were women.[12]

Although mechanization and capital and labor concentration did increasingly characterize Lyon's silk industry, the decline of handlooms in favor of mechanical ones was largely, but not totally synonymous with the disappearance of home production and the rise of factory production. For example, in 1914, 2,900 of the existing 17,270 handlooms were still operated out of the homes of that increasingly rare specie, the *canut*, while 1,300 of the 42,500 mechanical looms were operated in private homes—a vain effort to preserve traditional domestic production by using gas and later electrical motors.[13] Employment figures provided in reports drawn up by the prefect of the Rhône during strikes in the immediate postwar period reflect both the dispersal of the *fabrique*'s weaving activity into the often far-flung countryside, as well as the concentration of dyeing and weaving within Lyon and its immediate suburbs. These trends are even clearer when viewed in comparison with the prewar period. We have seen how there were 2,500–3,000 mechanical weavers in 1903. According to police reports drawn up during strikes in 1919 and 1922, there were still only 3,000 weavers in Lyon and its suburbs in the immediate postwar period. While the numbers of urban weavers reflect a stagnation of urban weaving, the 3,000 dyers and finishers increased to around 20,000 for much of that period.[14]

The decline of the traditional silk industry, which had centered on the *canuts*, meant that for the sons of weavers "occupational inheritance was no longer possible."[15] The uneven nature of the business cycle in the silk industry led to chronic unemployment in this industry. The weavers' *chambre syndicale* noted in 1900 that the workers in this trade lacked work for an average of two months a year.[16] Fortunately for the children of the *canuts*, a good deal of social mobility was possible in the prewar years. In these years, many weavers' sons born in the 1870s were able to become clerks and hence leave the working class for the increased status, security, and salaries of the lower middle class. Approximately half of the sons of manual workers of all trades born in these years were able to escape the proletarian condition.[17]

The development of the dyeing and finishing branches of Lyon's silk industry was, however, a far simpler and much more linear process than was the case for weaving. As we have seen, technological advances made dyeing in pieces after weaving possible. Unlike dyeing in hanks before weaving, this process was technically favorable to the development of mechanization, which favored large manufacturers like Gillet who dyed for foreign as well as local silk producers.[18]

From 1890 on, investment in mechanization for this sector of the textile industry equaled that devoted to weaving machinery.[19] After 1900, technological improvements permitted the application of these mechanized techniques to the pure silk cloth that previously had to be dyed in hanks but now could be dyed in pieces. By 1910, the value of products dyed in pieces, which had previously represented a third of the former method, now equaled that of dyed in hanks.[20]

By 1906, eighteen factories in the Lyonais agglomeration specialized in dyeing in pieces.[21] Closely connected to the dyeing sector of textile operations was finishing (*apprêt*). By 1906 there were ninety-six different finishing shops in the Lyonnais agglomeration.[22]

Figure 4.2 *Skilled male workers dyeing silk around 1900. By World War I, they had largely been replaced by semiskilled female workers employed in larger mechanized factories. Some former skilled male dyers were hired as foremen. Used with permission of the Lyons Municipal Library, SA18_2.*

For the dyeing and finishing sectors the first dozen years of the century were characterized by the proliferation of small shops employing between 15 and 85 workers. There were at least thirteen shops of this size in Lyon for most of this period. Medium-sized shops employing 100–450 workers were somewhat rarer. There were seven shops of this size during this period. Large factories employing over 900 workers were quite rare at this time; only the two factories of the Gillet Company had workforces of this size. There were some 3,500 muslin and fabric finishers in Lyon at the time of the great 1903 textile strike.[23] By 1912, 3,000 dyers and finishers were working in nineteen different shops.[24]

Work in dyeing shops and factories was not pleasant. The shops were humid and workers' feet were often covered by acid- and alkaline-saturated water, which, depending on the stage of the process, could be either extremely cold or boiling. Air circulation was poor and harmful vapors often permeated the workspaces.[25] Gillet in particular initiated a strict factory regime and met attempts to organize workers into unions with tough anti-union measures. Gillet's director of operations, Monsieur Marnas, agreed to hire ten workers in June 1911 on the condition that they quit the union, which they did.

World War I and Industrial Change

In the spring preceding the outbreak of hostilities in August 1914, the *fabrique* was in good economic health. Orders were abundant and profits were on the rise. But, as in other sectors of the economy, the effects of the declaration of war on the international silk industry were particularly disastrous in Lyon. While the metallurgy industry thrived, the traditional silk industry suffered greatly. Production over the rest of the year fell to 12 percent of that in the corresponding months of 1913. Long the city's leading economic sector, the silk industry was henceforth of secondary importance. The first few months of the war saw the region's workforce of three hundred thousand in silk production reduced by half. In the following year, however, business improved and production increased through the end of the war. Lyon's distance from the armed conflict saved it from the physical destruction suffered by the cotton and linen industries of the north. The large influx of female labor into the workforce of the *fabrique* in the preceding years saved it from the labor shortages that industries like metallurgy suffered. The hydraulic power that ran much of the silk industry spared those sectors the problem of fuel shortages that befell industries that relied on coal, although silk dyeing, which also used coal for fuel, faced problems by 1917. More generally, the war accelerated the modernization and concentration of this industry. Domestic weaving, once widespread in the Croix-Rousse, continued the decline begun well before the war. Shops in this sector underwent concentration and geographical relocation; many left the Croix-Rousse to establish themselves in the Brotteaux district near the finishing center of Charpennes. These adjustments helped restore some of the industry's past glory once the war ended. Besides the metallurgy industry, the war stimulated other sectors. A large portion of the shoes and clothing destined for French troops was produced in Lyon, likewise leading to the expansion of these sectors.[26] The signing of the armistice in November 1918 provoked a recession as prices immediately fell, but the situation improved by 1920.

The labor force in France's textile industry became even more markedly feminized in the postwar period. Nationwide, half of the 900,000 workers employed in this industry in 1929 were women.[27] In Lyon, women accounted for 2,500 of the 3,000 urban weavers present in Lyon in the postwar period. Seventy-five percent of the 300 tulle finishers working in 15 shops in 1919 were women.[28] Women were frequently found in leadership positions in local textile trade unions. Madame Bollen-County and Madame Ponsot (strike data omitted their first names) were important figures in the CGT weavers union, and Jeanne Chevenard continued to lead the CGT clothing workers' union.

Before discussing the many changes that occurred in Lyon's silk industry during this period, it is important to recall one aspect of the *fabrique* that remained unchanged throughout the whole period dealt with in this study: the division between *fabricants* who secured orders and the *façonniers*, the actual producers, who received raw silk and completed production of the various stages of finished silk. Under this system, most of the *fabricants* did not actually own or operate shops, factories, or tools themselves.[29] Those who did only owned small weaving factories. One of the peculiarities of the Lyonnais *fabrique* was that even fabricants who owned their own looms often had their orders filled by the *façonniers*, even as their looms completed orders for other *fabricants*. In 1924, more than half of the weaving looms and virtually all the dyeing shops and factories belonged to *façonniers*. Furthermore, the concentration and integration of various operations in the production of a given commodity, which became increasingly common in industries like metallurgy, continued to be exceptional in the silk industry. The structure of the *fabrique* continued, therefore, to involve large-scale institutionalized subcontracting.

The increased use of mechanical weaving looms that had begun well before the turn of the century continued up to and after the war. The 30,600 mechanical looms of the *fabrique* in 1900 grew to 42,500 in 1914 and 47,200 in 1924.[30] This did not, however, entail a complete elimination of handlooms. There were still 17,300 hand-powered looms in 1914 and 5,400 in 1924.[31] Concentrated production grew steadily during this period, but domestic production showed a surprising resilience as well. Similar factors explain both of these phenomena. While the new synthetic threads and new dyeing and impression techniques opened the way for mechanization, these same techniques actually favored hand weaving in certain cases. Although mechanical weaving was quicker and more precise, the cost of factory wages and equipment often closed this option off. In both cases, the movement of silk weaving outside of Lyon continued. Writing about the weavers in the Loire, the communist newspaper *Travail* noted that these "weavers seldom work in factories. Their labor takes place in family shops. They are not all grouped in large industrial centers. Many are peasants."[32] The few large silk factories, like those of Gillet, were largely associated with synthetic fibers.

Work in dyeing and finishing shops and factories continued to be difficult and dangerous. Workers were usually required to remain standing throughout their shift. Artificial silk workers often spent most of their shifts in leg-high water filled with dangerous chemicals and breathed harmful fumes.[33] Workers' hands became yellow and deformed from being dipped in chemicals. Harmful vapors caused lung damage. Dyers and finishers working on machines often labored in temperatures reaching 50–55 degrees Celsius in summer. Vaporizing acid stung lungs and eyes.[34] Against the backdrop of this review of the uneven evolution of silk weaving and the less complicated path of silk dyeing and finishing, we can now narrow our focus and examine the ways in which industrial change affected the skilled workers who labored in these sectors.

Industrial Change and Deskilling

As early as 1903 changes in the organization of production reflecting both technological change and a changing balance of forces between the employers and their workforce had begun to dilute the monopoly that skilled dyers and finishers had enjoyed over the labor process and access to their trade. A former *contremaître,* or foreman, explained some of these changes to the Lyon daily newspaper *Le Progrès* during the great textile strike that shook the city in late 1903. While the workforce in the factories and shops was formerly dominated by skilled labor, he noted, it was now made up of 70 percent *maneouvres* (unskilled) and only 30 percent "professionals" (skilled). Furthermore, many of these *maneouvres* had come to work on tasks that should have been reserved for the professionals who had undergone long apprenticeships. As an example, he spoke of dyeing in tender colors—"a task in which practice can eventually bring the skills of an untrained worker up to par with those of a formally trained (that is, through apprenticeship) worker."

The situation of skilled finishers was even more precarious. "Unlike dyeing," he declared, "little time was needed to learn this trade. In order to get the cheapest labor the bosses do not hesitate to replace an older worker with a beginner as the older worker can command higher wages as his skill increases, which in turn swells the ranks of the unemployed and forces these workers to work for lower wages in other factories."[35]

Skilled dyers were threatened by the introduction of a technological innovation called *trempage de soupe*. Employers were paying unskilled workers using this technique four francs a day, rather than the five francs stipulated in the settlement following the great 1903 textile strike, which helped to provoke the 1909 strike. An article in the SFIO weekly *L'Avenir socialiste* explained that if adopted, this system would lead to the suppression of a majority of jobs in this sector.[36]

Elsewhere in the textile industry similar changes were threatening skilled workers' control over the labor process. The *tullistes* union set forth their grievances in a letter to the prefect of the Rhône in November 1903. The introduction of new machines in that trade required a process called "*chauffage de bobines*," which had led to a situation in which workers were now being paid less for work on a new loom of 5,000 threads than they were on the old looms that had only 2,800 threads.[37] By 1912 technological advances had developed to the point where looms with 10,000–12,000 threads and more had become common.[38] R. Portier, writing in the *Avenir socialiste,* claimed that over the previous ten years no industry had experienced as much rapid and "abnormal" mechanization as in the fabric-working sector.[39] According to an article in the socialist press in June 1912, employers in this sector violated agreements prohibiting night work.

The struggle for control over the labor process created a tense environment on the shop floor. This was reflected in battles over authority, which pitted workers against the enforcers of shop floor discipline, the foremen. In strikes in 1900 and 1905, workers demanded the firing of unpopular foremen. Conversely, strikers in 1900 and 1903 demanded the rehiring of sympathetic foremen fired presumably for overindulgence towards the workers.[40]

Apprenticeship

The evolution of apprenticeship programs is an important indicator of the changing status of skilled workers and changes in the organization of pro-

duction. Worker-controlled apprentice programs were a way for workers
to exercise control over access to their trade. Their presence was a positive
indication of the existence of a craft labor market. Likewise, their decline
in favor of systems in which the employers controlled access to training
for occupations was an important element in the rise of a capitalist labor
market.

Professional instruction in this period passed from the hands of the
workers in the trade to professional schools like the municipal weaving
school, the chamber of commerce school, Ecole de la Salle, and the Ecole
de la Martinière. But these schools were geared essentially towards future manufacturers, directors, and foremen, rather than to the apprenticed weavers.[41] The decline of apprenticeship programs signified a loss
of worker control over access to their trade, hence an important aspect of
their control over the labor process.

A report published shortly before the First World War by the Municipal Labor Office provides important information on the evolution of
labor in Lyon's various industries. This information confirms the retired
foreman's reflections on work in the dyeing and finishing trades. There
was never a formal apprenticeship for finishers. These workers were recruited among unskilled workers as they progressively gained the ability
to carry out the required work tasks. Young workers of thirteen to fourteen years old were initially employed as carters. Later they began to work
on machines at the salary of 1.50 to 2 francs a day. At the age of eighteen
after having learned all the operations, they were finally considered workers and paid at the rate of 4.25–5 francs. The four or five years that it
took a young worker who began at the age of thirteen or fourteen to be
considered a full-fledged worker paid full wages was clearly far more than
were required to learn the job. This is indicated by the fact that this trade
was a favorite temporary haven for unemployed carpenters and plasterers.
These workers were usually hired at rates below that of professional workers of this trade, which was greatly resented by the latter.

Apprenticeship for dyers, on the other hand, was two or three years,
depending on the age of the worker; in addition, professional courses
were offered for this trade. Nevertheless, by the early years of the twentieth century these programs were not sufficient to dissuade employers
from using unskilled workers to do work formally reserved for the professionals, as explained by the foreman.[42] A 1909 article by a dyer published
in *Le Travailleur syndiqué,* the *Bulletin official de la Bourse du travail,*
complained of the downward pressure on wages resulting from this practice. The problem was not that "an unskilled worker did the work of a
worker" per se, but that these "unskilled workers earn 4 francs a day when

they should have a minimum of 5 francs." It is interesting to note that the complaint of this dyer was not couched in terms of a defense of the honor or the narrow corporate interests of the dyers' trade, but rather, of the interests of both unskilled and skilled workers who should receive the same wage for the same work: "We must demand the tariff without worrying about professional capacities."[43] A similar complaint had been aired in the pages of the same organ in December 1907. A union official complained that unemployed workers were used to do the work of skilled dyers, also called colorists. But the anger was directed at the bosses, not the unskilled workers. "We professionals," he wrote, "do not demand to keep the title of colorist, we simply ask that if an unskilled worker does the work of a skilled worker, that he be paid the same salary."[44]

The evolution of apprenticeship for weavers paralleled the decline of handloom production by the *canuts* in favor of the more productive and easily learned mechanical looms. While the increasingly rare handloom apprentice spent three years learning the trade, those apprenticed to learn mechanical weaving required only six months. The historical importance of weaving to the Lyonnais economy in general, and the silk industry in particular, was reflected by the extended discussion given to weaving by the Municipal Labor Office. Thirty to thirty-five years earlier, apprenticed handloom weavers accounted for 10 percent of the workforce in this corporation. At that time "four years of apprenticeship were required to produce a good weaver." The apprentice was "guided and instructed daily by the bosses (most likely master craftsmen) and the journeymen (*compagnons*) to learn how to perfectly practice his trade." In doing so, he learned "all the secrets and could later become a master craftsman (*chef d'atelier*) himself." But "today, apprenticeship has fallen into complete disuse. The number of apprentices account certainly for less than 1 percent of all the workers in the trade," which was accompanied by "a considerable decline of the number of workers." The report offered explanations for this situation. Among the "many and complex" reasons for this was, "the transformation of the equipment, the search for cheap labor through relocating shops in the countryside, which in turn leads to frequent unemployment, and the progressive lowering of wages." Furthermore, the terms of the apprenticeship were no longer an attractive option for a working-class family of modest means hoping to steer their son into a solid occupation. While under the old system the apprentice was given room and board and was made "part of the family," by the First World War, the youth was "neither fed nor lodged."[45] As for mechanical weaving, the report explained that "ten or so years before, apprenticeship was certainly more developed than today. ... There were always two or three apprentices in each factory." But currently, "there is no organization of apprenticeship, no contract." As a result of these and other developments, "workers look increasingly towards other better-paid occupations."[46]

Apprenticeship for fabric workers had flourished forty years earlier but had since greatly declined. Earlier, apprentices went through a three-year program, carrying out increasingly complex tasks and receiving higher wages at regular intervals. At the end of the apprenticeship, the worker received a *livret* stipulating professional competence. But in recent years, young fabric workers were rushed through rapid employer-controlled training periods without "instructions on the preliminaries of preparation, which was vital for the correct fabrication of the tulle." In fact, many "small time *chefs d'ateliers* no longer have the knowledge to correctly instruct the apprentices whom they are instructing." Instruction was even more lacking in the big factories than in the small shops. Such a situation had become "harmful for all the workers of the corporation, by the fact that workers instructed in such a way settle for low salaries and thus contribute to the overall lowering of wages."[47]

Accounts of apprenticeship programs for female textile workers suggest that the golden age of nineteenth-century apprenticeship was reserved for young male workers. Rules stipulating a six-hour limit for girls apprenticed in various textile trades were often grossly violated, with the actual working day extending to as much as twelve hours.[48] While extended apprenticeships for males was generally a sign of the quality of the professional instruction they received, female apprentices were held as apprentices longer in an effort to exploit the low wages they received. For example, female weavers were often kept as apprentices as long as four years when six months would have sufficed to train them for the tasks they were to carry out.[49]

Apprenticeship for textile workers was largely an institution of the past by the time of the First World War. The 1919 Astier act establishing government-sponsored apprenticeship was never applied in the textile industry. Many young workers received a somewhat informal apprenticeship from older, more experienced workers. The highly organized and well-financed professional school established by Lyon's metallurgy employers' organization did not have a counterpart in the textile industry. Various firms had their own internal apprenticeship systems. Many of them seemed designed more to keep the wages of young beginning workers even lower than those paid to other workers, than as serious training programs, which is also indicative of deskilling. Apprentices at Gillet were prohibited under threat of dismissal from taking part in strikes or other forms of collective action.[50]

Industrial Change and Skill

The limited number of occupations in weaving, dyeing, and finishing establishments makes the task of charting the evolution of industrial change and work in the silk industry easier than in metallurgy, which involved a bewildering number of occupations and job titles. On the other hand, while the often universally accepted title of "skilled," "semiskilled," and "unskilled" used to describe metal workers, regardless of the actual (often-changing) reality in metallurgy, provides a solid starting point for examining this question in that industry, similar data offers far less information of this type for textile workers. The nomenclature used in prefects' reports does not distinguish between skilled and semiskilled. This was the same method used in prewar reports. As we have seen, a variety of indicators supported the claim of prewar workers, employers, and government officials that textile workers at that time were either skilled or unskilled, with the semiskilled element being virtually absent or of only ephemeral existence—a defining characteristic of industrial labor before and early in the Second Industrial Revolution.

Given the developments discussed above, it is highly unlikely that the weaving, dyeing, and finishing labor force remained divided between skilled and unskilled workers. How then can the existence or absence of an intermediate grade between skilled and unskilled worker be determined? As we have seen, craft apprenticeship, nearly extinct before the war, was definitely an institution of the past afterwards. Workers learned their tasks on the job. In her study of women's factory work in the interwar period, Annie Fourcaut cites a worker who reported that only one to three months were necessary to learn several occupations, and six months to a year to operate other mechanized posts with efficiency.[51] This is equivalent to the time considered necessary to become a semiskilled worker in other industries.

The installation of the machines discussed above most likely represented a dilution of skilled labor. For example, the Fumenter dyeing machines not only produced more with less workers; with their capacity to dye silk simultaneously in six colors, work that used to require six skilled colorists was now carried out with one "skilled" worker and one unskilled worker.[52] In the absence of more detailed information than is currently available, the effects in terms of skill for the remaining workers could point in opposite directions: if the machines themselves were complicated ones requiring extensive knowledge, the workers operating them could be considered as having gained new skills to compensate them for the loss of older ones. But if the necessary knowledge required for the operation of these machines could be acquired in a matter of days, weeks, or months, it would be more accurate to consider these workers as semi-skilled machine operators roughly analogous to the semiskilled machine operators who became so numerous in metallurgy during the same period, and therefore deskilled in comparison to their prewar counterparts. Since the term *colorist* occasionally appeared alongside *dyer* at this time, it is likely that dyers in the mechanized plants had indeed become semi-skilled machine tenders while the dyers in the establishments where these machines had not been installed remained skilled workers in the manner in which that status was traditionally understood. The fact that the collective bargaining agreements of 1936 did not list occupational specialties while titles such as *dévideuses* and *flotteuses* were widely used before, also suggests that industrial change had deskilled many aspects of silk production.[53]

The state of the available evidence makes it particularly difficult to measure the effects of the mechanization of weaving looms on the extensive skills that handloom weavers possessed. It is possible that the new mechanical looms installed in factories were more productive and required less skill than the converted handlooms used by the remaining *canuts* working at home. Rayon weaving was certainly highly mechanized and required less proficiency. But the existence of employer-managed training programs and surviving worker accounts indicates that even in factories, mechanical weaving was not learned overnight. Further research is necessary to determine if the knowledge required could be obtained in a matter of weeks or months, which would indicate that this work was semiskilled, or if it required a longer training period as was the case for skilled work. But together, these admittedly partial fragments of evidence suggest that industrial change after 1914 had the net effect of continuing the process of deskilling weaving, dyeing, and finishing and therefore transformed most work in these sectors into semiskilled, largely female labor, while drastically reducing the numbers of remaining skilled male workers.

Rise of Capitalist Labor Market

In terms of the balance of forces between workers and employers, these various aspects of labor in dyeing and finishing during this period all point in the same direction: the labor market position of skilled dyers and finishers, already greatly degraded by the First World War, continued to worsen. The virtual elimination of worker-controlled apprenticeship programs, an abundant labor supply, periods of serious underemployment and unemployment, and the degradation of skilled work through mechanization meant that these workers could no longer defend their interests through a monopoly of scarce skills or control over access to the trade. In other words, the steady decline of a craft labor market in the silk industry during the prewar period was virtually completed in the interwar period as a capitalist labor market arose in its place.

Industrial Change and Worker Collective Action

The profound changes in the organization of production in the various sectors of the silk industry and the negative effects they had on the skill level and professional autonomy of weavers, dyers, and finishers were responsible for provoking much of the industrial strife of the period. These conflicts took place on at least two different but related levels. On the one hand, the silk employers sought to take full advantage of the degraded labor-market position of the workers as a whole. On the other hand, their attempts to play some workers off against others led to sharp and often bitter conflicts between the skilled workers who had undergone apprenticeship programs and the lesser-paid unskilled workers who were increasingly being recruited to fill jobs previously reserved for skilled workers. These conflicts characterized virtually all of the prewar textile strikes and gave rise to a rich debate in the workers' movement around the question of relations between different workers across the skill divide.

The introduction of mechanical looms with their capacity to greatly increase production with less labor provides an excellent example of how conflicts arose between both the employers and their workers, and among workers themselves. The refusal to operate more than one loom at a time as demanded by the employers often figured prominently in strike demands. Likewise, workers who agreed to operate more than one loom at a time either as a result of employer pressure or the promise of higher wages were often the objects of bitter hostility from their colleagues. For example, a three-day strike in September 1906 in a weaving factory employing 102 predominantly female workers was prompted by the decision of a female weaver to accept working with two looms. The sole demand of the strike was the firing of this worker.[54] Elsewhere, strikers physically attacked nonstriking female clothing workers in February 1911.

The employers sought to take advantage of the continued existence of lower wage rates for apprentices and helpers even though changes in the organization of production had rendered these categories increasingly obsolete. Workers were hired as apprentices at apprentice wages, even though they carried out the same production tasks as professional workers. A textile strike in 1906 involving 1,638 workers in fourteen different shops had as one of its four demands a limitation of the number of apprentices.[55] A brief 1909 strike in a medium-sized dyeing plant saw the union demand the replacement of "helpers" by "workers."[56]

The 1903 Strike

Conflicts between workers were particularly evident in the great silk strike that shook the industry in late 1903. Behind the strike was one of the economic downturns that interrupted the period of overall growth that the industry experienced between 1885 and 1929. The increased production made possible through the technological advances discussed above placed an enormous strain on the remaining small artisanal shops on the left bank, which still dyed in sheets.[57] Workers voted to strike at an enthusiastic meeting on 9 November after employers refused the wage hikes demanded by the union. At the beginning the strike involved the dyers and finishers in the small shops that made up about a third of the six thousand dyeing shops. In mid-December, four thousand female mechanical weavers voted to make common cause with them. The prefect noted that the strike of the dyers occurred at the same time as that of the finishers, "went through the same phases, and was led by a commission composed half and half by workers of each trade." A partial return to work began on 23 December, and increased in the following days. "Completely demoralized," the strike committee accepted the intervention of the mayor on 26 December concerning the employer's propositions, and work began again on the morning of the 28th. The strike caused a large "perturbation" in the silk industry, with the result that much previously contracted work had to be sent to the countryside and to different towns of the region. According to this report, the strike was particularly hard on the workers' families in the new industrial quarters of Villeurbanne, Charpennes, and Brotteux.[58]

Socialist politicians offered political and material support for the strike. The socialist parliamentary group voted a 100-franc contribution to the strikers and local socialist deputies challenged the government on the use of military force against the strikers in late December. They also raised the question directly with the prime minister.[59] The radical-socialist mayor Victor Augagneur was bitterly criticized for his support for the employers during the strike. One local pro-worker newspaper complained that even under Mayor Gailleton, Augagneur's predecessor, "the capitalists and bosses never had so much police and armed forces at their disposal."[60]

As the strike progressed the employers played on divisions between skilled and unskilled workers. At one point the employers sent letters to the unskilled, calling on them publicly to ask for work. This created enough

anxiety among union leaders that they issued public warnings to any unskilled dyer who went along with the ploy that they would be expelled
from the union.[61]

Divisions between workers of different skill and pay levels were even
sharper when factories dominated by unskilled labor are compared with
those where the numbers of skilled workers remained significant. For example, in the Gillet factory—by far the largest dyeing factory in Lyon—
groups of workers, few of whom were skilled, began drifting back to work
well before the workers in the small- and medium-sized shops began to
do so. At the daily mass meeting of the strikers on 10 December 1903,
attended by 1,800 striking dyers and finishers, the Gillet workers were
sharply criticized for their failure to join the strike and the union. Tensions flared further when a Gillet worker stated that he and his fellow
workers were satisfied with their wages and saw no need to join a union
that they felt did not function properly.[62]

Similar divisions gave rise to another incident at a meeting two days
later, when a finisher from the Bouffier-Pravaz factory took the floor to
ask why the personnel of his shop were prevented from working by the
striking unions since they worked on muslin rather than the specialties of
the workers who were at the origin of the strike. This frank declaration
that the rules of solidarity did not apply to him or his colleagues was met
with cries of "Throw the cow in the water," "Throw him out," and "Renegade."[63] The daily meetings of strikers, which drew up to two thousand
workers, often voted to march on the Gillet plants and the other large
factories in an effort to pressure those workers into joining the strike.

The failure of the unskilled workers in the large shops where mechanization and technological change had made the most progress to engage
in the same level of social protest as the organized skilled workers of the
smaller establishments was clear well before these strikes. The first May
Day demonstration of 1890 was marked by a sharp contrast between
heavy participation in the traditional artisanal quarters of the city and
the newer large factories in neighborhoods such as Vaise. Of the estimated eight thousand demonstrators who marched in the rain that day,
at least three to four thousand were from the Croix-Rousse—the work
and residential center of the still-significant *canuts*. Only one hundred
people participated in the contingent that left from Vaise.[64] The forces of
order reported with a certain satisfaction that Monsieur Gillet was quite
touched by the fact that not a single one of his approximately 1,400 employers failed to show up for work that day.[65]

This was not merely a phenomenon linked to the first May Day. Future
demonstrations confirmed the contrast between the new, large industrial
units employing a majority of unskilled workers and the slowly declining

smaller units that were bastions of traditional skilled-worker militancy. Among those who failed to strike and demonstrate in the 1905 May Day demonstration were workers from Gillet and Vulliod, the two largest dyeing factories in the city. In contrast, the Bath dyeing shop and the Durant Jr. finishing shops, which employed fifty-five and forty workers respectively, were empty that day.[66]

The highly charged and well-documented 1906 May Day reflected these differences even more starkly. The strike involved 3,200 dyers in 47 factories. In nearly all trades and industries, the smaller units dominated by skilled labor almost always experienced total absenteeism, while the larger units where deskilling had advanced the furthest either failed to strike or saw only a minority strike and demonstrate. While dyeing shops like Bertrand, Clair and Alberti, Feydel, and Pierry and Rossignol that employed 20, 10, 30, and 60 workers respectively were completely abandoned that day, all 1,600 workers at the Gillet Villeurbanne factory and the 500 dyers at the Vulliod factory showed up for work. All 400 of the semiskilled mechanical weavers at the Gindre factory in the Croix-Rousse came to work. Medium-sized shops saw part of their personnel participate in the strike and demonstrations, while others, sometimes a majority, went to work. This was the case at Latruffe and Co. dyeing factory where 200 struck and 100 came to work, and at the Rivat finishing shop where 20 struck and 80 worked.[67]

This strike revealed deep divisions in the finishing trade. One thousand finishers working in twenty-five shops struck.[68] The fabric finishers rejected a tradewide strike call by a majority of four hundred. The muslin finishers called a meeting to protest the lack of solidarity of the fabric finishers. The agitated workers at this meeting decided to set up a special commission to split away from the fabric finishers and form an exclusively muslin workers' union.[69]

In the aftermath of the 1903 silk strike, a debate opened up within these trades over relations between skilled and unskilled workers and what type of union organization could best defend dyers and finishers. This debate was reflected in the pages of the monthly trade newspaper, the *L'ouvrier teinturier-apprêteur*, which had been called the *Teinturier* until September 1903. The January 1904 issue carried an article that outlined the debate. The author, René Claude, paraphrased one current of thought in the following way: some union militants have been saying "during the strike of 1890 and again in this one, we have noticed that unfortunately it was the *manoeuvres* who were the first to give up the fight." Those comrades who are partisans of a union limited to skilled workers ("*syndicat professionel*") claim, "if we were alone we would always win." But if we reflect on this we would see such a split would have "disastrous results."[70]

The line of the *teinturier-apprêteur* expressed in Claude's article and others over the next year rejected forming a union that would exclude the unskilled dyers and finishers, though impatience with the lack of union consciousness of many unskilled workers was also reflected in the newspaper. The articles advanced a number of arguments that called for radical tradewide solidarity that drew upon traditional radical trade union thought combined with a sharp awareness of the reality of the silk industry and the direction it was likely heading, and are therefore worth reviewing.

In the case of a long strike, Claude explained, the bosses could use unskilled labor to continue production, and the skilled would be forced to appeal to them. Likewise, supposing that the skilled workers are "morally" the strongest, wouldn't it be in their own interest to fight for higher wages for the unskilled and to thereby recognize the law of supply and demand?

> A boss always tends to reduce his overall costs; we have seen this over the last few years in many factories where the professional element has been almost completely eliminated. All the trades tend to specialize and, as a result of mechanization and chemical materials, have become less difficult to master, which means that an intelligent unskilled worker can harm a striking professional. And if the skilled did go on to found their own union, what would they say to the unskilled who stayed out on strike until the end and who have paid their union dues for the last several years? It was, in fact, the unskilled majority who launched the strike and who have maintained the union for several years. This is not to say that the professionals haven't done so as well—I don't doubt that at all. It's just that all the unskilled are not cowards ... therefore, a split at this time would be pure madness.[71]

The newspaper's editorial staff felt obliged to return to this theme several months later. A front-page article entitled "Ouvriers et Manoeuvres" continued the argument with the skilled workers who saw the solution to their problems in forming a craft union excluding the unskilled. Men of good will, the author explained, realize that "the demands of the skilled and the unskilled are identical, both have the same needs, the same responsibilities, expend the same amount of manual labor and experience the same insolence, the same vexations, the same unemployment, and are exploited in the same way." Here the author certainly exaggerated the degree to which the conditions of work and the labor market position of skilled workers resembled those of the unskilled at that time. This bending of the stick was most certainly a device to underline the larger point of the importance of industrywide worker solidarity in a difficult period. "The proud and vain worker has a double need of the solidarity of the unskilled on both the intellectual and manual plane where the skilled worker is even more exploited." After all, in the event of a conflict when there are two unions, and the unskilled worker demands a raise or any other demand, would an unskilled worker join in solidarity? "No, since he would not have anything to gain." And "don't you think that an unskilled worker would continue working with the foreman and a few renegades during a strike of skilled dyers?" So, "instead of calling for a split between the skilled and the unskilled, you'd do better to educate them if you are really conscious and sure of yourself and your rights"; in any event, "I know what the unskilled did in the last strike, but we better not just blame them, for there were skilled workers as well" who did similar things. "I would excuse an unconscious *manoeuvre,* but I would not excuse an *ouvrier;* the *ouvrier* knows the worker's demands, whereas the unskilled worker often comes from the countryside, doesn't know what a union is, and can therefore be excused." In sum, "we need a union where the skilled and unskilled can fraternize ... for we all have but one enemy: the exploiter."[72]

Citing continued calls for an exclusively "professional" union, the author of this article returned to this theme in the February 1905 issue of the *L'ouvrier teinturier-apprêteur.* Referring to the proverb "Divide and rule," he wrote that one must have their eyes closed or be blind to fall for such duplicity. He cited the proud history of the dyers' union and the role it played in the struggle for the ten-hour day and higher wages. Today, "all the workers' centers, and all the corporations are regrouping and forming single trade unions and federations. ... We must follow these great revolutionary movements, such as that in England, the metal workers and dockers in Germany, Chicago and throughout America, Italy, Spain, and France where there are unions grouping unskilled, skilled, and foremen together."[73]

The newspaper took a similar approach towards women. In an article entitled "Aux femmes," the April issue contained the following: "Since the progress of 'mechanization' has allowed you to do the same work as men and even to sometimes replace them in the factory, we want wages to be equal for all if we have the same jobs and the same needs."[74] Mistrust of and hostility towards female workers characterized, of course, the attitudes of many male workers in many trades and industries. However, there seems to have been a concerted effort—especially in the difficult period before World War I—of male militants to extend the hand of solidarity to female workers, particularly in the textile trades. Thus the well-known anarchist militant Sébastian Faure addressed a meeting of washerwomen in October 1901 in the following terms: "Any solution demands ... that women are finally considered the equal of men. ... This requires that she be educated and conscious, that she is interested in political questions."[75] In fact, female silk workers were found in as many leading positions in silk unions as men. Around the turn of the century, men occupied 61.5

percent of union posts to 38.5 percent for women—figures that corresponded to their numerical weight in the unions.[76]

The tendency of skilled dyers and finishers to promote solidarity beyond the horizons of their own trade expressed itself in other ways. Towards the end of the bitter 1903 strike, when it was becoming clear that
the strike would not be won, and workers and their families had begun
to suffer, members of the strike committee proposed the establishment of
"*soupes populaires*" open to all strikers regardless of their trade.[77]

Textile Workers and Politics

Lyonnais silk workers in our period were the inheritors of a rich associational life. Since the Middle Ages silk workers like artisans in many crafts
throughout France had joined together in trade associations (*corporations*) and journeymen's associations (*compagnonnages*). In mid-century,
the Second Empire had seen the establishment of numerous mutual aid
societies.[78] From 1870 on, the trickle became a flood as all the trades of
the *fabrique* were drawn into the movement.[79] In 1886, Guesdist militant and silk weaver Gabriel Farjat was instrumental in forming a union
of journeymen weavers.[80] By the end of the century silk workers had
established solid trade unions complete with full-time staffers and, more
importantly, strike funds.

These unions were often well organized and capable of battling the
employers with sophisticated strike tactics. Thus, the finishers obtained
the ten-hour day in 1890 following a strike that involved the use of the
mis-en-index, by which workers refused to work in shops owned by employers who refused to meet union demands. They used the same tactic
in 1894–1895 to win a 20 percent raise.[81]

In chapter 2, we saw that the Guesdist Parti ouvrier français was particularly influential among the *canuts* of the Croix-Rousse as well as the
mechanical weavers in La Guillotière. Gabriel Farjat consistently received
impressive electoral support in the electoral district that included the
Croix-Rousse. Silk workers provided many leaders for various socialist
groupings—especially the Guesdists. When the socialist vote abruptly declined in the traditional weaving quarter of the Croix-Rousse in 1900, silk
workers in the newly industrial quarters and suburbs of the city continued
this tradition. As we shall see in subsequent chapters, this socialist tradition played a role in postwar political developments.

The local anarchists also enjoyed some success amongst artisan weavers.[82] On the whole, however, through their association via the offices of
Farjat to the Guesdist-controlled unions, many silk workers were partisans

of the class collaboration, nationalist current and its expression in the radical-socialist alliance. At the time of the Bourse du travail affair, silk worker unions were amongst those who sided with Mayor Augagneur against the revolutionaries. And the radical-socialist slate registered its greatest success in the electoral districts where silk workers lived and worked.

The POF made serious concerted efforts to aid and recruit silk workers. These socialist politicians offered political and material support for striking silk workers during the 1903 strike. These efforts were not lost on silk workers. Knowing they had friends in parliament, silk worker union activists made periodic public appeals to them for help. The *Avenir socialiste* often opened up its columns to them. Further, the reformist socialists included silk workers on their electoral slates in all of the prewar municipal elections. This was the case both when the Guesdists were offered slots on radical lists as part of the radical-socialist alliance, and in the increasingly frequent cases when the radical turn to the right, discussed in chapter 2, forced the SFIO to run their own independent lists. For their part, the radicals made concerted efforts to make alliance attractive to silk workers. In his successful bid for reelection in 1908, Mayor Edouard Herriot specifically promised aid to the unemployed silk workers of the Croix-Rousse.

Conclusion

As we have seen, the traditional structure of the weaving, dyeing, and finishing trades in the opening years of the twentieth century underwent profound changes. While small shops remained the rule, larger industrial units slowly but steadily began to appear. Through technological changes and other changes in the organization of production, employers were able to weaken the position of weavers, dyers, and finishers. The decline of worker-controlled apprenticeship programs was both a cause and result of this.

Industrial change did not affect weavers, dyers, and finishers in exactly the same way. The weaving operations that remained in Lyon became an increasingly mechanized, semiskilled factory affair. Handloom weavers were faced with virtual extinction throughout this period. Dyers were faced with a much slower pace of deskilling and could draw on a rich corporate past to navigate the turbulent waters of an uncertain present and future. Finishers entered the twentieth century in a weaker position than the dyers; there was never a formal worker-controlled apprenticeship program for their trade and the nature of the work process did not favor great skilled worker control over the productive process. Industrial change further aggravated this situation. Taken together, this signified the gradual elimination of a craft labor market and the rise of a capitalist one. But these developments did not go unopposed by Lyon's silk workers.

How then can the developments of this period be summed up? In the years preceding the First World War, industrial change was gradually transforming a previously skilled, mostly male labor force into what would eventually become an increasingly homogenized and feminized semiskilled one. Although this was the overall trend, the gradual pace of this change meant that for an extended period skilled workers coexisted with the semiskilled—a situation that, as we shall see, highlighted many of the features of the French labor movement as it had developed throughout the nineteenth century. The *canuts* were a dying breed; the price of resisting proletarianization and surviving as independent *façonniers* was increased pauperization. The structure of Lyonnais society allowed many of them, or at least their children, to leave their profession for lower middle-class positions.

Skilled dyers and finishers in this period were the victims of industrial changes that altered their relation to the work process in favor of the employers. But, as we have seen, the nature of the work process and the industrial changes that occurred were somewhat different in these two cases. In dyeing, employers were able to take advantage of recent technological advances to decrease their reliance on skilled dyers, the colorists, by employing unskilled workers working under the supervision of foremen, who were often former colorists themselves. In doing so, employers were gradually seizing control of access to the trade. These *manoeuvres,* as all parties referred them, were actually becoming semiskilled workers or what would later be called *ouvriers specialisés* or *o.s,* through the acquisition of the technical knowledge necessary to carry out what was becoming much simpler work through technical change.

The nature of the finishing process facilitated an even more rapid and brutal reorganization of the work process than that which occurred in dyeing. The employers exploited the opportunity to dilute the traditional monopoly over the labor process that skilled finishers had traditionally enjoyed, in a far more aggressive manner than that which was possible for the dyers.

The pressures on these silk workers led to tensions between trades, between factories, and especially between skilled workers and the unskilled. Workers responded with a variety of responses to this situation. Some skilled workers responded with hostility to the unskilled. They saw self-defense as involving organizational separation from the unskilled in trade organizations. This reflex signaled a retreat into narrow craft organizations. But more authoritative voices in the labor movement of these trades, those of seasoned trade union militants, called for broad working-class solidarity, especially between the skilled and the unskilled throughout the industry. Though the debates were often heated, it was these voices that prevailed.

But this type of solidarity characterized dyers somewhat more than finishers. We have seen how the pressures on finishers—a trade where unskilled, unapprenticed labor overtook skilled labor more rapidly than was the case for the dyers—resulted in the type of dissension that saw muslin and fabric finishers turn against one another during the heated May 1906 strike.

The center of gravity of the labor movement remained firmly anchored in the organizations and traditions of skilled male workers. For the most part, unskilled workers remained marginal to the organized labor movement throughout these years. This was reflected by the sharp contrast in patterns of organization and collective action between the small shops—still the preserve of the skilled worker—and the larger, more mechanized industrial units where the workforce was dominated by unskilled factory hands. While the small units were the earliest and most energetic participants in strikes, and the longest to hold out, the participation of workers in the larger units with a declining skilled worker component was the least reliable. The workforces of these units were the most susceptible to employer manipulation, and were the first to end tradewide strikes. May Day demonstrations reflected this cleavage even more starkly. The smallest units had the greatest participation, while the larger factories had the least. The same phenomenon was seen at the community level as well. Until the beginning of the century, neighborhoods dominated by skilled workers like Croix-Rousse provided the largest number of demonstrators for the early May Day demonstrations, while the newly emerging industrial quarters like Vaise saw very little May Day participation in this period. When unskilled workers did play a militant role in trade organizations and collective action, it was usually those who worked alongside skilled workers in the smaller shops.

Lyon and the *département* of the Rhône should in no way be considered unique in these respects. Michael Hanagan's study of artisan, skilled worker, and industrial worker protest in the adjoining *département* of the Loire revealed similar processes at work. The industrial town of Rive-de-Gier in these same years was the scene of "an impressive example of artisanal worker solidarity with industrial workers."[83] Like the skilled textile workers and artisanal *canuts,* the artisans of Rive-de-Gier were threatened with industrial change. Their response, like those of the seasoned militants in the dyers' union, was to extend the hand of solidarity to the unskilled in defense of the common interests of all.

The examples of Rive-de-Gier and of turn-of-the-century Lyonnais textile workers indicate that in a context of slow industrial change involving the weakening of skilled worker control over the work process, skilled workers and artisans were capable of mobilizing their professional institutions and traditions in the service of trade- and industrywide solidarity, and thus lead newer, unskilled workers in united struggles in the interests of all.

Finally, we have seen that silk workers were among the most faithful supporters of local socialist groups promoting the class collaboration, nationalist program. They were firmly anchored in the alliance that linked the POF to the middle-class Radical Party and the radical-led municipal government that was at the heart of POF politics. The success of this current among silk workers and the concomitant failure of revolutionary socialists and revolutionary syndicalists to attract a large following of these workers can be understood by reviewing the following points that have been discussed in this chapter.

First, as we have seen, Guesdist activists had chosen to focus on recruiting textile workers from an early date. In Lyon, where they had a presence from the very beginning (1880s), their aggressive organizing in working-class quarters allowed them to establish links with silk workers from this time on. Early arrival on the scene gave this political force an advantage over its rivals who arrived later. But it wasn't only early arrival on the scene that accounted for their success in winning silk worker support. Reformist socialists strove to deliver real aid to the workers of this industry so central to Lyon's economy. During the 1903 strike, the socialist parliamentary delegation sent them a donation and challenged the government on its use of troops against the strikers. Reformist socialists therefore used their political power in parliament and locally to deliver tangible benefits to silk workers. At the same time, their radical partners also appeared friendly to silk workers.

Turn-of-the-century radical municipalities and politicians made gestures toward workers in general and silk workers in particular to keep them in the broad Republican alliance. The municipal governments of Victor Augagneur and Edouard Herriot embodied the spirit of social progress based on mild social reform and secularism that was at the heart of the Radical Party's political orientation in this period. Although Mayor Augagneur's actions during the 1903 strike underscored the limits of Radical Party solidarity with workers when the interests of employers were at stake, the overall balance sheet of the radical municipal government seemed to be friendly to worker interests.

But it wasn't only political factors that accounted for the success of reformist socialism among silk workers. The effects of industrial change on the sociological structure of the silk-working population weakened the social forces among silk workers, which often rejected this kind of politics in favor of revolutionary syndicalism and its refusal to collaborate with radical politicians. As noted by many historians, revolutionary syndicalism appealed to threatened skilled workers and called on them to use their power as a "conscious minority." In an industry like metals, where the pace of industrial change was continuous but slow and uneven, this could be expected to have an appeal (as it did). But skilled silk workers were so rapidly undermined by the processes outlined above that reliance on the "conscious minority" of skilled revolutionary workers wasn't a plausible option, because that element was rapidly disappearing and the semiskilled workers taking their places lacked the organizational experience and political culture that were associated with revolutionary syndicalism. The opposition that skilled workers promoting solidarity across skill levels had in winning their colleagues to this perspective (as seen in the debate in the union press after the 1903 strike) shows how limited the revolutionary syndicalist idea of class- and skillwide solidarity had developed among skilled workers in this industry. The rapid decline of skilled labor here thus had the effect of reducing the numbers of skilled workers who in the metal industry were the bearers of these ideas. This therefore helped clear the way for activists promoting the other program on the scene: class collaboration, nationalism.

This is how local and national political programs, coalitions, and the particular political and social climate in turn-of-the-century France intersected with the sociological effects of industrial change on silk workers in ways that drew these workers to reformist socialist forces and the alliances they advocated. In the next chapter we will see how a different mix of these factors resulted in a different political orientation for metal workers.

Notes

1. Yves Lequin, *Les ouvriers de la région lyonnaise* (Lyon, 1971), 1:190.
2. Lequin, *Les ouvriers,* 1:167.
3. Ibid.
4. Françoise Bayard and Pierre Cayez, eds., *Histoire de Lyon des origines à nos jours* (Lyon, 1991), 321.
5. Michel Laferrère, *Lyon, ville industrielle. Essai d'une géographie urbaine des techniques et des entreprises* (Paris, 1960), 169.
6. Bayard and Cayez, *Histoire de Lyon,* 324.
7. Lequin, *Les ouvriers,* 1:87.

8. Ibid., 84.
9. Bayard and Cayez, *Histoire de Lyon,* 325.
10. Lequin, *Les ouvriers,* 1:190.
11. Bayard and Cayez, *Histoire de Lyon,* 323.
12. Lequin, *Les ouvriers,* 1:190.
13. Bayard and Cayez, *Histoire de Lyon,* 325 and Lequin, 1:87.
14. ADR 10/Mp/C61, C64, C66, C67, C69, C70.
15. Jean-Luc Pinol, *Les mobilités de la Grande Ville: Lyon fin XIXe–début XXe* (Paris, 1991), 87.
16. Robert Chagny, "La presse socialiste à Lyon, 1896–1914." (Master's thesis, University of Lyon, 1960), 23.
17. Pinol, *Les mobilités,* 313–14.
18. Bayard and Cayez, *Histoire de Lyon,* 327.
19. Lequin, *Les ouvriers,* 88.
20. Ibid.
21. Ibid., 89.
22. Ibid.
23. These are figures cited in prefectoral reports of this strike. ADR 10/Mp/C24.
24. These are figures cited in prefectoral reports from strikes in 1912. ADR10/Mp/C48.
25. Chagny, "La presse socialiste," 22.
26. Pinol, *Les origines,* 68.
27. Annie Fourcaut, *Les femmes à l'usine en France pendant l'entre-deux-guerres* (Paris, 1982), 72.
28. ADR 10/Mp/C36.
29. Laferrère, *Lyon,* 88–89.
30. Lequin, *Les ouvriers,* 1:175.
31. Ibid., 179–80.
32. *Travail,* 12 May 1923.
33. *Travail,* 5 October 1930.
34. *Travail,* 9 November 1930.
35. *Le Progrès,* 18 November 1903.
36. *L'Avenir socialiste,* #145, 27 November–4 December 1909.
37. ADR 10/Mp/C25.
38. *L'Avenir socialiste,* #277, 8–15 June 1912.
39. Ibid.
40. ADR 10/Mp/C28.
41. Chagny, "La Presse Socialiste," 44.
42. Ville de Lyon, Office municipal du travail, *Statistique et renseignements sur diverses questions ouvrières et sociales, 1913–1914,* 64.
43. *Le Travailleur Syndiqué,* November 1909.
44. *Le Travailleur Syndiqué,* December 1907.
45. Lyon, *Statistiques et renseignements,* 74.
46. Ibid., 60.
47. *Le Travailleur Syndiqué,* January 1909.
48. *Le Travailleur Syndiqué,* December 1907.
49. Marie-Françoise Roux, "L'ouvrière du textile à Lyon, 1880–1914" (Master's thesis, University of Lyon, 1981), 52.
50. *Travail,* 16 Sept, 1931.
51. Fourcaut, *Les femmes à l'usine,* 74.
52. *Travail,* 9 November 1930.
53. Emmanuelle Bonnet, "Des femmes à l'usine: La société lyonnaise de textiles artificiels, 1924–1939" (Master's thesis, University of Lyon, 1990), 45.

54. Office du travail, *Statistique des Grèves,* no. 560, 1906.
55. Office du travail, *Statistique des Grèves,* no. 613, 1906.
56. Office du travail, *Statistique des Grèves,* no. 341, 1909.
57. Lequin, *Les ouvriers,* 1:189.
58. ADR 10/Mp/C24.
59. Ibid.
60. *Le Peuple de Lyon,* 20 December 1903.
61. ADR 10/Mp/C24.
62. Ibid.
63. ADR 10/Mp/C24.
64. Ibid.
65. Ibid.
66. ADR 10/Mp/C141.
67. Ibid.
68. ADR 10/Mp/C38; Office du travail, *Statistique des grèves,* 1906.
69. ADR 10/Mp/C38.
70. *L'ouvrier teinturier-apprêteur,* April 1904.
71. *L'ouvrier teinturier-apprêteur,* October 1904.
72. *L'ouvrier teinturier-apprêteur,* December 1904.
73. Ibid.
74. Ibid., April 1904.
75. ADR 10/Mp/C21.
76. Roux, "L'ouvrière du textile," 130.
77. ADR 10/Mp/C24
78. Lequin, *Les ouvriers,* 2:197–98.
79. Ibid., 202.
80. Madeleine Thévenet, "Le Guesdisme Lyon, 1882–1905" (Master's thesis, University of Lyon, 1971), 52.
81. Jacques Leschiera, "Les débuts de la CGT à Lyon, 1890–1914" (Master's thesis, University of Lyon, 1972), 109.
82. Michelle Marigot, "L'anarcho-syndicalisme à Lyon" (Master's thesis, University of Lyon, 1966), 24.
83. Michael Hanagan, *The Logic of Solidarity: Artisans and Industrial Workers in Three French Towns, 1871–1914* (Urbana, IL, 1980), 8.

CHAPTER 5

METAL WORKERS IN LYON, 1900–1921

By the opening years of the twentieth century, industries working with metals began to challenge the silk industry as the motor of Lyon's economy, and metal workers organized in a number of trades and union structures joined silk workers as the most important components of the city's labor movement. As a group, metal workers evinced a strong occupational identity that combined craft pride, class consciousness, hostility to parliamentary politicians and politics, and antinationalism. This was reflected in the strong support that anarchism, revolutionary syndicalism, and eventually communism found among metal workers in Lyon and in France generally.

This chapter examines the ways that political opportunity structure and industrial social relations combined to shape metal worker political identity. We will see how flash points of industrial conflict like strikes illustrate these processes and helped to crystallize political identity formation. We begin with a review of the structure of Lyon's metallurgy industry, the effect of industrial change on skill, and how it impacted the overall relations among and between metal workers and their employers. We conclude with an analysis of the relative appeals of the various political currents competing for influence among metal workers and how industrial social relations and political opportunity structure shaped metal worker political identity.

Structure of the Industry

As we have seen, the silk industry's traditional dominance over the of Lyon's industrial economy declined at the end of the nineteenth century in favor of a more diversified industrial scene in which metallurgy played a central role.[1]

Notes for this chapter begin on page 141.

   The Lyonnais metallurgy industry involved the transformation of
raw materials imported from elsewhere. Lyon's close proximity to the
Saint-Etienne coal basin and its geographical position at the crossroads
of European trade routes favored its emergence as one of France's most
important industrial centers. Many firms that had previously furnished
the silk industry with the metal products necessary for production in that
industry proved flexible enough to take advantage of the new opportunities offered by the changing economic and industrial climate at the end
of the nineteenth century. The Teste Company is a prime example of
this. Founded in nearby Vaise in 1841, it initially produced metal pins. In
1885, it began to produce industrial cables. From 1891 on it specialized
exclusively in cables for mines, bridges, etc. By the end of the century,
various firms were specializing in electrical tools, copper boilers, boilers
for the local chemical industry, machinery for the needs of the increasingly mechanized silk industry, naval equipment, and especially for the
nascent automobile industry. The latter became quite important to local
and even national industry.[2]
   The Rochet Schneider automobile shops were opened in 1894, and
the famous Berliet auto factory was founded in 1899. By 1905, no less
than five well-known automobile manufactories were located in Lyon.
They were accompanied by scores of small-time producers of motorized
scooters and the like. By that date, production had reached nine hundred automobiles per year, representing a business that had grown from
100,000 francs in 1896 to 12,000,000 in 1905. Business historian James
Laux estimates that by 1911 "the automobile industry had become the
largest single element in the French metal working trades which in 1911
employed 621, 592 men."[3]
   In spite of its rapid development, this industry continued to bear many
of the marks of artisanal production. Shops were usually of extremely
modest size. Only Berliet attained a large scale of production at this time:
by 1912, 1,250 workers were employed at this firm. Early automobile
manufacturing in Lyon was favored by "a broad foundation of metal-
working shops and skilled labor [which] had developed out of the textile
machinery, railway equipment, and river transport businesses. This complex and highly specialized industrial context made it possible for a firm
with little capital to assemble cars from components picked up here and
there in the city."[4]
   Many of the earlier automobile manufacturers had begun by producing
bicycles, carriages, or electrical equipment. In Lyon, Rochet Schneider
began his industrial career in the bicycle manufacturing business. Claude
Mieusset was a builder of fire-fighting equipment until 1895, when he
took up automobile manufacturing, later specializing in fire engines, and

Luc Court began building cars in 1898 after having operated an electrical equipment firm since 1892.[5] Marius Berliet began as a small-time, self-taught mechanic who had served a brief apprenticeship in a silk-weaving firm before being smitten with automobile fever in the early 1890s. Berliet became the city's biggest employer of metal workers and one of France's leading automobile producers.

Like the textile industry, the size of metallurgical shops and factories can be classified into small, medium, and large enterprises in terms of the numbers of workers employed. In the prewar years the majority of metalworking shops still employed less than fifty workers. Medium-sized factories employed between fifty and five hundred workers. Several large factories had workforces of over five hundred. By 1914, the Lyon Chamber of Commerce calculated that one-third of the city's workers were employed in the modern metallurgy and chemical factories.[6] Although the majority of metal workers in Lyon still worked in small shops, the trend was clearly in the direction of the large factory. According to Shorter and Tilly, the percentage of metalworkers in establishments employing more than one hundred on the national level increased from 39 to 51 percent between 1906 and 1926 while those working in smaller establishments decreased from 42 to 28 percent, "a rate of concentration more rapid than any other sector."[7]

The expansion of the industrial sectors connected to the war effort involved an influx of labor. This was seen in the capital as well as provincial industrial centers like Lyon. The increase in the number of metal workers in the Parisian region reflected the growing importance of this sector, especially in relation to industries less central to the war effort. On the eve of the war there were just fewer than 200,000 *métallos* in the *département* of the Seine, compared to 400,000 clothing workers. At the end of the war metallurgy was the largest employer in the region, employing 330,000 workers compared to 300,000 in the clothing industry. In Lyon, the workforce in metallurgy grew from 25,000 in 1914 to 30,000 in 1915 and reached 45,000 by 1917.[8] Berliet's workforce alone grew from 3,150 on the eve of the war to 5,882 by 1917.[9]

At the end of the nineteenth century, the small enterprises that dominated the metallurgy industry were often equipped with all of the branches necessary to complete the given item under construction. Shops of forges, foundries, and modeling, mechanical, and other aspects of production were often grouped under the same roof. Mechanical construction shops founded in the nineteenth century declined as their tools became obsolete in the face of the rapid technical evolution of machine tools that accompanied the rise of the electrical motor and automobile industries. Modern machine tool production in the service of these and other industries opened the way to the production of large quantities of standardized pieces. One result of this was that the tools and machines of the older enterprises and their highly skilled personnel became outmoded. In the automobile and electrical industries especially, unskilled labor gradually began to replace the skilled artisans who had hitherto dominated these shops.

Gender and Metalworking

Work in the metal industry in the prewar years was predominantly a male affair. The exclusively female personnel of fifty-four women working at a factory producing parts for mechanical looms in Villeurbanne at the turn of the century was a notable exception, although women were occasionally hired as unskilled or semiskilled workers in other metal plants.[10] The rarity of female labor in prewar metallurgy in Lyon differentiates this industry from the silk industry, where female labor was common.

Significant numbers of women were hired in metal-working establishments during World War I. This was generated by the labor shortage resulting from expanded industrial needs and the drafting of many male

Figure 5.1 *Male and female workers assembling shells at the Acières du Rhone plant in 1915. Used with permission of the Lyons Municipal Library, S1225.*

Figure 5.2 *Women workers soldering artillery shells at the Gillet dyeing plant in 1917. Like many industrial enterprises throughout the country, production at Gillet was converted from its original activity to production for the war effort. In this way, these women silk workers became, if only temporarily, metal workers. Used with permission of the French Ministry of Defense.*

workers into the army. The high wages paid in the metallurgy factories producing for the war effort also attracted women to the plants. This involved a large-scale transfer of female wage labor from industries like textile and garment making that had traditionally employed women.[11] The law of 5 August 1917 requiring breastfeeding rooms in war plants (a practice that survived the war) reflected government recognition of the importance of women's industrial labor. Of course, the fact that it took three years of war for this law to be enacted also reflected male dominance of state institutions. In 1917 Berliet employed 1,220 women representing 20.7 percent of the workforce.[12] As will be seen below, the sudden and massive introduction of a semiskilled female factory proletariat into the labor force had important consequences for the labor movement and the overall shape of the working class.

The end of the war saw women summarily driven from their jobs in metal-working factories. The government played an important role here, offering one month bonuses to any women willing to leave their factory jobs.[13] According to Jean-Louis Robert, at the end of the war "women were brutally turned out of the war factories to take their place in the home. Contrary to a widely spread legend, the Great War was not a durable vehicle for women's labor, but a simple parenthesis."[14] In her study of Citroën, Sylvie Schweitzer offers detailed information of female labor in the period immediately following the war. Only 10 percent of the three thousand workers on the payroll in 1919 were women. These figures remained steady for much of the period under study, at least at Citroën. In 1928, 9.5 percent of the workforce at Citroën's Clichy plant was female.[15] But while this represented a dramatic drop compared to war-time female employment in the metal-working factories, it was still greatly superior to prewar female metallurgy employment, which represented only 5.6 percent of metal workers in the department of the Seine in 1911.[16]

Female labor in Lyonnais metal-working plants for this period indicates that their presence in metal working was highly uneven throughout the industry. Where they were employed it was usually under the most Taylorized conditions. For example, although they seemed to have been completely or totally absent from production jobs in many local shops and factories, they constituted 40 percent of the workforce of eight hundred at the Zenith carburetor ring manufacturing plant in 1930.[17] At Berliet in the 1930s, exclusively female workforces worked two of the most automated—and dangerous—assembly lines.[18] This connection between gender, skill, and rationalization underscores the connection between skill and gender in general. There were 10 skilled female occupations in the mid-1920s as opposed to 115 male ones according to a metallurgy employer study.[19] A fuller picture reveals segregation as well as unequal

Figure 5.3 *Female metal workers like these at the Aciéres du Rhone metal plant in 1915 were a ubiquitous feature of war-time labor. Used with permission of the Lyons Municipal Library, S2511.*

access to skilled positions along gender lines. Only 10 percent of skilled positions were held by both men and women.[20]

The war, then, signaled a massive entry of women into an industry that had previously been virtually an all-male preserve. But the question of female employment has a far greater interest than merely determining how many female workers entered the industry and how many left after the armistice. Gender was an integral part of the recasting of industrial production, the fight over the production process that this entailed, and the new conceptions and practices of skill that evolved in this period. French labor historian Laura Lee Downs explained this process in her study of women in the French and British metal-working industries between 1914 and 1939:

> The army's insatiable demand for weapons forced employers in both nations to replace the old craft methods and technologies with a more mass-production organization of work, grounded in the "rationalization"—that is, subdivision, routinization, and mechanization—of formerly skilled jobs. At the same time, war destroyed the sexual division of labor, pressing thousands of women upon an industry that had hitherto all but excluded them. The new technical division of labor was thus expressed as a sexual division of labor from its inception. In the war-time

metal working plants—except for jobs requiring the heaviest labor (manipulation of the very largest shells)—all unskilled work was reserved exclusively for women, as were a number of semiskilled jobs involving smaller pieces.[21]

In this way, "gender was thus transformed from a principle for excluding women into a basis for dividing labor within a newly fragmented production process."[22]

War and Industrial Development

During the war, French industry was nearly totally reoriented towards efforts to maximize production for the war effort. By 1917, 1,500,000 workers were employed in the war industries.[23] The state aggressively intervened in the economy to advance this goal. Jean-Jacques Becker and Serge Bernstein sum up the effects of the war on French industry by noting that French industry, "known for its rigidity, demonstrated a remarkable flexibility towards adaptation." The war produced a boom in the mechanical manufacturing, electrical, steel, and chemical industries based on widespread introduction of mass production and Taylorism, rather than strictly technological innovation.[24]

The metallurgy industry was at the center of war production. Metalworking establishments of every size and scale were mobilized towards this end. But it was the largest factories that received the most attention and aid from government authorities. Large companies such as Citroën and Peugeot indeed date their rise to importance from this period. The corollary to the advances registered by industries dealing with metals was the stagnation and decline of industries that could not be directly adapted to the war effort, such as the clothing, textile, food, and lumber industries.

A local state official succinctly summarized war-time changes in Lyon's economy in the following way: "To the prewar local industry made up in large part by weaving, dyeing, chemical production, and luxury goods was added metallurgy, which, due to the circumstances, developed to the detriment of luxury production and somewhat monopolized available labor."[25] Important industrial enterprises in this sector such as Hotchkiss, which employed 1,800 workers, were established in Lyon during the war.

Industrial Change and Skill

Fordism, Taylorism, and the bitter struggles they generated underscore how the possession of skill is a source of worker power. For this reason employers have generally sought to reduce, neutralize, or eliminate skilled work. This has put struggles over control of the labor process at the center of workplace conflict. Establishing the evolution of labor in terms of the skill of the workers under study here tell us much about the industrial social relations in this industry. Surprisingly little is known about how industrial labor in many sectors evolved in France during the twentieth century. It was argued above that skill is a social construction dependent on a variety of factors going well beyond the actual technical knowledge of individuals. Taken together, the constituent elements of labor markets determine if work is "skilled," "semiskilled," or "unskilled." Although information is extremely uneven about different groups of workers, and the boundaries between skill levels were occasionally disputed, workers, employers, and government officials did often agree on whether work was skilled, semiskilled, or unskilled. This provides us with a benchmark to determine the composition of labor forces in terms of skill, which we shall supplement with available information concerning labor markets.

French automakers including Lyon's Marius Berliet consciously implemented Taylor's theories and Ford's assembly lines. For many metal workers the Second Industrial Revolution meant reduced shop floor autonomy, assembly line production, and subdivided work tasks, the sum total of which French industrial sociologist George Friedmann has called "fragmented work" ("*travail en miettes*"). Alain Dewerpe has argued that many metal workers in the period 1910–1950 had less technical competence then the previous generation. "The machine stripped them ... of a good deal of their capacity, not only to produce a complete item, but also to manage in an autonomous fashion the modus operandi."[26] However, this process far from typified all metal workers. As we shall see, for a variety of reasons, some metal workers managed to avoid this type of deskilling. And for those who were deskilled in this manner, the timing of the process varied considerably between trades. In the next section we shall see how industrial change affected several metal working specialties.

Table 5.1 lists metal-working occupations and pay scales in Lyon during the 1900–1914 period. This list was primarily assembled from information drawn from documents regarding strikes and is therefore an approximation, rather than an exhaustive list.

Information concerning the nature of these various job classifications is difficult to come by for this period. Christian Chevandier's book on rail workers, *Cheminots en Usine*, however, offers useful information about several of the most important metal occupations in Lyon during this period. He also shows how some evolved over time from the turn of the century through the 1940s. The object of Chevandier's study is the fac-

Table **5.1** *Metal-working occupations present in Lyon, 1900–1914*

Occupations (skilled)	Hourly Wages in 1906
Adjusters (*Ajusteurs*)	6–10 francs
Boiler Scalers (*Piqueurs de chaudières*)	4–6 fr.
Burnishers (*Burnisseurs*)	5–7 fr.
Capstan lathe workers (*Décolleteurs*)	5–6.75 fr.
Drillers (*Perceurs*)	4,50–5 fr.
Electricians (*Electriciens*)	6–7 fr.
Blacksmiths (*Forgeurs*)	8–10 fr.
Joiners (*Mortisseurs*)	5.50–7 fr.
Locksmiths (*Serruriers*)	5.50–6.25 fr.
Lampmakers (*Lampistes*)	6–7.50 fr.(1909)
Machine Tool Operators (*Conducteurs de machines-outils*)	6–8 fr.
Mechanics (*Mécaniciens*)	8 fr.
Millers (*Fraiseurs*)	5–6 fr.
Molders (*Mouleurs*)	5–7 fr.
Molders, copper (*Mouleurs sur cuivre*)	5.50–7 fr.
Molders, aluminum (*Mouleurs sur aluminium*)	6.25–7.50 fr. (1905)
Molders iron, (*Mouleurs en fer*)	5.50–6 fr.
Molders pig iron, (*Mouleurs en fonte*)	5.50–6 fr.
Nickel Workers (*Nickleurs*)	7–8 fr.
Pattern Makers (*Modeleurs*)	7.25 fr.
Piston Makers (*Pistonniers*)	10 fr. (1903)
Polishers (*Polisseurs*)	6.50–8 fr.
Riveters (*Riveurs*)	5.50–7 fr. (1912)
Sheet Iron Workers (*Tôliers, Tôliers-fumistes*)	5.50 fr. (1907)
Smelters (*Fondeurs*)	5–5.50 fr. (1905)
Turners (*Tourneurs*)	5.50–8.00 fr.
Valvemakers (*Robinnetiers, Tourneurs-robinnetiers*)	5.50–7 fr.
Wiredrawers (*Etireurs*)	4–6 fr. (1911)
Welders (*Soudeurs*)	5.50–7 fr. (1912)
Zincworkers (*Zingeurs*)	5–6 fr.

tory workers of the Paris-Lyon-Méditéranée (PLM) railroad in Oullins, an industrial suburb south of Lyon, charged with building and repairing locomotives from the turn-of-the-century through World War II.

While one of Chevandier's main theses is that these factory metal workers had a rail worker identity due to their employment by the PLM, they were metal workers in all other respects.[27] Boilermakers and blacksmiths in the pre–World War I period worked with hot metal. Bearers of extensive knowledge, their jobs were also physically demanding. These workers worked under conditions of extreme heat and deafening noise.[28] This description parallels David Montgomery's discussion of boilermakers in the United States who "toiled in teams, amid deafening noise, covered with sweat and often with filth."[29] Chevandier cites a former hammerman who became a coppersmith. This man explained that riveters and hammermen were "below" coppersmiths, had few skills, but were nonetheless proud to exercise a recognized craft.[30] The uniqueness—and prestige or lack thereof—of several of these crafts revolved around the character of the material worked. It was significant if molders and smiths worked on copper or bronze, but not on pig iron or iron.[31]

According to Shorter and Tilly, the term *mécanicien-constructeur* described a very different type of worker depending on the size of the plant in the period of industrial transformation before World War I. The assembly line, which made its appearance no earlier than the end of the prewar period, transformed these skilled workers into proletarianized machine-tenders, drill press operators and wheel-nut screwers-on.[32] In small shops, the term *mécanicien* most likely described the skilled machine builder who at least for the moment survived mechanization.[33] Data provided by police reports of metal strikes in prewar Lyon are broadly consistent with these descriptions. Mechanics received wages only slightly behind the most highly paid metal workers. For example, mechanics at a factory producing motors in 1904 were paid 6 francs a day while polishers and smiths received 6 francs 50. Mechanics at another shop at the same time were paid 6 francs 50, while fitters in the same plant—almost always the best paid metalworkers—received 7 francs.[34] The term *conducteurs de machine-outils* clearly was used to describe unskilled machine tenders. In 1906, eighteen workers in this category were paid 8 francs at the Mieusset automobile factory while eight mechanics in the same plant were paid up to 10 francs, the same as machine builders and fitters.[35] *Serruriers* or locksmiths were typical of a craft that survived industrialization. Nationwide, they worked in very small shops whose median in striking shops was only thirteen workers.[36] In 1906, 600 locksmiths in Lyon worked in 260 different establishments. Things hadn't changed much five years later; in 1911, there were 500 metalsmiths working in 270 establishments.[37]

Tool and die makers were also able to preserve the craft nature of their occupation. Their continued use of their own tools made during their apprenticeship underscored the failure of Taylorism to end worker control in this area.[38] *Mouleurs* or molders on the other hand, were typical of the skilled workers who saw their skills rendered obsolete through industrial change that, while not eliminating them altogether, reduced them to semiskilled machine tenders. Like artisans and skilled workers, the turn-of-the-century molder was proud of his technical prowess and what he considered as his artistic taste.[39] It was not surprising then, that molders were particularly sensitive to the effects of technological change on their world of work. A 1903 article published in the trade newspaper of the molders, *La Fonderie,* sharply counterposed the traditional skilled labor of the molders with labor carried out with machines. Traditional un-mechanized work contributed to the self-respect of the worker, but the machine molders often lost all dignity, caught as he was in the craziness (*folie*) of the machine.[40]

At the summit of the labor hierarchy in terms of skill and prestige was the fitter, the "prince of the worker aristocracy." In the case of the locomotive shop at Oullins, the place of the fitter became increasingly important throughout these years. Throughout metal-working plants in Lyon, fitters were the highest paid metal workers. The turners at PLM, Oullins were nearly as prestigious as the fitters and they were nearly as well paid.[41]

All of the trades just discussed were considered skilled by all parties involved in this period. Industrial labor forces dominated by skilled labor were typical of the "craft phase" associated with the nineteenth century that was discussed in chapter 1. French industrial development was such that skilled workers dominated labor forces in many sectors until well into the interwar period. Photographs taken around the turn of the century show the predominance of skilled work with little or no division of labor. The shop floor depicted in the photo of the engine assembly shop in the Hotchkiss factory taken in 1906 and reprinted in James Laux's study of the French auto industry before 1914 bears no resemblance to the as-sembly line production of the 1920s. There is almost one workbench for each assembly station. This indicates the lack of interchangeable parts and the need to fit parts to each engine individually. Other photos depict skilled workers at their benches serviced by unskilled *manoeuvres.* Also present were machine operators who can be considered "semiskilled" as their tasks required several weeks or months to arrive at a satisfactory level of performance and were usually paid more than *manoeuvres* but less than skilled workers.[42] As we shall see in chapter 8, the presence of such semiskilled workers (*ouvriers spécialisés* or "o.s." as they were called in the 1936 collective bargaining agreements) increased only slowly, and it was some time before they nudged skilled and unskilled workers aside as the dominant element in metal-working establishments. This is reflected in the composition of prewar factory labor forces in metallurgy. For exam-ple, highly skilled workers such as mechanics, fitters, and mounters made up a large proportion of the workforce at the Renault car factory at the beginning of the century. That proportion had fallen to only 70 percent by 1914 and barely under 50 percent by the 1920s. In 1920, 65 percent of the workers at Peugeot's Sochaux plant were considered skilled, 25 percent were semiskilled, and 10 percent were unskilled laborers.[43]

In prewar Lyonnais metal-working establishments, workforces were usually composed of a large majority of skilled workers spread out into different occupations along with a few unskilled laborers. The composition of prewar metal workforces underscores the dominance of the skilled worker and the rarity of the semiskilled. For example, the workforce at six striking Lyon automobile plants in 1905 included 863 skilled workers (547 fitters, 125 lathe operators, 152 milling machine operators (*fraiseurs*), 38 blacksmiths, and 80 unskilled laborers. Only 16 semiskilled machine operators worked alongside 59 fitters, 22 lathe operators, 21 coppersmiths (*chaudronniers*), and 21 unskilled "helpers" (aides) in a local machine shop making gas motors in 1904.[44]

In the prewar period, the percentage of unskilled workers varied greatly between different shops and factories. At PLM Oullins, censuses show that they accounted for from anywhere between a quarter and a third of the workforce between 1906 and 1936.[45] The least skilled were *journaliers* or day laborers hired and laid off as they were needed. The unskilled worker is one "who doesn't know how to do anything, therefore, the one who does everything." There were two types of *manoeuvres*. The "false" unskilled worker was the recently hired worker who might rapidly learn a specialized trade, or begin to exercise a previously learned one. The "real" unskilled worker never acquired a trade. *Aide-ouvriers* were future skilled workers who for the moment often did the work of *manoeuvres* while the *manoeuvres* often did the work assigned to the "professionals."[46] The skill divide was reflected in off-the-job social relations. For example, Chevandier found that among the workers at PLM Oullins, an unskilled worker was ten times as likely to have an unskilled colleague as a witness at his wedding than a skilled worker, while skilled workers too usually had other skilled workers as witnesses.[47]

Industrial work during the First Industrial Revolution was largely the preserve of artisans and skilled laborers. Unskilled laborers were often employed in the same shops as aides and helpers charged with transporting material throughout the enterprise, heating ovens, and the like. Rare before the twentieth century, semiskilled workers were largely associated with the Second Industrial Revolution. They were differentiated from laborers by higher pay and specialized work tasks. The modest but real place they occupied in the classification of workers in terms of skill in interwar Lyon metal-working plants indicates the importance of a nuanced view of the progress of industrial change in this period. Industrial change had clearly made serious inroads on the dominance of skilled labor, but the skilled worker element was far from eliminated.

Industrial Change, Metal Worker Resistance, and Solidarity

Having examined the nature of industrial change in this period and how it altered the composition of the labor force in terms of skill in Lyonnais metal-working plants, we now look at ways in which industrial change shaped the types of demands workers raised as well as the effect of these changes on relations between workers and their ramifications for the ability of workers to engage in collective action.

Until the turn of the century most of these skilled workers enjoyed a large measure of control over the labor process through the technical capabilities they possessed and the control over access to their trade flowing from their control over supply networks. In other words, they benefited from the existence of craft labor markets. French employers sought to wrest control over the labor process from skilled workers not only through reorganizing production on the shop floor but also through a wider dismantling of craft labor markets and the establishment of capitalist ones. In these transitional years before the First World War, the immediate effects of industrial change involving both the introduction of new technology and the reorganization of the labor process using existing or slightly modified machinery, as well as attempts to control supply networks, forced metal workers into a long series of defensive strikes.

The most concerted attempt to increase capitalist profits and reduce worker control over the labor process was the methods of scientific management pioneered by the American Frederick Winslow Taylor, which, as we noted in chapter 1, began to be widely applied in French automobile plants around 1910 after an initial period of hesitation on the part of French industrialists. The introduction in 1912 of stopwatch monitoring in the auto industry was resisted by auto workers in Lyon as well as in more well-known auto plants like Renault in the Parisian region. In Lyon, the introduction of the stopwatch provoked a strike of the one hundred mechanics, one hundred fitters, sixty turners, and thirty laborers employed at the at the Auto-Buire plant that lasted from 20 February to 12 March 1914.[48] Even before the introduction of the stopwatch, speed-up campaigns inspired by Taylor's time-motion studies had provoked strikes in the auto industry. As early as May 1905, 1,025 auto workers working in seven different factories struck against the firing of a worker at the Berliet plant accused of taking ten minutes to finish a task that Berliet claimed should have only taken six.[49] Likewise the system of *pointillage* or punching the time clock was greatly resented. The local socialist weekly *L'Avenir socialiste* published a bitter complaint about this practice in a series of articles it ran on abuses at the Berliet plants in late 1910 and early 1911. The same series also spoke out against the system of production bonuses instituted by Berliet as well as the forced overtime that extended the work day from ten to twelve hours. Other strike demands reflecting resistance to these employer-inspired innovations demonstrate the intensity of the struggle for control over the labor process and in defense of craft labor markets.

Relations between workers and foremen reflect the anxiety of skilled metal workers faced with deskilling in this period. Several of these strikes demanded that a foreman be fired or, more rarely, objected to the dismissal of a sympathetic foreman. Demands for the firing of a foreman figured in twenty strikes in metalworking establishments in Lyon between 1900 and 1914, and another in October 1919; in two strikes workers demanded the rehiring of a foreman.[50] French historian Michael Hanagan has argued these that demands often "concealed protests against work discipline."[51] In Lyon, the demand to fire a foreman was particularly frequent in auto strikes in 1913 and 1914—a period when Taylorist methods were beginning to be introduced. The links between Taylorism and demands for the firing of a foreman were unmistakable in the strike at the Auto-Buire factory that took place between 20 February and 12 March 1914. The strikers called for the dismissal of a foreman considered responsible for introducing the stopwatch.[52] The role of foremen in enforcing work discipline gradually became clear. The secretary of the copper molders' union in Lyon related his own experience to the newspaper of the molders' federation. He accepted a job as a foreman in 1900. He soon learned that his job consisted primarily of hiring some workers, firing others, lowering wages, and enforcing strict discipline in the shop. After sixteen months of this, he quit his job and returned to his old position as secretary of the union.[53]

Workers were particularly offended by foremen who ordered workers to carry out tasks that they themselves were incapable of doing. Metal workers often sought a subtle type of revenge by asking foremen technical questions whose answer they knew perfectly well, but sensed ignorance on the part of the foreman. Workers, especially the highly skilled fitters and turners, particularly resented being asked to carry out tasks usually reserved for unskilled workers.[54]

The introduction of piece work was typical of the drive towards reduced skilled worker autonomy. Though piece work was an integral part of Taylor's scientific management methods in the form of bonuses tied to production norms that were established through the use of stopwatches, various forms of piece work were already present in the nineteenth century. Where it hadn't existed before, skilled metal workers in Lyon and elsewhere fought against attempts to institute piece work. During an industrywide auto strike in Lyon in 1905 in which one of the demands was the suppression of piece work, a delegate from the Federation of Metals told strikers that metal workers throughout France supported them in their struggle against this practice.[55] All told, demands for the elimination of piece work figured prominently in no less than seventeen metal strikes in Lyon between 1902 and 1913. Turners and valve makers; copper workers; fitters; engine mounters; drillers; smiths in all metals; blacksmiths; slag removers; pig iron, iron, copper, and aluminum molders; metal polishers; capstan lathe workers; locksmiths; and hammermen all struck to demand the suppression of piece work.[56]

Employers used subcontracting to avoid the concentrated and organized power of industrial workers to advance their claims around wages, hours, and working conditions. Strike demands against the introduction of piece work in metallurgy often occurred alongside demands to end this practice. In Lyon, seven metalworking shops employing two hundred workers struck unsuccessfully for three weeks in the strike-ridden month of May 1906 for the eight-hour day, but also for the suppression of piece work and subcontracting.[57] Automobile workers successfully struck against these practices in January 1910, as did 500 locksmiths working in 270 different industrial establishments in June 1911.[58]

Apprenticeship

As was the case in the silk industry, the decline of craft labor markets in the metallurgy sector in the opening years of the twentieth century was reflected in part in changing patterns of apprenticeship. The 1913–1914 Lyon Chamber of Commerce report offered information on several of the most important metal trades. By that date, sheet metal workers (*tôliers-fumistes*) for example, still received a traditional apprenticeship. Most of the approximately 150 apprentices of this trade went through a two-year non-paid apprenticeship. Those who spent a third year as apprentices earned .50 centimes a day. Things were different for zinc workers, however. According to the report, apprenticeship in this trade had been more developed earlier. At that time "apprentices received no remuneration but became accomplished workers. Today, remuneration is immediate, but most of the time the young people are employed as laborers to the great detriment of their technical education."[59] The survival of many occupations requiring theoretical and practical knowledge and training meant that apprenticeship could not be completely eliminated. Berliet solved this problem by establishing his own internal apprenticeship programs.[60]

The increasing simplification of skilled labor through mechanization and division of work in some sectors—which is both the cause and effect of the decline of craft labor markets—made it more and more technically possible for employers to use poorly paid apprentices to do the same jobs as fully qualified workers having gone through traditional apprenticeship programs. Employers sought to do this in order to lower labor costs, but especially to circumvent the shop floor power of skilled workers. As such, it was bitterly resisted. The molders' union complained specifically of this practice in their trade publication, *La Fonderie*.[61] An examination of strike demands in the metal trades in Lyon between 1900 and 1914 reveals the full extent of this practice. In May of the industrial strife–ridden year of 1906, 250 striking workers in fifteen shops demanded a 10 percent cap on the employment of apprentices. A general strike of bronze workers including molders, turners, and burnishers that occurred at the same time also demanded a 10 percent limitation of the number of apprentices employed in that industry.[62]

This problem afflicted the metalworkers in the city's luxury trades as well. As early as 1902, a small shop of several jewelers struck to demand a limitation of the number of apprentices.[63] These examples reflect not only the decline of apprenticeship and the anger it provoked amongst the metalworkers but also the fact that access to many trades had passed out of the hands of the workers and their organizations. The demands of these frequent and intense strikes give an idea of the scale of the employer offensive in these years.

The particular circumstances of the war involved labor struggles that often posed the question of worker solidarity across trades, skill, and genders. Mass, continuous-process production involving increased division of labor and mechanization was given a boost by the regime of war production. Though these developments could have helped break down divisions between workers in terms of skill and craft, government labor policy erected new barriers between workers. The most obvious of these was the distinction between mobilized and nonmobilized workers. Mobilized workers were considered soldiers and were thus subjected to military discipline. The metalworkers' union published a study revealing the superexploitation of the mobilized workers. As for the nonmobilized, these workers, often refugees from invaded regions and Belgium, were victimized by the employers "who abuse their unhappy situation by paying them low wages and often lower these even more with the threat of replacing them with mobilized workers."[64]

Absenteeism, which was considered a fortiori striking, could result in court martial leading to imprisonment or transfer to the front. This naturally chilled labor struggles among mobilized workers, who numbered 30,000 of the 80,000 workers employed in Lyon's war industries. As mobilized and nonmobilized workers often worked side by side in the same plants, divisions were inevitable. The 350 workers at the Société Elec. Paris Rhône plant in Lyon who struck in May 1918 were all non-mobilized workers. Not one of the remaining 150 mobilized workers in the plant joined the strike. But these divisions were eventually overcome. By the end of that year mobilized workers were frequent participants in the growing number of strikes.[65] Becker and Bernstein have written that mobilized workers rarely participated in the first large-scale strikes in the war industries that occurred in May and June 1917. Mobilized workers in Lyon were precocious in this regard. As early as June 1917, 50 mobilized workers joined 160 nonmobilized men and women in a sit-down strike that ended two hours later when the workers' demand for the immediate application of the government's wage guidelines, the *bordereau,* was granted. The police report named four mobilized workers as the leaders.[66]

A striking feature of the wartime labor movement in Lyon was the effort taken by union activists to protect the most vulnerable layers of the workforce and to avoid letting government and employer policy divide workers along skill, gender, or specialty differences. For example, the Hotchkiss workers took care to propose that demands around piece rates be applied to women, those who found speed-up drives difficult, those working for daily wages, unskilled workers, and other categories.[67]

Skilled male workers' attitudes often reflected hostility to women on the shop floor. The former were alarmed by the connections between new techniques and the ever-growing wave of female labor flowing into the factories. However, the historical record reflects both much hostility towards women from male workers and examples of authentic solidarity across gender lines. Further, the official position of the CGT was "equal wages for equal work." This was a slogan that could unite men and women workers in defense of the interests of all. Whatever their attitudes concerning female labor, male workers could support this demand.

The Fédération des métaux took the question of female labor seriously. On 17 March 1915 it sent out a questionnaire concerning female labor to thirty trade unionists in various trades. In addition to soliciting the overall opinions of these male trade unionists, the questionnaire aimed at gathering information concerning the specific work tasks performed by women. It also asked the respondents whether women working in metallurgy should be organized, and if so, whether they should be organized in specifically female unions or in the already existing unions. In fact, women were organized in both female and mixed unions. In 1916, the Fédération des métaux founded a mixed union.[68] "By July of 1917, women, who formed nearly 30 percent of all workers in the Parisian metals and munitions industries, also made up about 30 percent of the region's unionized metal workers."[69] In May 1918, a meeting in Lyon of the

Union des syndicats du Rhône voted to establish a permanent delegate slot representing the women's unions to the UDSR.[70] Aware of the long hours and difficult working conditions under which women worked, the secretary of the metal workers' union, Antoine Garin, called for an active campaign to win a half-day rest per week for women workers—a demand that reflects both their working conditions as well as the solidarity that could be extended by male workers to their female colleagues.[71]

Female workers were unmistakably at the forefront of the labor struggles that erupted in the war industries in May 1917. But they left their mark much earlier. The first strike in the metallurgy and arms industries involving women began when 110 women workers struck the De Dion plant on 29 June 1916.[72] The issues surrounding this strike highlighted the superexploitation of women in the war factories as well as the incessant drive for greater production, efficiency, and profits. The strikers were all employed in the rifle shop, where the division of labor was extremely advanced. There were forty-one different operations for each rifle produced. The workers were paid piece rates for each operation. These rates were constantly being reduced, and the working conditions at the plant were atrocious. A day shift toiled for ten-and-a-half hours, followed by a night shift that worked eleven hours. The direct cause of the strike was a new management decision requiring the women to tend three machines at once instead of two.

The situation at De Dion was emblematic of the situation in war industries throughout the country. Wartime labor struggles in Lyon consistently revealed the hyperexploitation and unbearable working conditions of women working in the war plants. Female workers proved to be particularly sensitive to the continuous rise in the cost of living provoked by wartime inflation. A female striker made the link between the low wages paid to these women and the high cost of living for which they bore the brunt, when she complained to the military commander of the region that restaurant owners "do not distinguish between men and women when it comes to prices."[73]

The 1917 spring strikes were marked by the high participation of female workers. Laura Lee Downs has pointed out that this, coupled with the fact that overt antiwar demands only appeared somewhat later, led unionists, police observers, and historians to belittle the importance of these strikes. But as she points out, "if French labor first recovered its voice in 1917—and the burgeoning protest that followed in the autumn of that year suggests this was indeed the case—then May–June marks an important passage from invertebrate silence to vocal opposition."[74]

During the strike wave that shook Lyon in 1918, militant women strikers declared that if the men were too timid to join the strike, the women would drag them out of the factories.[75] The cry "Plus d'obus, nos poilus" (No more shells, we want our doughboys) raised by female munitions workers in 1918 throughout the country succinctly linked factory protest with opposition to the war. Although the overall balance sheet concerning the solidarity extended to female workers by their male colleagues was mixed, the role of women in wartime labor protest was not lost on militant male workers. During a meeting of workers from Berliet's factory C in January 1918, a skilled worker pointed to the struggle of striking female workers at the local industrial exposition as an example to be emulated.[76] Through their massive presence in the plants producing for the war effort and their heroic militancy, female workers won the respect of their male colleagues.

Metal Workers and Politics

In chapter 2 we saw how the class independence, antinationalist program in turn-of-the-century Lyon was represented by revolutionary syndicalists, anarchists, and the small wing of the Blanquist socialist current that did not fuse with class collaboration, nationalist socialists. In the same way that turn-of-the-century textile workers were often identified with Guesdist socialism, French metal workers of the day were closely associated with revolutionary syndicalism. Nationally, metal worker unions were mainstays of the revolutionary syndicalist tendency within the CGT from its beginnings.[77] This was certainly the case in Lyon, where organized metal workers were often red-hot revolutionary syndicalists. Metal worker unions in Lyon played an important role on the national level as well. For example, the trade publication of the important Federation of Copper Workers was published in Lyon in the 1890s, and leading trade unionists like Alphonse Merrheim of the Metal Workers' Federation were in close contact with local trade union activists.

As we have seen, revolutionary syndicalism had deep roots in Lyon. Many of the early revolutionary syndicalist militants came from the anarchist-Blanquist current, which had a solid presence in the southeast. This current was able to establish a strong base in the 1880s in the newly industrialized neighborhood of La Guillotière where many metalworkers lived and worked. Along with construction workers, the city's metalworker unions were the most favorable to revolutionary syndicalism and its glorification of the general strike.[78] According to a police report, the corporation of copper workers, polishers, and nickel workers was made up exclusively of militants and revolutionaries. Revolutionary syndicalist metal workers in Lyon were organized into a metallurgy action committee made up of the ten most revolutionary unions: jewelers, mechanics, slag removers, blacksmiths, coppersmiths, nickel polishers, foundry molders, locksmiths, and ironsmiths. This committee was the "vanguard of revolutionary syndicalism" in Lyon.[79] A February 1904 police report stressed that it was "seriously organized" and played a "preponderant role in all the revolutionary and worker's actions." It was led by one Mermier, a jeweler, and Blum, a mechanic.[80] The majority of these militants were also members of the International Antimilitarist Association. Revolutionary syndicalists also animated the committee for the eight-hour day and the committee for the general strike.[81]

Revolutionary syndicalism significantly influenced the forms of industrial organization and collective action present among metal workers. As shown above, many metal workers were threatened with deskilling or even outright elimination. The changing composition of the workforce in terms of skill that this entailed could be problematic for relations between workers across the skill divide. In a period of industrial change when the traditional control workers exercised over the productive process was being slowly eroded, craft pride and traditions could easily translate into short-sighted, backward-looking defensive reflexes. One feature of revolutionary syndicalist thought bore directly on this question of working-class solidarity. The theory of the "active minority," stressed by syndicalist theoreticians, "appealed to threatened artisans, who were often the leaven of the trade union movement."[82] In theory, "syndicalism preached solidarity and cooperation between artisanal and industrial workers."[83] In fact, many metal workers responded to the challenge of capitalist assault against them by taking institutional measures to protect all the workers of their industry. Foremost among these was all-grade industrial unionism, rather than narrow craft organization. Skilled revolutionary syndicalist metal workers actively worked for industrial unionism. The 1909 fusion of the still-small industrial federation and the federation of crafts was largely the work of revolutionary syndicalists.[84] Metal worker union leader Alphonse Merrheim himself was a strong partisan of this form of unionism. In practice it took many forms. Unions were founded that organized workers across skill levels within the same craft, and others that aimed at uniting various crafts in the same union. Following its unification congress in 1909, the federation leadership called on craft metal unions throughout the country to dissolve and combine together into industrial unions.[85] The text prepared by the molders' union for its unification with the nationwide metal workers' federation in 1905 justified its action as a response to the "incessant development of mechanization" in the industry, developments that threatened the very existence of many crafts.[86]

In Lyon the links between metal workers, revolutionary syndicalism, and industrial unionism were clear. The unions of mechanics and iron-smiths were involved in both fusions of craft unions into industrial unions and the metallurgy action committee. A mechanic named Chabert known for his activity in antimilitarist and antipatriotic work was thanked by Mer-rheim for being instrumental in bringing about the fusion of capstan mill workers, electricians, blacksmiths, and mechanics discussed above.[87]

Lyonnais industrial unions were part of a nationwide effort by many unionists in the metal trades to create large industrial unions. Already by 1891 seven Lyonnais metallurgy unions were members of the Fédéra-tion métallurgique whose headquarters was at the Bourse du travail.[88] By 1913 thirteen craft unions had fused.[89] Among the many fusions of metal craft unions into multicraft industrial unions in prewar Lyon was the uni-fication of capstan lathe workers, electricians, smelters, and mechanics into a single union.[90]

The steady progression of craft union amalgamation in the direction of industrial unionism, and the existence of antimilitarist, general strike, and eight-hour day committees with strong metal worker participation, reflected the considerable influence that revolutionary syndicalists en-joyed among early twentieth-century metal workers in Lyon. In addition, a careful examination of prewar metallurgy strikes in Lyon reveals inter-esting information about the links between craft, skill, organization, and strike solidarity that bore the marks of revolutionary syndicalist influence. One measure of the influence of ideas of labor solidarity is the rate of worker participation in strikes.

In forty, or approximately half of all strikes in this sector, 100 percent of the workforce participated. This was especially true for small shops employing fewer than fifty workers where the workforce consisted of one craft and a few aides or unskilled workers. Workers in these shops struck ten times in this period. Three medium-sized metal-working shops em-ploying workers of one trade and their aides also saw all the workers down their tools. The high rate of organization among metal workers contrib-uted to unanimous strike participation in eleven strikes where workers of one craft were spread among several shops. This included such impressive examples of coordination and organization as the 500 metal smiths work-ing in 270 different shops who struck in June 1911, and the 150 black-smiths working in 16 different shops who struck during the strike wave of May 1906.[91] But perhaps the most impressive display of metal worker solidarity across skill and craft was represented by the eighteen strikes that saw workers of several categories strike together. Strikes of this nature were distributed throughout the entire prewar period, from the strike at the Alioth machine building factory in 1902 where 80 mechanical fitters,

60 turners, 60 mechanics, and 50 unskilled workers all struck together, to the Auto-Buire strike in early 1914 where mechanics, fitters, turners, and unskilled workers struck in unison.[92] One of the most striking examples of the capacity of metal workers to carry out strikes involving widely different types of metal workers was a not quite unanimous strike that took place at the Berliet auto plant in January 1912. Though only 61 of the 170 unskilled workers participated in the strike, all of the other workers distributed into no less than fourteen crafts struck together.[93]

The highly developed sense of working-class solidarity promoted by metal worker militants was also reflected in their ties to workers in other countries. The strikers at the Alioth machine building shop in May and June 1902 received a letter of support and a 10,000-franc contribution from the US International Association of Machinists. During the same strike, the workers sought support from worker delegates from the company's flagship enterprise in Basle, Switzerland. The union treasurer reported with satisfaction that contributions from other metal workers in Lyon put a considerable sum at the disposal of the strikers.[94]

The ability of metal workers to conduct strikes across factories, skill levels, and crafts as well as develop international ties of solidarity with workers across national boundaries was truly remarkable. The links between revolutionary syndicalism, skilled workers, industrial unionism, and general labor solidarity are further underscored when the activity of workforces with significant skilled worker presence are contrasted to those were the skilled worker element was minuscule or nonexistent. An example of this was the auto strike that took place in May–June, 1905. The secretary of the Federation of Metal Workers, Alphonse Merrheim, came personally to Lyon to help coordinate the strike. Though the entire personnel at seven auto plants totaling 1,025 workers struck, Merrheim complained publicly on several occasions of the paucity of support and solidarity from other metal workers. Merrheim and other union leaders were particularly disappointed with the metal workers from the newly industrialized quarter of Vaise where industrial plants tended to be newer and where seasoned skilled workers were found in lesser numbers than elsewhere.[95] Nickel workers and polishers, unions under heavy revolutionary syndicalist influence, complained of the attitude of the Lyonnais proletariat in general at the time of their strike, which took place in the highly charged atmosphere of May 1906.[96]

Revolutionary syndicalists were not the only labor activists whom metal workers in Lyon encountered in metal working establishments and labor organizations and institutions. Two other types of socialist activists were also present. Both proposed a broader political strategy than the revolutionary syndicalist reliance on action limited solely to the economic arena.

The small revolutionary socialist Blanquist group offered metal workers an instrument to express support with class struggle–independent politics in the electoral arena. In 1900, that current received a small but respectable 12.7 percent citywide in the municipal elections, which increased modestly to 16.7 percent in 1904. But the combined ticket of left radicals and reformist/class collaborationist socialists proposed by the Guesdist POF won 39.7 percent citywide in 1900 and 55.8 percent in 1904. Significantly, it was the third arrondissement—the neighborhood of La Guillotière where many metal workers lived and worked—that gave the radical-socialist coalition its largest vote percentage with 63.4 percent in the 1904 municipal elections.

We have seen how the strategy of craft amalgamation and industrial unionism that was part of the program of revolutionary syndicalism was put into practice by many craft metal unions in Lyon under the aegis of revolutionary syndicalist militants who also animated the committees for the eight-hour day, the general strike, antimilitarism, etc. Given the large number of crafts and skill levels present in metallurgy, which increased the advantage that employers always enjoy in industrial conflict, organizations linking workers across craft and skill were essential to the defense of metal worker's interests. However, as effective as revolutionary syndicalists were in promoting worker solidarity as a strategy to defend metal workers, the combination of the employer offensive on the shop floor and government repression eventually eroded support for this current. Labor militants faced repression on and off the shop floor. A worker named Gourin was fired from his job in an auto plant in May 1902 for collecting money for the strikers at the Alioth machine building shop.[97] In 1905, a union militant working in the Berliet auto plant was victimized for his role as a fund collector.[98]

A large number of the strike demands reflecting resistance to the employer offensive of these years occurred in the strike-ridden year of 1906, which saw the largest strike wave France had ever experienced up until that point. Eight, or fully half of the strikes in metallurgy that took place in Lyon between 1900 and 1914 having demands for the elimination of piece work took place in that year.[99] One of three strikes having elimination of subcontracting as one of its demands in those years took place in 1906, as did three of the five strikes where metal workers demanded that apprentices receive the same wages as skilled workers. Nearly all of these strikes took place in May of that year. This is significant because May Day 1906 was the occasion of the great CGT offensive for the eight-hour day. As will be recalled, the campaign for the eight-hour day failed miserably and worker militants suffered brutal repression. Such respected labor historians as George Lefranc writing on a national level and Yves Lequin in his work on Lyon have held that 1906 marked the beginning of the end for revolutionary syndicalism.[100] This defeat was particularly crushing for the Lyonnais metal workers who, as we have seen, were in the forefront of revolutionary syndicalism in Lyon.

The class independence, political independence current represented by revolutionary syndicalists and revolutionary socialists therefore enjoyed much support among Lyon's metal workers. But in spite of their heroic fidelity to their program discussed above, and their proclaimed abhorrence of political alliances, the broader political and social climate began to drive some metal workers to turn to the political sphere for allies as the shortcomings of revolutionary syndicalism and the electoral weakness of the revolutionary socialists became apparent.

We have seen how middle-class reformers and some socialists were allied in these years around a program of defense of republican values and support for a socially progressive republic and how this coalition was unusually strong in Lyon. For its part, the radical-socialist municipality in Lyon was ready to assist workers who wished to act in a reformist rather than revolutionary manner. This was one of the lessons of the Bourse du travail affair, a message not lost on some metal workers. Thus, striking metal workers from the Alioth plant cried "Vive Augagneur!" and sang the "Internationale" in a noisy street demonstration on 23 May 1901.[101] Faced with the failure of industrial action alone to prevent employers from using poorly paid "apprentices" to do the work traditionally carried out by skilled workers, Raoul Lenoir, the leader of the molders' union in Lyon, broke with revolutionary syndicalist doctrine in June 1903 by calling for legislative measures to protect workers against this abuse.[102] So, in the same way that the revolutionary syndicalist unions who left the Bourse du travail after their defeat by the combined forces of the radical-led municipality and their reformist union allies later felt obliged to return to the reformist-controlled bourse in order to avoid total marginalization, revolutionary syndicalist metal workers were forced to seek help from the very forces they considered to be their opponents.

The political and social environment nationally and locally thus played a big role in the appeal of different political programs and practices to workers. The increasingly repressive actions of radical-led governments exercised a contradictory effect on the success of the political currents appealing to workers. Government repression, especially when administered by supposedly worker-friendly radical governments, confirmed revolutionary syndicalist propaganda about the inevitable hostility of "bourgeois politicians" to workers. But at the same time, the repression meted out to workers associated with revolutionaries, juxtaposed to the modest but real benefits extended to reformist worker organizations, aided the latter.

The failure of the 1906 May Day campaign for the eight-hour day combined with other defeats did not work to the advantage of those advocating the revolutionary syndicalist program. As we have seen, the revolutionary unions affiliated with the Union locale, which included metal unions, were first isolated in the battle around municipal subsidies to the Bourse du travail and the struggle with radical Mayor Augagneur. And as we have also seen, reformist control of the bourse that followed that affair closed off the possibilities of revolutionary syndicalists, with metal workers at the forefront, to use this working-class institution to advance antimilitarist propaganda—a key plank of revolutionary syndicalist doctrine. Revolutionary syndicalist methods of the active minority and reliance solely on industrial action, then, were insufficient to defend metal workers in this difficult period. As a result, some metal workers felt obliged to ally themselves with political and social forces that they mistrusted.

Conclusion

Turn-of-the-century employers in the auto and other metal-working industries aggressively sought to wrest control of the labor process from skilled workers through shop floor rationalization including mechanization and Taylorist methods, as well as eliminating worker-controlled apprenticeship programs. This offensive provoked a long series of strikes in which metal workers struck against piece work, subcontracting, and the use of poorly paid apprentices to perform the labor traditionally reserved for better-paid skilled workers. The aggressive use of scientific management rationalizing techniques on the eve of the war put skilled workers on the defensive. The outcome of these struggles was quite uneven. In some cases, employers were able to go very far in dismantling craft labor markets and the high degree of shop floor autonomy this entailed, while in others, workers were able to maintain a large measure of control over the labor process. By 1914, however, the balance sheet was a mixed one. Rationalization and mechanization made a much-publicized but in fact quite limited impact. Though craft labor markets in a number of trades were eliminated and capitalist labor markets were beginning, large pockets of skilled worker control still remained.

During the war, French employers—with metallurgy industrialists at the forefront—received unprecedented help from the state to step up their offensive. The war mobilization temporarily removed much of the seasoned skilled worker element, while the militarization of labor neutralized that which remained. After the war, industrial change resumed its uneven course. The information available suggests that skilled labor control gradually declined, matched by a slow but steady increase in semiskilled labor. An examination of the demands raised in strikes suggests that the advance of capitalist labor markets had reached the point that the very nature of worker demands had begun to change. This is apparent in the near disappearance of the type of demands aimed at preserving the shop floor strength of skilled workers that were so frequent before the war.

The reconstituted practices and notions of skill that emerged from the tug of war between metallurgy employers and workers had profound ramifications for female workers. During the war the drive of the state and the arms industry to assure adequate supplies of labor, boost production, and eliminate skilled worker control over the labor process involved radically new policies toward female labor. While women had been effectively shut out of the metal-working industry before the war, they were now recruited into the semiskilled positions that occupied increasingly significant portions of the labor force. This trend continued in the interwar period.

Like metal workers throughout turn-of-the-century France, many metal workers in Lyon were attracted to the revolutionary syndicalist current that enjoyed much influence in their industry. The struggles of the period put this program to the test. Many craft metal unions in the city drew on revolutionary syndicalist support to build craftwide unions and industrial unions. This strategy served the metal workers well in overcoming the potential divisions resulting from the existence of over fifty different crafts and occupational titles. Skilled revolutionary syndicalist workers in particular were at the center of large strikes across scattered industrial enterprises involving many crafts and extensive skill divisions. The impressive solidarity that characterized many of the struggles of metal workers in these years was not, however, systematically extended to the few female metal workers who worked in this sector. The metal industry employed very few women during this period. Though some women were employed in early mechanized metal-working plants, their numbers were few and the industry as a whole was largely associated with skilled work, which was limited to men. The great acceleration of the trend toward mass production that began in 1914 involved a campaign by employers to reconstitute prevailing notions of skill along gendered lines. Traditional views of women's social role and innate characteristics sharply limited their employment in prewar metal plants. As women were needed and recruited into metal-working plants after 1914, these views were recast from excluding to including them. In fact, gender was an important part of the newly emerging division of labor in fragmented production and was integral to the reworked concept of skill that developed in this period. Women entered the metal-working force in large numbers during the First World War and played an important role in the collective action of that period. Though many were forced out after the war, substantial numbers remained. The flood of women into the war industries during the war and their continued presence in metal-working plants forced the male-dominated labor movement to take into account women as workers.

The political practices and affiliations of metal workers in this period were outlined in the narrative of this chapter. That history poses two important questions. The first is why class independence, antinationalist politics in the guise of revolutionary syndicalism, and to a lesser extent revolutionary socialism, were initially so well rooted among metal workers. The second is to explain why some of these same workers occasionally abandoned their declared courses of action for the road taken by their reformist socialist opponents.

As we have seen, anarchists—one of the main components of revolutionary syndicalism—chose metal unions in the 1890s when Pouget and others decided to work in the unions. So they had the advantage of an early start on their reformist opponents in the same way that Guesdists had an advantage with textile workers.

In the early years of the twentieth century when relatively worker-friendly governments were turning to the right and betraying their worker allies, the force of governmental repression fell unevenly. Revolutionary workers were the target of greater state repression, while reformist unions were treated less harshly. This could only confirm the propaganda of revolutionary syndicalists and socialists in the eyes of many workers.

Revolutionary syndicalist propaganda and strategy were particularly well geared to workers confronted with the particular pace and rhythm of industrial change in the metal industry. As we have seen, metal workers' shop floor prerogatives were under attack during this period. But the particular mix of technological change available and worker power meant that while skilled workers were under steady attack, the actual pace of undermining their positions of strength (and indeed survival) was much slower than was the case for the silk workers. On the one hand, these attacks gave workers much to rebel against. But on the other hand, the fact that their positions were not rapidly eliminated, nor was their industry flooded with cheap, semiskilled labor uneducated in the doctrines and practices of the labor movement, meant that much of the skilled worker element that led militant strikes survived the employer onslaught. Yet some metal workers were led in spite of themselves to find accommodations with the reformist middle-class radicals whom they opposed. Why? In spite of impressive displays of solidarity, the revolutionary syndicalist program of struggle solely on the industrial plane was inadequate. To the failure of strike action alone to stem the tide of the degradation of skills in the metal trades was added the crushing defeat of the May Day 1906 attempt to win the eight-hour day and the isolation of revolutionary syndicalists within municipal labor organizations and institutions. Together, these experiences underscored the shortcomings of the revolutionary syndicalist program. Revolutionary socialists of Blanquist origin sought to fill this gap by fighting for working-class independence from middle-class politicians in a broader political arena that included participation in elections. Their electoral efforts were significant, but modest. However, the activity of revolutionary syndicalists based in the workplace and the revolutionary socialists in the electoral arena did not amount to a division of labor between two forces working in harmony. Revolutionary syndicalists certainly did not view these socialists as close allies. Rather, they viewed them as politicians no different from the reformists or even the middle-class radicals. So the forces representing class independence, antinationalist politics were badly divided. This, coupled with a repressive political environment, imposed sharp limits to the type of defense they could provide to workers in a difficult period.

While the strategy of class independence that was central to the programs of both revolutionary syndicalists and some revolutionary socialists proved unequal to the challenges of the period, the strategy of alliances with middle-class radical politicians offered a modicum of relief. The radical-controlled municipality, which owed its existence to an electoral coalition between reformist socialists and radical politicians, proved to be sympathetic to workers who refrained from promoting revolutionary politics. Though it certainly could not bring about the abolition of the wage system, participation in this broad alliance linking middle-class and working-class republicans through the Radical Party and some socialist formations seemed to be the only option to some revolutionary syndicalists in turn-of-the-century France as their preferred strategies fell fall short of their goals. Modest but real, social legislation was passed during this period. Thus leading metal worker militants such as Lenoir of the molders' union, in spite of their broad revolutionary syndicalist culture, called on the state to protect workers. On the local level, municipal governments provided meeting space for workers as long as their activity did not upset the radical-led municipality. The Bourse du travail affair clearly demonstrated how labor activists who agreed not to compromise the Radical Party were awarded with the material benefits of meeting space, while unions under revolutionary syndicalist control found themselves excluded from these benefits and isolated from other workers.

For different reasons, then, class struggle and independent working-class politics in either its revolutionary syndicalist or revolutionary socialist version was unable in the years before the First World War to attract large masses of workers. Constraints in the political arena and the limitations of a strategy limited to the economic arena led many revolutionary syndicalist workers, among them many metal workers, to set their ideology aside and enter into alliances with middle-class radical politicians. This does not mean that these ideas were abandoned altogether; on the contrary, revolutionary syndicalism constituted the embryo of an independent revolutionary working-class party from which the French Communist Party (PCF) later drew many of its members. And in Lyon, we will see how revolutionary syndicalist propaganda before the war paid off during the war as the city became a center of antiwar activity. On the whole, however, the failure of revolutionary syndicalism and independent socialist politics limited its appeal to a minority of dedicated worker militants in the metallurgy industry.

How did the experiences of metal workers differ from silk workers in this period? Workers in both industries experienced a frontal assault on their working conditions from employers anxious to monopolize control over the labor process. As a result, workers in both industries found themselves in a long series of defensive strikes. But industrial change reduced the role of skilled dyers and finishers in favor of semiskilled factory labor at a faster rate than was generally the case for most metal workers. Though small groups of devoted skilled silk worker activists promoted solidarity across craft and skill divisions, it was often difficult to involve unskilled dyers and finishers in industrial protest. This was especially the case in the large plants where semiskilled workers were rapidly replacing skilled workers. The early and rapid success of employers in the dyeing, finishing, and mechanical weaving sectors in reducing the power of the skilled workers rapidly eliminated the element that was so decisive in promoting worker solidarity in the metallurgy industry.

In metallurgy, the uneven pace of industrial change meant that many skilled metal workers with a broad working-class culture survived to impart the ideas of class struggle and independent politics to the semiskilled workers who gradually took their place in the ranks of labor. These skilled workers were the decisive element in metal worker protest in particular, and left-wing political protest in general. In this they resembled the Russian workers studied by Victoria Bonnell for this same period, much more than the image handed down by the Commons school of US labor history in which skilled workers were politically conservative and hostile to less-privileged workers. An important characteristic of most of the shops and factories that worked on the various facets of metal working was that in nearly every case, workers belonging to various trades found themselves working side by side in the same shop. If class formation consists, in part, of organization and collective action, these years were extremely important. Metal workers of all skills and crafts throughout the city went through common struggles together through strikes, demonstrations, mass meetings, and the like, and were frequently joined together in the same unions. While repression made union organizing difficult in the big auto plants like Berliet, skilled metal workers who were experienced union activists and dedicated to all-grades solidarity were often able to unite workers across skill and craft divisions in industrial protest. At the large Gillet dyeing plant, however, where semiskilled workers rapidly became a majority, unions were unable to implant themselves in this period and the workers at Gillet consistently lagged behind skilled workers in smaller establishments in terms of strike behavior and participation in May Day and other demonstrations. The frequent failure of Gillet workers to strike in unison with dyers and finishers in other shops and factories weakened the effects of silk strikes as a whole.

Textile workers nationally had a long tradition of attachment to Guesdist politics. The Guesdists were strong partisans of electoral politics and entered frequently into electoral alliances with left republicans. Silk workers reaped modest but real benefits from their participation in electoral coalitions with socialists and radicals. While the experiences of the metal workers revealed the weakness of the revolutionary syndicalist program that many had embraced, those of the silk workers confirmed the logic of participation in the broad republican alliance linking middle-class republicans with socialist politicians until the right turn of the Radical Party in general, and the local radical-led municipality in particular, undermined support for this alliance.

Notes

1. *Metallurgy* here refers to all industries featuring the use of metals. The following quote is from the introduction in Laura Lee Downs's *Manufacturing Inequality: Gender Division in the French and British Metalworking Industries,1914–1939* (Ithaca, NY, 1995), 1: "Metal working embraces the iron and steel industries, machine building of all varieties, automobiles, bicycles, airplanes, electronics (lampmaking, radios, batteries, and the automobile accessory trades), and small metal working (chain-and nailmaking, screw cutting, cutlery, hollow ware and file cutting). Some branches, notably autos and airplanes, include processes that involve working with fabric or wood, but these workers generally worked within the same integrated production process as those who machined parts or assembled the bodies."
2. See Yves Lequin, *Les ouvriers de la région lyonnaise, 1884–1914* (Lyon, 1971), vol. 1, and Michel Laferrère, *Lyon, ville industrielle* (Paris, 1960), 216.

3. James M. Laux, *In First Gear: The French Automobile Industry to 1914* (Liverpool, 1976), 179.

4. Ibid., 62.

5. Ibid.

6. Ville de Lyon, Office Municipal du Travail, *Statistiques et renseignements diverses questions ouvrières et sociales, 1913–1914*.

7. Edward Shorter and Charles Tilly, *Strikes in France, 1830–1968* (Cambridge, 1974), 211–12.

8. Ibid., 69.

9. Alain Pinol, "Travail, travailleurs, et production aux usines Berliet, 1912–1947" (Unpublished master's thesis, University of Lyon II, 1980), 37.

10. ADR 10/Mp/C17.

11. Downs, *Manufacturing Inequality*.

12. A. Pinol, "Travail, travailleurs, production," 37.

13. Catherine Omnès, *Ouvrières Parisiennes: Marchés du travail et trajectories professionnelles au 20e siècle* (Paris, 1917), 113.

14. Jean-Louis Robert, "1914–1920," in *La France ouvrière*, ed. Claude Willard, vol. 1 (Paris, 1995), 438.

15. Sylvie Schweitzer, *Des engrenages à la chaine, les usines Citroën, 1915–1935* (Lyon, 1982), 109.

16. Ibid., 57.

17. ADR 10/Mp/C76.

18. A. Pinol, "Travail, travailleurs, production," 153.

19. Omnès, *Ouvrières Parisiennes,* 27.

20. Ibid., 140.

21. Downs, *Manufacturing Inequality,* 41.

22. Ibid., 2. Diane P. Koenker makes similar points in her article on the printing industry in early Soviet Russia, where "'skill' itself was considered a male attribute." "Men against Women on the Shop Floor in Early Soviet Russia: Gender and Class in the Socialist Workplace," *American Historical Review* 100, no. 5 (December 1995): 1446.

23. Robert, "1914–1920," 163.

24. Jean-Jacques Becker and Serge Bernstein, *Histoire de la France du vingtième siècle* (Paris, 1994), 77.

25. Quoted in Jean-Luc Pinol, "Les origines du communisme à Lyon." (Master's thesis, University of Lyon, 1972), 65.

26. Alain Dewerpe, *Le monde du travail en France, 1800–1950* (Paris, 1989), 147.

27. Christian Chevandier, *Cheminots en usine, les ouvriers des ateliers d'Oullins au temps de la vapeur* (Lyon, 1993).

28. Ibid., 76.

29. David Montgomery, *The Fall of the House of Labor* (Cambridge, 1987), 192.

30. Chevandier, *Cheminots,* 77.

31. Ibid, 79.

32. Shorter and Tilly, *Strikes in France,* 210–11.

33. Ibid.

34. ADR 10/Mp/C30; Office du travail, *Statistique des grèves* (Paris, 1904).

35. ADR 10/Mp/C39.

36. Ibid.

37. ADR 10/Mp/C40; C45.

38. A. Pinol, "Travail, travailleurs, production," 157.

39. See Christian Gras, "Presse syndicale et mentalités, l'ouvrier mouleur à travers le journal de sa fédération: La Fonderie, 1906–1909," *Le mouvement sociale,* no. 53 (1965): 51–68.

40. *La Fonderie,* August 1903.

41. Chevandier, *Cheminots,* 67.

42. According to the definition established by the 1936–1938 collective bargaining agreements, which will be discussed in greater detail in chapter 8.

43. Gérard Noiriel, *Les ouvriers dans la société française XIXe–XXe siècles* (Paris: 1986), 130–31.

44. ADR 10/Mp/C35; Office du travail, *Statistique des grèves,* 1905.

45. Chevandier, *Cheminots,* 73.

46. Chevandier, *Cheminots,* 74. The hierarchical attitudes that prevailed among workers of various crafts was not a specifically French phenomenon. In his memoirs published in 1926, Charles Stetzle, an American worker, recalled that there were "at least a dozen grades of 'society' among the men" at his plant. Skilled mechanics would never dream of allowing unskilled laborers to "eat their sandwiches and drink their beer in the same corner in which they ate. The draftsmen considered themselves much superior to the pattern-makers, the pattern-makers thought they were better than machinists, the machinists looked down upon the tin-smiths," etc. Quoted in Montgomery, *House of Labor,* 196.

47. Chevandier, *Cheminots,* 108.

48. Office du travail, *Statistique des grèves,* 1914.

49. ADR 10/Mp/C34.

50. Office du travail, *Statistique des grèves,* 1900–1914; ADR 10/Mp/C37.

51. Michael P. Hanagan. *The Logic of Solidarity: Artisans and Industrial Workers in Three French Towns, 1871–1914* (Urbana, IL, 1980), 68.

52. ADR 10/Mp/C31.

53. Gras, "Presse syndicale et mentalités," 55.

54. Chevandier, *Cheminots,* 95.

55. ADR 10/Mp/C35.

56. 13 May–11 July 1901, ADR 10/Mp/C28; 17 April–23 May 1902, ADR 10/Mp/C 30; 18 May–19 June 1905, ADR 10Mp/C34; 13 June 1905, ADR 10Mp/C34; 18 May–19 June 1905, ADR 10Mp/C35; 7 May–11 June 1906, ADR 10Mp/C40; 2–19 May 1906, ADR 10Mp/C 40; 1–25 May 1906, ADR 10Mp/C 40; 2–22 May 1906, ADR 10Mp/C 40; 24 February–26 May 1906, ADR 10Mp/C 40; 2–23 May 1906, ADR 10Mp/C 40; 2 May–1 June 1906, ADR 10Mp/C 40; 7–14 May 1906, ADR 10Mp/C 40; 4–14 May 1906, ADR 10Mp/C 40; 4–22 April 1910, ADR 10Mp/C 44; 6–16 June 1911, ADR 10Mp/C 50; 2–29 March 1912, ADR 10Mp/C 51.

57. Office du travail, *Statistique des grèves,* 1910; ADR 10Mp/C34, C35.

58. ADR 10/MP/C/44.

59. Ville de Lyon, *Statistiques et renseignements,* 174.

60. See Didier Cazzelles, *Apprenti à Berliet* (Lyon, 1999).

61. *La Fonderie,* March 1904.

62. ADR 10/Mp/C40.

63. Office du travail, *Statistique des grèves* (Paris, 1902).

64. Alfred Rosmer, *Le mouvement ouvrier pendant la première guerre mondiale* (Paris, 1993), 1:448.

65. Becker and Bernstein, *Histoire de la France,* 111.

66. ADR 10/MpC57.

67. ADR 10/Mp/C55.

68. Quoted in Rosmer, *Le mouvement ouvrier,* 411.

69. Downs, *Manufacturing Inequality,* 119.

70. ADR 10Mp/C59.

71. Ibid.

72. See Rosmer, *Le mouvement ouvrier,* 114, and Downs, *Manufacturing Inequality,* 126.

73. Rosmer, *Le mouvement ouvrier,* 391.

74. Downs, *Manufacturing Inequality,* 37.

75. ADR 10/Mp/C62.
76. ADR 10/Mp/C59.
77. Claude Willard, *Les Guesdists* (Paris, 1965), 38.
78. ADR 10/Mp/C29.
79. ADR 4M 235.
80. ADR10/Mp/C29.
81. Jacques Leschiera, "Les débuts de la CGT à Lyon, 1890–1914" (Master's thesis, University of Lyon, 1972), 71.
82. Hanagan, *Logic of Solidarity,* 24.
83. Ibid., 71.
84. Ibid.
85. Gras, "Presse syndicale et mentalités," 36.
86. Not all metal worker union activists, however, were partisans of industrial unionism, and there were different appreciations of the concept among those who were. Christian Gras has identified three main currents within metal unions around this issue in the prewar period. A right wing centered around the mechanics favored the maintenance of craft unions; a center around Merrheim and Lenoir favored the building of industrial unions and the launching of a vast campaign of education and agitation towards this end. A left wing hoped to abolish totally the craft framework and build a concerted drive to organize the unorganized mass of workers in the automobile industry. The Merrheim wing envisioned industrial unions organized in six sectors based on the following industrial subbranches: metals, foundry work, turners, and electrical. Ibid., 34–35.
87. Ibid., 38.
88. Leschiera, "Les débuts de la CGT à Lyon," 19.
89. Ibid., 98.
90. Ibid., 93.
91. ADR 10/Mp/C29; 10/Mp/C31.
92. ADR 10/Mp/C27; 10/Mp/C34.
93. ADR 10/Mp/C32.
94. ADR 10/Mp/C27.
95. ADR 10/Mp/C34.
96. ADR 10/Mp/C29.
97. ADR 10/Mp/C27.
98. ADR 10/Mp/C34.
99. Office du travail, *Statistique des grèves,* 1900–1914.
100. George Lefranc, *Le mouvement socialiste sous la Troisième République* (Paris, 1963), and Lequin, *Les ouvriers,* vol. 2.
101. ADR 10/Mp/C26.
102. ADR 10/Mp/C27.

CHAPTER 6

POLITICAL OPPORTUNITY STRUCTURE
1921–1935

The war and its immediate aftermath signaled a changed industrial and political scene in France. French manufacturers with aid from the state had used the wartime mobilization to accelerate Taylorist rationalization in their factories. The changed industrial social relations that those developments brought about interacted with a reconfigured political opportunity structure to shape worker political identity. This chapter outlines the ways that the organized political currents that represented established worker political identities in France fared in the political climate from 1921 to 1935. We begin, however, with a few general points on industrial change for that period.

Massive state intervention into the economy during the war provided French industrialists with unprecedented opportunities to continue their campaign against the relatively large remaining pockets of skilled worker control over the labor process. Mechanization and Taylorization were used to advance these goals. More broadly, state regulations placed control over labor supplies and access to trades firmly in the hands of the employers. Skilled workers were faced with dilution of their technical knowledge and semiskilled machine-driven labor increased markedly. In this way big advances were registered in the direction of establishing a capitalist labor market in metallurgy. Once again, therefore, the war accelerated trends that were present before the war.

Another important change for the composition of the working class was the increased numbers of women working in industrial jobs where few had been present before the war. The specific conditions created by the war were closely connected to the question of female labor in at least two ways: on the one hand, the war created a shortage of the male workers who had traditionally filled certain industrial jobs. At the same time, women found themselves hired in precisely the sectors that had been the most mechanized. While the war accelerated certain trends associated with industrial labor, the question of female labor is more complex. Many of the women recruited to industrial jobs, particularly in metals, found themselves driven out of these sectors once the war ended, though some of them, as we will see, were later rehired as semiskilled factory operators in metal-working plants in the 1920s and later. Therefore, as far as female labor was concerned, the war was more a parenthesis than an accelerator.

Two Currents

Accounts of the post–World War I French labor movement tend to emphasize rupture with the prewar movement. The forms of the two currents whose organizations, ideologies, programs, and practices represented the two political identities under question here *were* certainly altered by wartime and postwar developments. However, the basic orientations of each concerning questions of class independence versus multiclass alliances, and attitudes towards the nation and Republic were carried over into the latter period. The emphasis here, therefore, is on continuity with the prewar movement. In general, the occupational groups whose political identities were allied with these currents continued to identify with them into the interwar period. That was certainly the case for Lyon's silk and metal workers. In the following section we will see how the class collaboration, nationalist and then class independence, antinationalist currents evolved.

The abandonment of internationalism, antimilitarism, and antinationalism by the leadership and much of the rank and file of the CGT and the Socialist Party in August 1914 and its embrace of the policies of the Sacred Union can be seen as a sudden reversal of the trends towards working-class autonomy that seemed clear in the period before the war. By the end of the war, however, most workers had rejected the Sacred Union and the war, and a majority had repudiated the class collaborationist union leadership in the CGT and SP that continued to support the war. In other words, the promoters of class collaboration, nationalist politics enjoyed near total hegemony for the first part of the war, while the isolation of supporters of class independence, antinational politics was never greater. By the end of the war, the balance of forces between these two currents had sharply shifted in favor of the latter. This changing balance of forces found an organizational expression in the split within the SFIO in 1920 that led to the foundation of the French Communist Party (PCF) and the CGTU. The PCF and the CGTU represented the continuation of the class independence, antinationalist current. The SFIO (also referred to as the Socialist Party or SP) and the CGT continued to embody the class collaboration, nationalist program.

The Socialist Party continued the policies of electoral alliances with progressive republican political formations that parts of the French socialist movement had practiced since the early Third Republic. Theoretically, it was characterized by a gradualist or evolutionist approach to socialism along the lines of the turn-of-the-century thinking of such German social-democratic thinkers and leaders of the Socialist International as Edward Bernstein. It was often promoted by former revolutionaries who had gone through a thorough transformation during the war.

The main political expression of this evolutionism was the heavy stress that the SP placed on parliamentarianism and especially alliances with left-leaning bourgeois political parties. In 1924 it entered into a *Cartel des gauches,* an alliance with the radicals in the chamber of deputies led by the Radical Party leader and mayor of Lyon, Edward Herriot. That alliance ended in 1926, but the socialists joined with the radicals in a new cartel again in 1932. The CGT unions preferred arbitration and negotiation to sharp industrial conflict. While strikes were the favored form of struggle for the unions affiliated to the CGTU, the CGT sought to convince "the government and the employers of the reasonableness of the reforms it proposed."[1] In these ways the postwar Socialist Party continued its prewar program and strategy with similar implications for the political identities of the workers who identified with it.

Broadly speaking, the class independence, antinationalist program found its roots in prewar revolutionary syndicalism and more recently in identification with the experience of the Russian Revolution, as it was understood in France. Its program of revolutionary class struggle and international proletarian solidarity represented a continuation of revolutionary syndicalist thought and practice and more generally the program of what is called here the class independence, antinational program. There were some significant changes as well. The prewar revolutionary syndicalist movement that dominated the CGT for a period before the war had opposed electoral participation. While the PCF program envisioned a road to socialism that would result from a decisive revolutionary upheaval involving a proletarian dictatorship, rather than a gradualist road to socialism through parliamentary channels as the socialists envisioned, the PCF did not reject electoral participation. It maintained, however, strict political independence from bourgeois political formations such as the middle-class Radical Party, the frequent electoral partner of the SP.

By promoting and carrying out sharp confrontations in industrial disputes, the CGTU also continued the traditions of revolutionary syndicalism. But at the same time, its close ties with the PCF contradicted the principles of the 1906 Charter of Amiens requiring strict trade union independence, a principle held particularly dear by revolutionary syndicalists. It was the connection with the prestige of the Russian Revolution, however, that helped many former revolutionary syndicalists like Pierre Monatte and Alfred Rosmer overlook those issues and sign onto the PCF and CGTU.

In one form or another, this program guided the PCF and the CGTU up until the mid-1930s when it was reversed by the policy of the Popular Front, a strategy initially imposed by the Comintern that involved the end of the PCF's class isolationism in favor of broad "antifascist" alliances with "democratic" capitalist forces. In the next section we review the working-class political and trade union organizations in Lyon that represented the two currents.

The Communist Party in Lyon

While a large majority of the delegates at the SFIO congress held in Tours in 1920 voted for affiliation to the Third International, most of the party's cadres, journalists, and elected officials remained in the SFIO.[2] The majority had a high proportion of young workers without experience in the labor movement. In the Rhône, George Lévy was the only one of the region's three parliamentary deputies to join the PCF. In the Lyon city council only three of the twenty-five socialist city councilors joined the new party.[3]

Soon after the founding of the party, its local activists embarked on an ambitious program of organization and propaganda. By the time of its first congress in April 1921, the Rhône Federation of the Communist Party had organized thirty propaganda meetings, recruited three hundred new members and established thirty-five sections throughout the area surrounding Lyon. Plans were discussed for the establishment of a party print shop.[4]

The first years of the French Communist Party were turbulent ones, especially in the Rhône. The difficult negotiations between the pro–Third International forces in the SFIO and the leaders of the International drove away most of the elements that had been the most implicated in the wartime Sacred Union before the party was founded in December 1920. Nevertheless, opinions on a number of matters including the possibility of reforming and uniting with the Second International, the fate of centrist elements, and party–trade union relations continued to divide the French Communists. These differences were reflected in several factions.

Even after the founding of the party and the weeding out of the elements most unacceptable to the Bolsheviks, conflicts continued between Moscow and the PCF. In 1922 a number of editorial board members of *l'Humanité*, the Masons, and members of the League of Human Rights were forced out. In 1923 L. O. Frossard, the party's first general secretary, resigned from the leadership and later from the party.

In Lyon, the very first congress of the Rhône Federation of the Communist Party saw sharp conflicts over a number of questions including the role of the party in relation to consumer cooperatives and the proper attitude to take towards the upcoming May Day celebration. The first secretary general of the Rhône Federation, Felix Metra, left in 1922. The next leader, Charrial, also left after a brief period. Divisions became so bad in these early years that the central party organization sent in national leader Pierre Sémard to try to calm factional activity.[5] The degree of local internal strife as well as the importance that the national organization assigned to Lyon was underscored by the fact that party leader Benôit Frachon was sent to become the local leader from 1926 to 1928. Frachon later became general secretary of the CGT. Likewise, Waldeck Rochet, who became regional leader of the party in the Rhône in 1932, later became PCF secretary general. By 1922 the Rhône Federation had already lost half of its founding membership. Its membership remained at 1,500 for the next ten years.[6] Throughout the period from the founding of the party to the Popular Front, the Rhône section of the PCF was an active but embattled and often marginal political force. This can be seen through an examination of the fortunes of its press, its election campaigns, and its organizational structures.

In April 1922, the *Cri du peuple* was replaced by a new newspaper, *Travail,* the weekly organ of the Communist Party in the southeast. The newspaper was beset by frequent financial troubles. At several junctures financial constraints forced it to briefly suspend publication. At other points it was reduced to one page.[7] In 1931 it was even transferred briefly to St. Etienne following the refusal of its Lyon printer to continue to publish it on credit. These problems were compounded by the repression that the PCF suffered from the government. Early in 1930, the editor in charge of *Travail* was jailed for three months for publishing antimilitarist articles.[8]

But as the political fortunes of the PCF rose from the eve of the Popular Front on, its press became more stable. In 1932, *Travail* gave way to a new weekly, *La Voix du peuple.* Its initial press run of 4,500 increased to 7,000 in 1935, 14,000 in 1936, 18,000 in 1937, 18,400 in 1938, and 23,000 by the following year.[9] At a party conference held in 1935, distribution figures by neighborhood were reported. While 165 copies were sold in the first arrondissement, 150 in the reactionary stronghold of the second, 160 in the sixth, and 190 in the former center of the *canuts,* the fourth, 450 were sold in the third, 210 in the fifth, and 225 in the seventh.[10]

A look at the structures of the Communist Party tells a similar story. The party sponsored a number of antimilitarist, veterans', and youth committees. It also held frequent conferences, most of which produced more enthusiasm than solid results. An attempt to organize a party school failed for lack of resources.[11] Financial constraints forced the party and the CGTU to send a smaller delegation than it had hoped to Moscow for a meeting of the ISR in 1930.[12] Although the local communist youth organization was quite active, publishing a weekly brochure devoted to antimilitary activity, the number of its members seems to have been quite modest. Events planned as part of an internationally coordinated week of activity of Communist Party youth groups in September 1931 were canceled due to lack of participants.[13] A police report noted with astonishment that a September 1932 meeting of the local PCF youth was attended by only seven people.[14]

In 1924, the party had 40,000 members nationally. That same year, following the line of the Comintern, the PCF reorganized itself into factory cells. This represented a break with the traditions of French socialism, which had always organized its local affiliates in neighborhood organizations. The attention that the party paid to activity within the plants and its efforts to report on this through its practice of *rabcors* or worker correspondents permits a close look at party efforts within the plants. The *rabcor* reports are often invaluable sources of information on a variety of subjects concerning changes in the labor process and allied shifts in the professional activity and status of the workers involved.

By 1936, there were 894 members in 47 factory cells in Lyon and its nearby industrial suburbs (not including Villeurbanne). For all the importance that the party attached to its factory cells, neighborhood cells continued to exist. In fact, with 1,216 members organized in 53 cells in 1936, a higher proportion of the membership was organized in this fashion than in the factory cells.[15] The PCF built up its working-class audience and membership considerably during the labor upsurge that was the backbone of the Popular Front. By 1938 the party factory cells in Lyon had outdistanced the neighborhood cells 71 to 47.[16]

The SFIO in Lyon

With 80 out of 101 delegates the pro–Third International majority in Lyon was larger than the national average. Those who remained with the

SFIO included, however, a large majority of the party's elected officials, including twenty-two of Lyon's twenty-five city councilors.[17] There were no SFIO equivalents for the PCF-led veterans and antimilitarist committees or factory cells. Furthermore, the party's de facto alliance with the radicals was apparently at least part of the reason why it did not reestablish its party press until 1929; it looked to the *Progrès* to articulate its positions. The SFIO organ, the weekly *L'Avenir socialiste,* claimed continuity with the prewar socialist newspaper of the same name. In its first edition since it reappeared, it carried an article sharply criticizing the Communist Party with language similar to that used by the right-wing press. Its critique centered on the PCF orientation towards municipal politics. It sought to present the SFIO as responsible municipal administrators as opposed to the communists' manipulation of elections and elected posts to advance the cause of revolution. The very same issue, which appeared on the eve of that year's municipal elections, also carried an article critical of its electoral allies, Herriot's radicals, an explanation perhaps for the timing of the reappearance of *L'Avenir socialiste.*[18]

The CGTU and the CGTSR

Just as the French Communist Party nationally and locally traced its roots directly to the wartime Zimmerwaldian current, the CGTU was largely built on the anti–Sacred Union current in the CGT. The Rhône had been one of the *départements* with the highest number of subscribers to *La Vie ouvrière.*[19] At first, many revolutionary syndicalists joined the CGTU, where they found themselves in alliance with the communists. Adherence to the Red International Union became a divisive issue in the CGTU in 1923, and many anarchists left at this point. In 1924 Monatte, Rosmer, and many revolutionary syndicalists left the party. Some returned to the CGT. In 1926 the CGTSR was founded, following the initiative of the building workers' union of Lyon that had left the CGTU in 1924.

Within Lyon's CGTU, revolutionary syndicalist sentiment in favor of trade union independence was particularly strong. This was reflected during the first congress of the CGTU held in St. Etienne in 1922. The question of adherence to the Moscow-based ISR was at the center of the debates at that congress. Pierre Besnard defended the classic position of absolute trade union autonomy, holding that the trade unions should not only be independent from all political organizations but were also the sole revolutionary force that would organize management and production in the future postcapitalist society. His resolution was opposed by Monmousseau, a long-time revolutionary syndicalist who had only recently joined the Communist Party on the basis of his being convinced, partially through his discussions with Lenin, that the communists were an authentic revolutionary force completely different from the reformist politicians whom revolutionary syndicalists had always opposed. Monmousseau also claimed continuity with the Charter of Amiens, holding that it was consistent with the charter for the unions to enter into close working relationships with all authentic revolutionary forces in what would be periodic, rather than permanent, collaboration. Monmousseau's motion won a large majority, which gave the communists control over the CGTU. But a majority of the Rhône delegation, thirty-four delegates, voted for the Besnard resolution versus twenty-seven for that of Monmousseau.

From its inception the CGTU in Lyon had a stormy existence. Although they were a minority on the national plane, the partisans of union independence were a local majority. At the St. Etienne congress most of the building trades delegates, as well as all of the metal worker union delegates, voted for the Besnard motion (ten out of thirteen). Among the most prominent supporters of the autonomist unions in the Rhône CGTU were Nury, Henri Raitzon, Théophile Leclaire, and Ruault, all metal worker union leaders who had been prominent antiwar, anti–Sacred Union activists during the war. The secretaries of the USR were "autonomists" and the partisans of the ISR were held in check in the first years of the decade as long as the national leadership of the CGTU did not officially intervene.[20] The August 1923 departmental congress of the CGTU confirmed the hegemony of the national minority as well as the sharp differences separating the two camps.[21] The depth of the bitterness between the two camps was once again underscored in the USR general committee meeting in January 1924. Heated words and an exchange of insults between the two camps led to the communists walking out of the meeting.[22] The next month an attempt by the national CGTU organization to intervene in the Rhône further exacerbated the tensions, an exercise repeated in June. By the end of the year the two camps had parted ways. In December 1924, the pro-ISR unions—a majority nationally, but a minority in Lyon—left the CGTU to found the CGTU-ISR. It included 2,500 dues-paying members in eighteen unions and individual members from opposing unions.[23]

The Lyon autonomists went on to found a third CGT, the CGTSR, in 1926 that affiliated with the International Association of Workers (IWA) founded in Berlin in 1922 The constitution of a third CGT did not reduce tensions between the two revolutionary trade union organizations. On 12 December 1926, CGTU and CGTSR militants meeting in different rooms of the same Bourse du travail building fought each other with iron bars and benches. One of the rooms was completely destroyed.

Several CGTSR workers were badly injured and the bourse nearly burned down after a bin full of hot coals was thrown down the staircase. The next day, the departmental secretary of the CGTU brandished a revolver during the visit of a CGTSR delegation that came to demand explanations for the previous day's events.[24] Similar incidents occurred regularly until the reunification in 1934.

The CGT

After the 1921 split leading to the formation of the CGTU, the CGT was spared the bitter divisiveness that wracked the CGTU. While the CGT retained the majority of unions, the CGTU had a majority of individual members. Furthermore, most of the younger, dynamic members joined the CGTU. George Lefranc describes the atmosphere in the CGT in the period after the split as one of "lassitude and inaction."[25] The split greatly reduced the ranks of the CGT. Before the split, 3,996 unions belonged to the CGT; after the split, only 1,296 remained. However, in the following years, these numbers rose regularly. Between 1925 and 1931, the number of unions affiliated to the CGT increased from 1,802 to 2,359.[26] In terms of individual membership, the CGT's 373,400 members increased to 884,000 by 1930.

The strength of the revolutionary current in Lyon meant that the Rhône CGT in the period after the split was greatly reduced in size and influence. As the police were far more concerned with the activity of the CGTU and the CGTSR, organizational information about the local CGT is much sparser. Among the leading unionists of the pre-split CGT to remain was the leader of the clothing workers' union, Jeanne Chevenard. Henri Bécirard was a local example of a seasoned revolutionary syndicalist who joined the CGTU for its revolutionary orientation, only to later return to the CGT in the name of trade union independence.[27]

These were then the two sharply opposed working-class political currents that competed with one another for worker support in factories, the streets, and elections. In the next section we look at how they fared in the electoral arena.

Programs in Action: Lyon 1919–1935

The 1919 legislative elections—the first held after the war—saw the victory of the broad right-wing coalition known as the Bloc National. This coalition was "conceived as the continuation in times of peace of the

Sacred Union."[28] It consisted of an alliance of the right and the center right integrating formerly excluded nationalists and Catholics. The unity of the right, the divisions of the left, and the generally agitated social climate in the country as well as the international situation, particularly the question of German reparations and the Russian Revolution, helped the Bloc National score a decisive victory in the name of the fight against Bolshevism.

Opposition to the conservative policies of the National Bloc and its "failures to maintain the preponderance of France on the international plane, to resolve the monetary crisis born of the war, to make Germany pay, to maintain national unity" laid the foundation for the constitution and victory of the electoral alliance known as the Cartel des gauches or Left-Wing Alliance (LWA) in the 1924 legislative elections.[29] This alliance of the Radical Party and the SFIO—largely the fruit of the efforts of Radical Party leader Edward Herriot, who sought to detach his party from the Bloc National and once again anchor his party as a one of mildly progressive social reforms—can be viewed, in the words of Becker and Bernstein, as a "reconstitution of the republican tradition, of the turn-of-the-century Left Bloc which remained its model: socialists, radicals, moderate republicans, united against reaction and clericalism."[30]

These elections, which were the first important ones held after the organizational crystallization of the two working-class programs described above, were an opportunity for each to put their respective strategies into practice in the electoral arena. The victorious LWA managed to actually put together the full range of party alliances in seventy-four of the country's ninety-seven electoral districts. Fifty-seven lists united socialists and radicals. In the remaining seventeen, radicals and socialists ran alone but unopposed by the other formation. While in some of the twenty-three electoral districts where the alliance failed to materialize the radicals and the SFIO put forward their own programs, in most cases "they settled for a violent denunciation of the policies of the National Bloc, defining themselves solely by opposition to it."[31] True to its program of class independence, the Communist Party refused to join the LWA. It presented candidates on lists called the Worker and Peasant Bloc, which won 875,812 votes giving the PCF twenty-six seats in parliament.

The municipal elections held the next year illustrate how these two programs were implemented in the electoral arena in Lyon. Well before the 1925 citywide elections, the socialists and the communists had indicated what their local strategy would involve. As early as 1921, the communists were denouncing the coming LWA. They charged the local SFIO with "opening flirting with the old radical group," and outlined their own electoral strategy. Local party leader George Lévy, one of the few

local elected SFIO office holders to join the new Communist Party, explained party electoral strategy in an article published in the local communist press in the summer of 1921. "The Communist Party," he wrote,
"considers that participation in electoral activity in the commune, the
department, and the nation is useful in the current phase of its development."[32] Communist electoral strategy saw elections as a platform to
denounce the capitalist system and the limitations of parliamentary democracy, rather than as a means of attaining power. This explains why the
PCF occasionally presented women as candidates, even though women
did not have the right to vote or hold office at this time. In the summer
of 1921 the Lyon communist Merlin ran in a special by-election held to
fill a vacant seat in the working-class seventh arrondissement. He received
a respectable 1,800 votes in the first round.

The 1925 municipal elections saw close collaboration between the radicals and the SFIO. In a speech given on 3 May, the day of the first round,
Herriot summed up the political tenor of his campaign by declaring in the
tradition of Lyonnais center-left radical republicanism that his campaign
opposed the two "reactions" of the right and far left.[33] After strong show-
ings in the first round by all the components of the LWA (the slate headed
by Herriot himself in the first arrondissement won an absolute majority),
the two parties concluded agreements between the two rounds. Each
withdrew its candidates in favor of the other, depending on the balance of
forces in specific arrondissements. For example, in the fourth arrondissement the SFIO withdrew in order to assure the support of the radicals.
In the seventh, the radicals withdrew in favor of the SFIO. In the second
and fifth an agreement was struck by which a united radical-socialist list
was drawn up to represent the LWA. The results were a clear victory for
the radical-led LWA. Significantly, the LWA triumphed in the conservative stronghold of the second arrondissement—the first left-wing victory
in that district in a quarter of a century. These elections made it clear
that "the feudal-like support of the Lyonnais SFIO to Herriot was even
stronger and more durable than that of the radicals to Augagneur" at the
turn of the century.[34]

These elections confirmed not only the electoral strategy of the socialists but that of the communists as well. The PCF ran its own slate in all
seven arrondissements. In the third and the seventh a dissident communist slate presented lists as well. The results, however, were quite modest.
Nowhere did the PCF or the dissident slate win even 10 percent of the
vote.

In the following municipal elections held in 1929, these political orientations persisted, but the balance of forces began to change somewhat.
The SFIO hoped to capture city hall while avoiding an alliance of the

radicals with the moderate right.[35] In the second round, united lists of the radicals and socialists were only assembled in the sixth and second arrondissements. In the latter, the right recaptured the seats it had lost in 1925. Though the SFIO held twenty-seven seats in the new city council compared to twenty-three for the radicals, Herriot was able to conserve the mayoral seat thanks to the tacit support of the seven moderate republicans.

The elections underscored the strengths and limits of SFIO electoral strategy and its reliance on moderate support, as well as the class independence, antinational orientation of the PCF, which presented its own slate in both rounds. Further, these elections also marked a modest electoral breakthrough for the latter. In the seventh, George Lévy, the head of the PCF list in this working-class district, received nearly 15 percent of the vote. In nearby Vaulx-en-Velin, the Worker and Peasant Bloc won the elections giving that commune a PCF mayor, and in Villeurbanne George Lévy received more than 35 percent in the first round. From that date on, the PCF made steady electoral progress in Lyon and throughout the Rhône. Its advances in the 1932 and 1934 legislative elections were superior to those registered by the party on the national level. As we shall see, it was the PCF that made the most spectacular gains during the Popular Front.

In the late 1920s the various national sections of the Comintern followed Stalin's abrupt change in orientation called the "Third Period." This strategy—which had its roots in Stalin's struggle against the "right" around Buhkarin after having eliminated the left opposition around Trotsky—involved an exceptionally hard line against the social democracy which was considered "social fascist" by the Comintern. The label *Third Period* was intended to mean that the international situation was headed in a revolutionary direction after a second period of capitalist stabilization (the first period was the revolutionary one opened up by the October Revolution). The Communist Party in the Rhône followed this strategy as well. During the 1932 legislative elections, *Travail* ran a sharp response entitled "The Voice of the Enemy" to a local Trotskyist who had proposed the united front tactic of calling for a vote for the SP in the second round.[36] The critical tone of the PCF against the SP during the Third Period did not, however, represent a qualitative change in the overall class independence, antinational program of the PCF.

The Communist Party followed this strategy not only during electoral campaigns but through the tribunes provided by electoral office and through extraparliamentary action. Municipal councilor George Lévy brought his party's positions into the debates of the council, which were later circulated through its press. For example, in the course of a discussion in the city council in 1922 about erecting a monument to France's dead in World War I, Lévy told hostile municipal councilors that the best way to honor the fallen soldiers was to take better measures to provide for the disabled survivors rather than spend money on "bellicose monuments." Several months later Lévy took the floor during a council meeting to propose a motion condemning police brutality during a recent strike, the activity of the employers' organization (the Comité des forges), and the government's repression of strikers in the port city of Le Havre during a bitter strike at that time. While the SP identified with the Republic seeking to conquer power using parliamentary methods, the PCF rejected the Republic as a form of "bourgeois democratic" rule. During the solidarity campaign with the Le Havre strike, *Travail* published a cartoon of the republican icon Marianne as a prostitute.

Although communists participated in elections, it was in extraparliamentary activity that the differences between their program and that of the socialists can most clearly be seen. This extraparliamentary political activity can be divided into (1) shop floor campaigns such as strikes, often conducted in collaboration with the unions belonging to the CGTU, and (2) public political activity such as meetings and demonstrations that were implemented in alliance with sympathetic local single issue committees such as veterans' groups, antimilitarist committees, and the like. Workplace activity will be examined in greater detail in the following chapters devoted to the silk and metal workers; the focus here will be on the second type of extraparliamentary activity.

Throughout this period the Lyon communists carried out sustained work among the substantial numbers of foreign workers in the city. This was consistent with their program that relativized electoral activity, privileged agitation among highly exploited manual laborers, and highlighted international proletarian solidarity over nationalist chauvinism. Even before the founding of the Communist Party, Lyonnais supporters of the Third International made this type of activity a priority. In February 1920, they organized a meeting for foreign workers. One thousand Italian, Spanish, and Greek workers listened to internationalist speeches hailing the Russian Revolution and denouncing the "national chauvinism provoked by the international bourgeoisie." Several Spanish and Italian workers took the floor as well. The Communist Party and the CGTU sponsored a committee called the Main d'oeuvre coloniale, which sought to recruit "colonials" (especially Algerians) to the local organizations.[37] The Lyon communists also cooperated with pro-Bolshevik expatriate Russian workers.[38] Indeed, in the numerous political strikes that the local PCF and the CGTU called in conformity with national and international directives throughout this period, foreign workers were often overrepresented. This was the case, for example, for a twenty-four-hour strike called by the CGTU and the PCF in October 1925. The police reported large numbers of foreigners participating in this strike, which saw four thousand to five thousand workers cease work.[39]

Though most veterans' groups in interwar France pursued decidedly right-wing politics, the Communist Party sponsored the Republican Association of Veteran Soldiers, the ARAC, which was quite active in Lyon. The local communist youth organizations were also heavily involved in antiwar activity, publishing a brochure listing current antiwar meetings and other activities.

Thus the relations between the CGTU and the Communist Party were such that they can be considered as the trade union and party components of the same current, embodying the same program. There was also a close organizational match between the two. The factory unions corresponded to the political cells, the union locals had their party equivalents and the regional union structures of the CGTU corresponded to regional party structures. These connections became increasingly explicit. In 1929, Communist Party leader Marcel Cachin addressed the Rhône CGTU congress as an official representative of the PCF.[40]

In practice, the class independence, antinational program of the CGTU operated on two levels. On the one hand, the PCF and the CGTU both sought to mount strikes, street demonstrations, and public meetings against French imperialism, in defense of the USSR, or in solidarity with labor struggles elsewhere. On the other hand, the two organizations sought to defend the most immediate demands of manual workers. This included opposition to rationalization and struggles for better wages and working conditions. Actions of the second type will be examined in the following chapters in the context of how this program was applied in the silk and metallurgy industries.

Actions of the first type met with mixed success. Some were successful to the degree that many of the workers affiliated with the CGTU unions or in industries where the CGTU was present participated. In others, however, the actions failed to mobilize more than small numbers of workers, suggesting that these issues were apparently too remote from the preoccupations of the workers and/or the strikes were called under unfavorable conditions. In all cases, the factional atmosphere between the CGTU/PCF and the CGT/SP handicapped the success of the actions. Several examples drawn from the experience of the labor movement in Lyon during the period running up to the Popular Front illustrate these different variations.

In August 1922, the CGTU and the Communist Party called for nationwide twenty-four-hour strikes in solidarity with the general strike in

Le Havre. In the Rhône the strike was supported by the USR, the Bourse du travail, and the Action league of the building trades. The prefect reported that 12,000 workers struck in the Lyonnais region on 29 August. The strike was nearly general among the building trades, the clothing workers, and the shoe workers. It was "partial" in the metal industries and a virtual failure in the silk weaving, finishing, and dyeing sectors. At three o'clock in the afternoon, four thousand strike supporters demonstrated in front of the Bourse du travail and listened to speeches by Merlin, secretary of the Communist Party; Riboult of the masons' union; Accary of the painters and plasterers' union; Natto of the dyers' union; and Raitzon of the metal workers.[41]

These facts and figures reveal much about the conditions under which a program can appeal to workers. While in retrospect it is clear that the wave of worker protest opened up internationally by the Russian Revolution and the strikes in France at the end of the war was on the wane, this was less clear for contemporaries lacking the benefit of hindsight. In 1922, many believed that revolution was still a possibility in the West. In such an environment political solidarity strikes called by revolutionary forces were salient, as demonstrated by the 29 August 1922 action. However, strike participation varied considerably by sector. The industries with unions that were part of the class independence current—building and shoe workers—where anarchism and revolutionary syndicalism had a broad following, were able to mobilize virtually all the workers, unionized or not, in favor of the action. In the industries where the CGT and the CGTU competed for the allegiance of the workers, the strike was either only partial, as was the case for the metal workers, or followed not at all, as was the case for the weavers, dyers, and finishers.

In September 1925, the local communists and the CGTU began to agitate for a twenty-four-hour general strike planned for 12 October, to protest against the prospect of war in Syria and Morocco. From the beginning, the strike was handicapped by the refusal of the Bourse du travail and the CGT to support an action they considered as a purely political maneuver led by the PCF. Even the unions who were part of the class struggle current were far from enthusiastic about this action. The building workers' participation owed more to the fact that the action coincided with a masons' strike than genuine enthusiasm for a political strike at that moment. As it turned out, fewer than five thousand workers joined the strike. Those who did were predominantly metal and construction workers.[42]

Unlike the 1922 strike, which took place in a context of labor upsurge, the 1925 action took place in a context unmistakably less favorable to radical action of a political nature. Divisions within the labor movement were far more salient by 1925 than in 1922. This was reflected in the weeks before the strike by the refusal of the CGT unions and the Bourse du travail to support an action they considered to be a PCF political campaign; at the time of the strike itself, the bourse leadership refused to grant use of its premises for strike meetings. The tensions within the class independence, antinational wing of the local labor movement were such that even other organized components of that current refused to lend it support. The speeches given that day were all made by local communists like George Lévy and CGTU leaders like Cellier, the secretary of the rail workers' union. The masons who were already on strike did not support the action. It will be recalled that the building unions had left the CGTU in 1924 in disagreement over communist influence in the confederation. Other strikes of a similar nature called by the PCF and the CGTU were even more isolated and unsuccessful.[43]

PCF and CGTU strategy was therefore sharply opposed to that followed by the SP and the CGT. While the CGTU sought to organize aggressive mass strikes and mobilize workers in the streets around a variety of issues and PCF elected officials used elective office as a platform to broadcast its ideas, the CGT and the SP preferred negotiation, cooperation, and traditional parliamentary channels as means to defend workers.

Although the CGT felt obliged to maintain a revolutionary discourse to resist the competition of the CGTU, its practice was clearly reformist. An example of this was its campaign for social insurance. The prewar CGT had strongly denounced social insurance, but this reform became the focus of an extensive campaign by the postwar CGT under Jouhaux. The CGTU sharply criticized the CGT for this, using prewar revolutionary syndicalist arguments, especially concerning the provisions of the reform that involved worker payments to the social insurance fund. Another example of the reformist orientation of the CGT surfaced during the 1920 rail strike in the context of a debate around the question of nationalizations. The Economic Council of the CGT favored a form of nationalization that would not represent a clear break with capitalist property relations. It called for management of the railroads by a council consisting of representatives of the state, rail worker delegates, technicians, industrialists, and other businessmen. This was criticized by the revolutionary left as involving "no suppression of the least parcel of capitalism."[44] Throughout the 1920s the CGT also fought—unsuccessfully—for other reforms such as mandatory collective bargaining and paid vacations.

CGT collaboration with the state took on institutional forms. Its federation secretaries were charged with establishing contact with parliamentary groups and ministers, the secretaries of the Departmental Unions (UDs) were in contact with the prefects, and the confederal secretariat sought to influence the (governmental) president of the council.[45]

The CGT attitude towards strikes was one of the most ubiquitous differences between CGT and CGTU strategy. Lefranc explains CGT strike strategy in the following way:

> The strike continued to be considered by the unionists of the CGT as a unique working-class weapon, but it was not used as before. In the heroic period, it was hoped that the vigorous launching of an action, carried out with enthusiasm, would force an employer to give in. But once solidarity and industrial counter-organizing among employers took place, things became more difficult. The strike became less a means of obtaining direct satisfaction than a means to attract the attention of the public powers and encourage them to offer to arbitrate in a conflict in which they would otherwise not dare intervene.

> Strikes made the CGT leadership nervous, for they offered the CGTU an opportunity to try to build a "united front" among the rank and file which the CGT wanted to avoid at all cost.[46]

May Day Demonstrations

The practice of the unions affiliated with the CGT, CGTU, and CGTSR in Lyon illustrates how these strategies were applied on the local level. While these practices in specific industries will be examined in the following chapters, we can get an overall view of them on the citywide level through an examination of the practices of each during May Day demonstrations—a holiday widely recognized as belonging to workers of all tendencies, organized or not.[47] Plans for the 1923 May Day celebrations were dominated by the factional atmosphere between the SP and the PCF and the CGT and the CGTU. Overall it was a successful action in that thirty thousand workers in Lyon and its surroundings struck. But the CGT and the CGTU each demonstrated separately: 4,500 marched in the action organized by the Communist Party and the CGTU, while only 1,000 marched with the CGT. In 1924, 1925, and 1926 united street demonstrations were held. But in 1927, the factional atmosphere, which had never fully disappeared, flared up and prevented the organization of united demonstrations for the rest of the period leading up to the Popular Front and the reunification of the CGT. At the same time the CGT abandoned the streets to the CGTU. While the PCF and the CGTU managed to mobilize 2,500–3,000 in the streets in May Day marches between 1928 and 1932, the CGT settled for indoor meetings. Even when the CGT resumed street demonstrations in 1933, the superiority of the PCF and the CGTU in this type of action was clear; only 450 participated in the CGT march while 1,500 marched with the CGTU. On May Day 1934, only 500 marched with the CGT in spite of the presence of Leon

Jouhaux, while 1,800 marched with the CGTU. The superiority of the CGTU over the CGT in mobilizing its members was clear up until the unification in 1936. On May Day, 1935, the last before reunification, only 500 workers turned out for the meeting held by the CGT while 1,500 heard speeches at a meeting organized by the CGTU at the City Hall of the sixth arrondissement following a march.

Conclusion

The postwar period saw a reconfigured labor movement that, in spite of the changes, continued to represent the two political currents whose content constituted worker political identities. The class independence, antinationalist current now represented by the PCF and CGTU promoted classwide, international solidarity in factories, meeting halls, the streets, and (unlike the earlier period) in electoral campaigns and from the floor of parliament. The class collaboration, nationalist current represented by the Socialist Party and the CGT, following the split in 1921, continued to work with middle-class political forces to bring about social reform. That current approached the political system as capable of recognizing and integrating workers into the nation and Republic. The political opportunity structure of the time allowed multiclass alliances and the possibility at certain junctures to obtain some social reforms, but also harsh repression of labor and political radicals.

The prevailing political opportunity structure and industrial social relations continued to attract silk workers to class collaboration, nationalist politics and metal workers to class independence, antinationalist politics, as we will see in greater detail in the next two chapters. But as we will see, by the mid-1930s the combined effects of industrial change and an evolving political opportunity structure worked to alter existing patterns of political identity.

Notes

1. René Mouriaux, *La CGT,* crise et alternatives (Paris, 1982), 62.
2. See in particular, Annie Kriegel, *Aux origines du communisme français* (Paris, 1969), and Jean-Louis Robert, "1914–1920," in *La France ouvrière,* ed. Claude Willard, vol. 1 (Paris, 1995).
3. R. Chevailler, B. Girardon, V. T. Nguyen, and B. Rochaix. *Lyon: Les traboules du mouvement ouvrièr* (Paris, 1980), 118.

4. Ibid.
5. Ibid., 121.
6. Françoise Bayard and Pierre Cayez, eds., *Histoire de Lyon des origines à nos jours* (Lyon, 1991), 369.
7. Chevailler et al., *Les traboules,* 126.
8. *Travail,* 5 April 1930.
9. Chevailler et al., *Les traboules,* 126.
10. Ibid.
11. *Travail,* 30 January 1930.
12. ADR 4M235.
13. Ibid.
14. Ibid.
15. Chevailler et al., *Les traboules,* 127.
16. Ibid., 125–26.
17. Ibid., 111–12.
18. *L'Avenir socialiste,* 9 August 1929.
19. Chevailler et al., *les traboules,* 112.
20. Claire Auzias, *Mémoires libertaires: Lyon 1919–1939* (Paris, 1993), 71.
21. Sixty-five delegates voted for Robert Fourcade's motion defending trade union autonomy versus twenty-four for a pro-ISR motion and five abstentions. Ibid., 72–73.
22. Ibid., 76–77.
23. Ibid., 82.
24. Ibid., 98.
25. George Lefranc, *Le mouvement syndical sous la Troisième République* (Paris, 1963), 279.
26. Ibid., 280.
27. Auzias, *Mémoires,* 113.
28. Jean-Jacques Becker and Serge Bernstein, *Histoire de la France du vingtième siècle* (Paris, 1994), 190.
29. Ibid., 241.
30. Ibid., 244.
31. Ibid.
32. *Le Cri du Peuple,* 30 July 1921.
33. Bayard and Cayez, eds., *Histoire de Lyon,* 366.
34. Ibid., 365.
35. Ibid., 367.
36. *Travail,* 27 March 1922.
37. Chevailler et al., *Les traboules,* 139.
38. Ibid., 140.
39. ADR 10/Mp/C40.
40. Lefranc, *Le mouvement syndical,* 277.
41. ADR 10Mp/C37.
42. ADR 10Mp/C38.
43. Ibid.
44. Edouard Dolléans, *Histoire du movement ouvrièr* (Paris, 1967).
45. Lefranc, *Le mouvement syndical,* 283.
46. Ibid., 284.
47. Information for May Day comes from ADR 10/Mp/C44–46.

CHAPTER 7

SILK WORKERS IN LYON, 1921–1935

This chapter focuses on Lyon's silk workers for the period 1921–1935. It picks up the thread examining silk weavers, dyers, and finishers that began in chapter 4 for the period 1900–1921. The chapter first reviews the technological and industrial evolution of the silk industry up to 1935, then turns to its effects on workers in terms of skill and working conditions, as well as the forms of collective action that change generated. It concludes with an analysis of the comparative success or failure of the class collaboration, nationalist, and class independence, antinationalist programs.

Structure of the Silk Industry

In chapter 4 we saw how the war accelerated the trends that had already relegated Lyon's silk industry to secondary importance behind the metalworking industries. In the 1920s, the silk industry experienced a series of short, cyclical downturns, a result of the frequent changes in national monetary policy and the rise and fall of international prices and currencies. By the late 1920s, however, it was becoming increasingly clear that interwar clothing styles associated with the Jazz Age, such as shorter skirts, favored cotton and other cheaper materials over the more expensive silk that was so well adapted to the elaborate dresses of the belle époque.[1] The nature of the French economy meant that the effects of the worldwide economic crisis provoked by the stock market crash of 1929 were not felt by most sectors until 1931. Here, however, Lyon's silk industry was the exception. Between 1929 and 1937, trade fell by 75 percent. The export value of Lyon's silk industry declined by 83 percent between 1928 and 1935. The number of establishments was reduced from 119 to 69 and the workforce declined from 16,800 to 6,450.[2] By 1930, 60 percent of the looms in Southeast France were idled.[3]

Notes for this chapter begin on page 183.

Before discussing the many changes that occurred in Lyon's silk industry during this period, it is important to recall one aspect of the *fabrique* that remained unchanged throughout the whole period dealt with in this study: the division between *fabricants* who secured orders and the *façonniers*, the actual producers, who received raw silk and completed production of the various stages of finished silk. One of the peculiarities of the Lyonnais *fabrique* was that even *fabricants* who owned their own looms often had their orders filled by the *façonniers*, even as their own looms completed orders for other *fabricants*. In 1924, more than half of the weaving looms and virtually all the dyeing shops and factories belonged to *façonniers*. Furthermore, the concentration and integration of various operations in the production of a given commodity, which became increasingly common in industries like metallurgy, continued to be exceptional in the silk industry. The structure of the *fabrique* continued therefore to involve large-scale institutionalized subcontracting.[4]

The increased use of mechanical weaving looms that had begun well before the turn of the century continued up to and after the war. The 30,600 mechanical looms of the *fabrique* in 1900 grew to 42,500 in 1914 and 47,200 in 1924. This did not, however, entail a complete elimination of handlooms. There were still 17,300 hand-powered looms in 1914 and 5,400 in 1924.[5] Concentrated production grew steadily during this period, but domestic production showed a surprising resilience as well. Similar factors explain both of these phenomena. While the new synthetic threads and new dyeing and impression techniques opened the way for mechanization, these same techniques actually favored hand weaving in certain cases. Although mechanical weaving was quicker and more precise, the cost of factory wages and equipment often closed this option off.[6] In both cases, the movement of silk weaving outside of Lyon continued. Writing about the weavers in the Loire, the communist newspaper *Travail* noted that these "weavers seldom work in factories. Their labor takes place in family shops. They are not all grouped in large industrial centers. Many are peasants."[7] The few large silk factories, like those of Gillet, were largely associated with synthetic fibers.

Most of the remaining independent urban weavers and some of the mechanical weaving factories remained in the traditional neighborhood of the *canuts*, the Croix-Rousse. The 1936 prefectoral lists of establishments, unfortunately most likely incomplete, names twenty-one weaving establishments, most of which were very small scale *façonniers*. At least fifteen of these were located in the first and fourth arrondissements, which corresponded to the slopes and plateau of the Croix-Rousse. There were also scattered textile operations in this quarter.[8]

Figure 7.1 *The Gillet dyeing factory in 1930. Used with permission of the Lyons Municipal Library, SV77.*

A close look at this list helps shed light on little-known aspects of the structure of Lyon's silk industry at this time. Information for nineteen of the twenty-one included the numbers and gender of those employed in these enterprises. Seven of these were *canuts* working alone. Another 7 had between 2 and 5; 4 employed between 7 and 13; and the largest had only 17 workers. Some of the larger of these were specifically listed as mechanical weaving enterprises, while some of the smaller ones were specifically designated as *façonniers*. This suggests that some of the larger shops were in fact small mechanical weaving factories paying wages to proletarianized mechanical silk workers, while others were traditional independent artisanal establishments filling weaving orders provided by *fabricants*. Most would have worked on mechanical looms, although some may have worked by commission on the handful of handlooms still in existence at this late date. The nineteen enterprises for which size of workforce is available totaled seventy women, and only fourteen men. The presence of only one male in most of the larger enterprises suggests that the lone male was a foreman or mechanic or perhaps both. The two enterprises in which one man and two women worked may have been vestiges of a quite older form of organizing silk weaving in which a male artisanal weaver was assisted by female workers, perhaps family members who were responsible for preparing the silk for weaving. The tasks of separating hanks of silk yarn into single threads (*dévidage*), rolling them onto spools called *canettes*, and setting these into the shuttles (*navettes*) that were then placed in the looms was traditionally female work.[9] Spoolers (*dévideuses*) and woof winders (*canetteuses*) sometimes worked under the supervision of weavers, though in most cases at home alone on a piece

Figure 7.2 *Semiskilled female workers at the mechanized Ducharne silk-weaving factory in 1930. Used with permission of the Lyons Municipal Library, SA1305.*

work system.[10] While nearly all of the workers in what were probably small mechanical weaving factories were women, three of the seven weavers working alone were also women. The division between independent artisan and proletarianized wage worker was, therefore, not exclusively structured around gender.

The evolution of silk dyeing and finishing in the period running from the end of the war to 1929 also continued along the trajectory begun after 1885. Unlike weaving, however, dyeing became an increasingly mechanized and urban branch of the *fabrique*. As we have seen, technological changes that led to dyeing in pieces after weaving rather than the older method of dyeing the yarn before weaving, along with evolving women's fashions, were at the heart of these developments.

One of the most significant developments in the silk industry was the introduction of a new raw material, rayon, which appears in the records as "artificial silk," increasingly used from 1922 on. By 1926, consumption of artificial silk equaled that of natural silk. By 1928, 35 percent of French artificial silk production (6,500 metric tons) was produced in the region surrounding Lyon.[11] In 1929, fifteen of France's thirty-two artificial silk factories were located in the Lyonnais region.[12] Artificial silk, which could be produced by the expanding chemical industry, had the advantage of reducing the reliance of French production on expensive foreign imports

Figure 7.3 *End of shift at the Ducharne silk factory on a rainy day in 1925. Used with permission of the Lyons Municipal Library, S1218.*

Figure 7.4 *End of shift at Ducharne in 1930. Used with permission of the Lyons Municipal Library, S1311.*

of raw silk at a time when international commerce was becoming increasingly unstable. The rayon thread was also easier to weave than the "noble thread," which provided the added advantage of relieving the *fabricant*'s dependence on skilled silk weavers.

Large-scale unemployment and underemployment hit the silk industry during the depression. From November 1929 on, hours began to be reduced in weaving factories. In the dyeing and finishing factories, employers responded to the crisis with waves of layoffs. Between January 1931 and March 1932 alone, 2,367 were laid off, a figure that represented over 11 percent of the local dyeing and finishing labor force. At various points during the depression, the local situation seemed to improve slightly only to rapidly deteriorate shortly thereafter. For example, a rayon factory in nearby Vaulx-en-Velin hired an additional one hundred workers in August 1933, only to lay off five hundred at the end of October of the same year.[13]

In several respects the effects of the crisis were contradictory. While yarn dyeing—a technique associated with older and more expensive methods—practically disappeared from Lyon, and the mechanization of looms became nearly total, other features of silk production became more decentralized. Factory weaving *declined* in favor of home production, both within but especially outside of Lyon. Indeed, most of the factories built rapidly after the wars were abandoned between 1930 and 1934.[14] Many of the new mechanical looms bought by factory owners in the 1920s were sold at cut-rate prices to rural family weavers. In addition to the economic crisis, the factors promoting this return to decentralized forms of silk weaving were reflected in the collective bargaining agreements of 1936. Those agreements permitted the Lyonnais weaving industry to expand to thirteen mainly low-wage *départements* in the southeast at a time of rising social charges for factory owners.[15] The spread of electricity to rural areas also favored the decentralization of silk weaving by making possible the shift from hand to mechanical looms. For dyeing and finishing, however, the crisis slowed but did not reverse the movement towards mechanized factory production. And unlike weaving, these sectors remained within Lyon and the immediately surrounding suburbs.

Employment figures provided in reports drawn up by the prefect of the Rhône during strikes also reflect the dispersal of the *fabrique*'s weaving activity into the often far-flung countryside, as well as the concentration of dyeing and finishing within Lyon and its immediate suburbs. These trends are even clearer when viewed in comparison with the prewar period. We have seen how there were 2,500–3,000 mechanical weavers in 1903. According to police reports drawn up during strikes in 1919 and 1922, there were still only 3,000 weavers in Lyon and its suburbs in the immediate postwar period. While the numbers of urban weavers reflect a stagnation of urban weaving, the 3,000 dyers and finishers increased to around 20,000 for much of that period.[16]

Rationalization in the Silk Industry

In chapter 4 we saw how silk workers in early twentieth-century Lyon experienced a steady degradation of the high degree of control over the labor process they once enjoyed. The decline of a craft labor market where skilled workers enjoyed a large degree of shop floor autonomy and control over entry to their occupation and the rise of a capitalist labor market in which the balance of forces on and off the shop floor shifted dramatically in favor of the employers was quite advanced by the First World War. Employers conducted this assault on the prerogatives of skilled workers by instituting technological change and other measures. The decline of worker-controlled apprenticeship programs was both a cause and result of this. Taken together, this meant that there was an uneven process of deskilling in silk weaving, dyeing, and finishing during this period. Here we will extend the earlier analysis of this process into the postwar period. This will be done by examining how employers used technological change and other rationalizing methods including payment systems as well as hiring practices to deepen their assault on remaining pockets of workers' control, and how this amounted to the completion of a capitalist labor market and a further deskilling of work in these sectors. Against the background of this broad examination of industrial change and its effects on labor, it will be possible to draw some conclusions about industrial change and skill. Having done this, we will look at how these changes shaped worker protest during this period.

In the dyeing sector, mechanization and speed-up were increasingly instituted in the 1920s. In 1914, a typical dyer working in either yarn or pieces dyed four loads in a ten-hour day. In 1928, a dyer working with the method known as *trempage de soupe,* the institution of which provoked a strike in late 1909, and which seems to have been perfected and generalized in the 1920s, was responsible for ten to twelve loads. Measured in weight and length, this increase represented fifty kilos and 1,400 to 2,000 meters in 1923, as opposed to only six kilos and 140 meters in 1914. And while workers were responsible for operating one or two machines in 1914, the norm grew to eight to ten per worker by 1928. It was estimated that these changes represented a tenfold increase in production while wages only increased sixfold for the same period.[17] By 1930 a new generation of machines was capable of preparing 12,000 meters of fabric a day with three dyers as opposed to the 2,500 meters prepared by eight workers operating the old machines.[18] In the finishing sector, the installation of new American machines increased the amount of fabric processed to 25,000 meters a day in the same period as opposed to the 4,000 meters processed daily on the old machines with twice the personnel.[19] Mechanization, then, had considerably advanced in this sector.

But as in other industries, rationalization meant far more than the mere introduction of labor-saving technology. Speedup drives were often conducted independently of mechanization. As was the case in the metallurgy industry, debilitating work paces were often the result of the various pay systems imposed by employers. A variety of pay systems were used in French textile enterprises during the interwar period. Hourly as well as weekly, and on occasion monthly salaries often coexisted with piece work and bonus systems. For example, in 1928, female dyers at Gillet were paid hourly salaries ranging from 2.45 francs for beginners, which increased to only 2.55 for workers after six months and 2.60 after a year.[20] In addition, bonuses were paid according to the number of pieces dyed. This is where the wage differentials between workers with and without skilled titles appeared. Workers who were considered skilled, like colorists, received higher bonuses than those who were not.

The shop floor regime in silk enterprises during this period was also characterized by the presence of strict foremen charged with overseeing the work process. While foremen in the metallurgy industry after the war were no longer the unpopular enforcers of strict shop floor discipline as they had once been, their counterparts in textile factories seem to have continued to play this role. These foremen (there were also occasionally forewomen) had wide powers. At Gillet, foreman eliminated the bonuses of young female apprentices if they failed to complete forty or fifty bolts of silk a day.[21] The Gillet factories were filled with "a veritable army of spies and fascists."[22] The fact that foremen's duties included technical tasks like mixing different combinations of chemicals and other operations necessary to prepare the dyeing "baths" with which the workers worked suggests that they were former skilled colorists themselves.[23]

Employers of dyers and finishers seem to have little or no difficulty in finding adequate supplies of labor at this time, for the working-class population of Lyon and its immediate suburbs was expanding rapidly. Widespread unemployment at various times during this period worked in their favor. At the Société lyonnaise de textiles artificiels in the industrial suburb of Décines, young female workers were often recruited by their mothers. In 1926, 17.7 percent of the women worked alongside their daughters. By 1931 this figure rose to 69.6 percent.[24] That same company also established solid labor supply networks with Armenian immigrants.[25]

There were, however, periods of labor shortages in the early 1920s for *fabricants* who relied on rural weaving. This was due to several factors, including rural migration to cities with their promise of high wages in metal and chemical factories as well as rising prices for agricultural goods, which permitted many peasants to eschew the supplementary income provided by rural home weaving and devote themselves exclusively to agricultural work.[26]

Apprenticeship for textile workers was largely an institution of the past by the time of the First World War. The 1919 Astier act establishing government-sponsored apprenticeship was never applied in the textile industry.[27] Many young workers received a somewhat informal apprenticeship from older, more experienced workers. The highly organized and well-financed professional school established by Lyon's metallurgy employers' organization did not have a counterpart in the textile industry. Various firms had their own internal apprenticeship systems. Many of them seemed designed more to keep the wages of young beginning workers even lower than those paid to other workers, than as serious training programs, which is also indicative of deskilling. Apprentices at Gillet were prohibited under threat of dismissal from taking part in strikes or other forms of collective action.[28]

The eight-hour day had been finally won as part of the big strike wave at the end of the war. But this turned out to be of short duration for many workers. After the employer offensive of the mid-1920s, many dyers and finishers found themselves working ten or more hours a day. Weavers in factories and in home industry worked even longer. Forced overtime was practiced on a wide scale. Female workers in this now predominately female industry often left work to come home to a long round of household chores. A woman working at Gillet reported that many of her colleagues rose at five or five thirty in the morning and were unable to go to bed before eleven in the evening because of household responsibilities.[29] For their part, the independent weavers were driven to fourteen- and fifteen-hour work days in order survive on the ever-diminishing *tariffs* paid to them by the *fabricants.*

Industrial Change and Worker Protest

In what ways did the industrial change described above shape worker collective action during this period? An examination of the issues at stake during strikes indicates that an initial period of offensive action by silk workers around wage and hours issues soon gave way to an employer offensive in which workers were reduced to defending previously won gains. Silk workers only struck twice during the war (November–December 1915 and 15–16 June 1917).[30] Both were offensive actions demanding wage increases. In 1919, weavers, silk testers, dyers, finishers, fabric workers of various specialties, spoolers, and others all successfully struck for higher wages.[31] These struggles took place in the context of the general working-class offensive that was local, national, and international in scope. But Lyon's textile workers soon found themselves on the defensive. In June, 1920, the tulle employers announced that economic constraints forced them unilaterally to rescind the recently signed tariff on wages and reduce wages for men to 140 francs a week and 98 francs weekly for women.[32] Most of the few strikes that took place in Lyon's weaving, dyeing, and finishing establishments after 1919 were unsuccessful attempts to oppose wage cuts. Typical was the three-week strike of fifty weavers at the Guichard weaving factory in September 1922, in which the forty-six female and four male weavers saw wages of 20–22 francs for the men and 16–18 for the women cut to 19–21 and 15–17 respectively.[33]

Not only were most strikes in these sectors of a defensive nature, virtually all of them were limited to protests against wage cuts, or occasionally for wage increases. Before the war, however, silk workers frequently raised demands that reflected struggles over shop floor control. As seen in chapter 4, workers demanded the firing of unpopular foremen on at least two occasions and the rehiring of sympathetic ones on two others during that period. But even though the evidence presented above suggests that foremen were resented as repressive company agents after the war, demands concerning foremen are completely absent from strike data for the second period. One of the few examples of textile workers struggling around shop floor issues was a strike of tulle workers at the Prylli Company in Villeurbanne in November 1932.[34] Workers protested against modifications in company production norms that involved having to operate two instead of one machine at a time. But although they won this demand, the ensuing reduction in wages seriously compromised this victory. How can the virtual absence of demands around foremen or any other issue relating to discipline, mechanization, or any other shop floor issue be explained?

As we have seen above, the process that eliminated the large measure of shop floor control over the productive process that skilled silk workers enjoyed during the first industrial revolution steadily advanced in the years before the First World War. Industrial change after the war greatly accelerated this process, weakening the position of women and men workers at all levels while reducing the numbers of skilled workers whose exceptional technical proficiency still helped provide them with a measure of bargaining strength. The absence of shop floor demands while the shop floor regime was repressive, dangerous, resented, and clearly tilted in favor of the employers, suggests that these changes made the once well-established prerogatives and practices of skilled workers in these branches of the textile industry a thing of the past to the degree that struggles in their defense, or for a return to them, were no longer realistic. The most immediate and obvious point of conflict between workers and employers was around wages. Furthermore, wage demands united workers of both sexes and all skills and specialties.

Many of the 1919 strikes also demanded the eight-hour day, in many cases successfully. But, although like the wage increases, this victory was soon rescinded in favor of work days of ten or more hours plus forced overtime, demands around hours rarely appeared after 1919. Why did this demand, so ubiquitous before the war, practically disappear afterwards? Demands for a reduction of the work day would have represented an offensive demand, ill-suited to the overall situation facing these workers: high unemployment and low wages. Cuts in the work day would have represented a cut in wages for an already impoverished labor force. Demands for the reduction of hours for dyers and finishers who were struck by layoffs would have made more sense. But again, the overall balance of forces worked against such an offensive campaign.

Under such conditions it is not surprising that silk workers did not participate in great numbers in militant street demonstrations that could have jeopardized their already precarious job situations. These workers were often underrepresented in May Day street demonstrations. In 1922, for example, very few struck or marched on May Day and police reports indicate that silk workers were virtually absent from the 1923 May Day activities as well. In 1924, few silk workers were among the two-thirds of the city's workforce who observed May Day. In 1925 once again, few silk workers participated in May Day activities while half of their metal-working counterparts did so. Police reports tell the same story for the 1931 and 1934 May Days.[35]

Industrial Change and Worker Solidarity

What were the ramifications of industrial change for relations among workers across skill and specialty divides? In the prewar period it was seen that worker resistance to the employer offensive was seriously hampered by the rifts between skilled and unskilled workers revealed during strikes, particularly that of November 1903. As we saw, some skilled, unionized dyers and finishers greatly resented the failure of unskilled workers to engage in the same level of strike activity as themselves, while other skilled-worker trade unionists held that by failing to educate unskilled workers and include them in their organizations, skilled workers were themselves partially responsible for the shortcomings of the unskilled. For the period running from 1914 to 1935, however, there is no evidence of divisions among workers in terms of skill, specialty, or gender. The only suggestion of such a rift was the claim by the Communist Party newspaper *Travail* that the German management of the Seux-Charrel factory successfully divided workers by granting a 25-centime raise to the skilled workers and nothing to the unskilled during a strike in 1930.[36] But this does not seem to have had significant or lasting importance. Participation in strikes was far from unanimous in many of the few strikes of the period. But there is no evidence that those who did strike and those who did not were separated by skill, specialty, or gender. It is reasonable to explain this as at least partially the result of the growing importance of semiskilled machine tenders in weaving factories and dyeing and finishing plants, and the concomitant decline of the skilled worker element. These changes largely eliminated the yawning gap in skill between skilled and unskilled dyers and finishers that was at the root of the conflicts between them in the prewar period.

The varied paths of weavers throughout this period involving proletarianized factory work for some, the maintenance of artisanal home production for others (until 1929), and the dispersal of both into the countryside as the depression hit the silk industry may have leveled skills in the factories, especially the mechanical rayon-weaving enterprises. But the continued isolation of independent artisans and proletarianized weavers working for master artisans did not favor unity among them. In fact, the competitive nature of this system, in which the survival of both *fabricants* and *façonniers* demanded that the design of fashionable patterns remain secret from competitors, appeared to link the two to each other at the expense of ties between weavers.

Silk Workers and Politics

Activists promoting the programs and strategies of the currents represented by the Socialist Party and the CGT on the one hand, and the Communist Party and the CGTU on the other, which we have termed class collaboration, nationalist and class independence, antinationalist, both actively sought to extend their influence among Lyon's silk workers.

The differences in strategy between the two currents were particularly clear in the textile sector. The CGT unions consistently sought to defend their members through negotiation with employers and government officials, while the CGTU sought to mobilize workers in energetic strike activity. Following the split in the CGT in 1922, at least two trade union leaders who had played important roles during Lyon's wartime radical trade union movement chose the reformist Jouhaux wing of the CGT. These were Auda, a former Guesdist, and Jeanne Chevenard of the clothing workers' union. Even before the 1922 CGT split, trade unionists like Auda preferred negotiation to strikes. In 1919, when many French were striking to make up for ground lost during the war, he organized negotiations with Mayor Herriot and mechanical weaving employers.[37] CGT trade union leader Madame Bollen-County complained that CGTU "extremists" were undermining negotiations with weaving employers to maintain the eight-hour day and win a 10 percent wage hike in the autumn of 1922.[38] Earlier that year the national CGT textile union centered its strategy of defending the eight-hour day on appeals to the minister of labor. The results of CGT strategy in this period of an unfavorable balance of forces for textile workers were quite meager. Typical was the negotiated settlement engineered by local CGT leader Vivier-Merle in 1935. Rather than mobilizing workers to try to force the cancellation of the 8–10 percent pay cuts decreed in shop floor notices at the Salmona factory in Villeurbanne, the settlement simply provided that the cuts would be staggered over time: 4–5 percent immediately, and 4–5 percent three months later.[39] We have also seen how the rolling back of the eight-hour day did not give rise to strikes in its defense. While this was largely the result of a deteriorated balance of forces, CGT strategy would also have dampened any rank-and-file sentiment in favor of more aggressive tactics like strikes.

This strategy was routinely attacked by the CGTU and the Communist Party in the PCF press and within textile establishments. These organizations sought to defend silk workers through a strategy of worker mobilization and strikes. The Communist Party tried, with mixed success, to build factory cells in weaving, dyeing, and finishing plants. In 1926, there were PCF factory cells in four local textile plants. In 1928, after much difficulty, a cell was finally established in the large Gillet dyeing and finishing plant, though it seems to have had an ephemeral existence.[40] The PCF press also mentioned the existence of a party cell at the Mathieu textile plant in 1929.[41] In addition to selling the regional PCF newspaper, *Travail,* and soliciting articles by worker correspondents, the *rabcors,* the party launched several factory bulletins such as the *Teinturier Rouge* aimed at the Teinture Lyonnaise factory, and the *Volontaire* for the Gillet workers. The PCF tried to reach workers in plants even where they didn't have members. A communist militant was arrested on May Day 1930 as he passed out leaflets at a rayon weaving plant in nearby Vaulx-en-Velin.[42]

The PCF also organized factory congresses for dyers and weavers. In October 1930, one such congress brought together 105 delegates, which *Travail* claimed represented several thousand workers from thirty different local factories. Algerian, Italian, Greek, Armenian, and Spanish workers accounted for twenty of these. But the extreme gender imbalance—only ten delegates were women in this overwhelmingly female industry— severely limited the scope of the Communist Party's implantation in this sector.[43] Several series of detailed, in-depth articles in *Travail* about the structure of the regional silk industry underscore the importance the PCF attached to the industry.[44]

Interestingly, the PCF did not limit its organizing efforts to the dyers and finishers in the big mechanized plants like Gillet. There was also a concerted effort made in the direction of the few remaining independent *canuts* of the Croix-Rousse. Articles in *Travail* signed the *"Red Canut"* exhorted these artisans to join the PCF and the CGTU and polemicized against "parliamentary action."[45] The party also tried to connect with, and keep alive, the historical memory of the fighting tradition of the *canuts.* The PCF organized meetings and a street demonstration (which was banned) featuring national party leaders Jacques Duclos and André Marty in November 1931 to commemorate the 1831 revolt of the *canuts.*[46]

The basis upon which the Lyon communists sought to appeal to the *ca-nuts* was quite consistent with the "class against class" strategy promoted by the Comintern at that time. The communists sought to convince the *canuts* of the advantages of proletarianization over the continuation of the independent family shop. They argued that the independent status of the *canuts* meant self-exploitation and fifteen-hour work days in order to eke out livings on the ever-shrinking prices offered by the *fabricants*. The *canut*'s interests lay with both their proletarianization and the future "communist regime" of short work days and weeks, rather than a vain defense of their independent status; "Long live the family shop and the independence that is leading us to the most vile slavery" ironized the "*Canut* Rouge."[47]

The relations between the Communist Party and the CGTU were particularly tight in this industry. The strategy promoted by the CGTU was the trade union variant of the class struggle/political independence program that the Communist Party applied through its cells, press, public campaigns, and electoral activities. Sixty-five of the 105 delegates who participated in an October 1930 congress of dyers and finishers organized by the PCF were CGTU members.[48]

Both currents, therefore, were active among silk workers. But how successful were they in attracting support from the workers they sought to win to their respective banners? Nationally, the CGT textile sector had 39,000 members in 1934, while the CGTU claimed 24,674 workers in its textile unions in 1931.[49] While no evidence has been uncovered that would indicate the precise numbers of weavers, dyers, or finishers who belonged to these organizations in Lyon, available evidence suggests that the Communist Party and the CGTU seem to have begun their existence with far less influence among silk and other textile workers than with metal workers. Dyers and finishers were absent from the political demonstrations organized by the Communist Party and the CGTU in support of the Le Havre general strike in 1922 and against French imperialism in October 1925.[50] The CGT and the SP, on the other hand, enjoyed considerable success among these workers throughout the 1920s. But by the early to mid-1930s the balance of forces between the two currents was reversed. While as late as June of 1933 the CGT clothing union led by Jeanne Chevenard organized more workers than its CGTU counterpart, police reports indicate that by July of that year the "*unitaires*" of the CGTU began to recruit at the expense of the CGT. The prefect noted that the CGTU and Communist Party were having success in extending individual strikes throughout the industry.[51]

This history raises two interrelated questions: (1) Why did the current represented by the CGT and the SP enjoy more success than its CGTU and PCF counterparts from the beginning of this period up to the early 1930s? and (2) What accounts for the decline of CGT and SP influence and the rise of CGTU and SP influence from approximately 1933 on?

SP and CGT influence among these workers in the 1920s and early 1930s was partly an extension of the success that reformist socialist and trade union forces enjoyed in the prewar period. Once again, long-term implantation helps explain the continuing success of a political current even in a radically changed environment. Second, prewar developments in this industry had nearly wiped out the skilled worker element, and developments in the industry after 1914 accelerated this trend. By rapidly eliminating the last vestiges of a craft labor market (at least in dyeing and finishing), industrial change eliminated the skilled worker element that had traditionally been most susceptible to class independence worker politics, thus leaving the field open for its rivals. At the same time, the PCF and CGTU strategy of militant strike action was far less suited to the silk industry than to metallurgy because strikes in enterprises with low rates of capital investment are less susceptible to strike action than those with heavy capital investment (as in metallurgy). When faced with militant labor forces, silk employers had the option of moving operations to the countryside. In addition, an abundant, easily trained reserve army of unemployed labor during a period of high unemployment made such tactics risky. These are the reasons why the SP and the CGT enjoyed greater success in attracting silk worker support until the early 1930s than their rivals. We now turn to an explanation of the reversing fortunes of the two currents around 1933.

From the early 1920s on, the PCF and the CGTU made concerted efforts to reach silk workers. These included *rabcor* reporting, the organization of industrywide congresses, and the difficult task of building PCF factory cells and organizing trade unions in the face of severe company repression. Lacking deep roots in this industry (their revolutionary syndicalist ancestors were never well implanted in the silk industry) was a major obstacle for PCF and CGTU organizers. After a decade, however, their efforts began to pay off. Silk workers in and around Lyon could see the sustained commitment of this current toward fighting to defend their interests.

The local CGTU was also adept in adapting the national program to local conditions and balance of forces. Nationally, the CGTU textile union elaborated a program that called for defense and extensions of wage gains; the seven-hour day without wage reductions; twenty-one paid holidays a year; worker delegates to assure hygienic and safety standards; minimum unemployment payments of 20 francs a day; social insurance for accidents, sickness, injury, old age and unemployment to be paid for by the employers for all workers, immigrant or French; equal work for equal pay; maternity pay; and safe working conditions.[52] We have seen how the actual demands raised by silk workers in Lyon during strikes were far more modest and therefore better geared to local conditions than the ambitious program drawn up in Paris. The modification of the national CGTU program to Lyon's local conditions also helps explain CGTU influence in this sector.

On a more general level, the gradual concentration of fixed capital in the dyeing and finishing sectors in the late 1920s made silk employers more vulnerable to the aggressive strike tactics advocated by the CGTU and the PCF than they had been earlier. The favored strategies of this current were therefore increasingly well geared to the actual conditions in this industry.

Conclusion

Industrial change had different effects on the different types of silk workers during the period under examination here. For the closely allied trades of dyeing and finishing, prewar trends towards mechanization, concentration, and feminization were greatly accelerated in the postwar period. Besides a few remaining skilled colorists, most had become semiskilled, proletarianized factory workers. The situation for weavers was somewhat more complicated. Up to 1929, weaving too was increasingly mechanized and factories became more common. However, the economic crisis led to a situation in which as in the early nineteenth century, many weaving operations were dispersed throughout the surrounding countryside. Weavers within Lyon were divided between an increasingly proletarianized and feminized factory workforce intimately connected to a few closely allied female trades like garment making, and a few surviving male and female *canuts*. As independent artisans, the *canuts* managed to resist the proleterianization that became the lot of their factory counterparts. But their situation vis-à-vis the *fabricants* continued to deteriorate. It was the weavers who bore the brunt of the periodic crises that befell the industry, and they who bore the costs of maintaining their looms. The declining prices paid for their work in this industry, characterized by a form of institutionalized subcontracting, forced many to work extremely long hours. Their "independence" was maintained at a high price. The skill of female "helpers" employed in the preparatory stages of the weaving process in small independent artisanal shops seems to have been conserved. But these skills did not give them a privileged labor-market situation.

If the above hypothesis concerning their place in the production process in home industry is correct, these women were employed at highly subcontracted labor. Portions of the work and payment given to the male weaver by the *fabricant* were in turn distributed to them. This means that for dyers and finishers, the movement away from a craft labor market and towards the completion of a capitalist labor market that was highly advanced by the First World War was virtually completed in the postwar period. Some weavers too found themselves working under a capitalist labor market. The few remaining artisans managed to stave off the coming of a capitalist labor market, but widespread subcontracting and the features of the system that shifted the burden of the industry's frequent crisis onto their backs meant that the surviving aspects of a craft labor market offered them little protection.

Silk workers in Lyon in this period had much to protest against. Wages were low, and the factory regime was harsh and dangerous, a situation constantly made worse by the seemingly endless employer campaign of rationalization and wage cutting. But it proved quite difficult to coordinate aggressive strike action around work issues. Moreover, silk workers were largely absent from May Day demonstrations and other extraparliamentary actions. This was in sharp contrast to the city's metal workers, who engaged in widespread collective action when faced by similar attacks from a more powerful and united group of employers. How can these divergences be explained?

The general situation for all French workers until the Popular Front was a difficult one. It took years for the damage of the defeat of the postwar labor upsurge to be overcome, and police repression was liberally applied by successive governments. Furthermore, worker collective action was negatively affected by the bitter division of the CGT into two wings and hostility between the socialist and communist parties. But repression was equally harsh for workers in all industries. The difference between metal and silk workers can be at least partially understood as flowing from the rhythm of industrial change and its effects on the composition of the labor forces in terms of skill in these two industries. In metallurgy the postwar attacks on workers' control was a continuation of the unfinished prewar employer onslaught against skilled workers' prerogatives and strength. Different types of metal workers were touched in different ways and at different rates. Rationalization contributed to the slow but steady rise of a semiskilled factory proletariat, while touching other metal workers more slowly or not at all. In the silk industry, however, skilled workers were virtually eliminated in dyeing and finishing by the early 1920s. The elimination of this element, which played a critical role in metal worker collective action in general, certainly weakened the struggles of silk workers as a whole. The same was true for rayon workers and at least partially for other mechanical weavers.

The particular hardships faced by female workers in this predominantly female industry further weakened silk worker capacity to engage in powerful collection. Lower wages for women in an industry already characterized by very low wages in comparison with other industries, and the double working day associated with the lives of working women, were not conducive to building and maintaining unions and carrying out strikes. Finally, the depressed wages and generalized poverty of workers in this sector made it difficult for them to maintain union structures and build up war chests to sustain them through strikes. Metal worker collective action on the other hand, was still often led by skilled workers, including many who had accumulated militant experience in the labor battles of the war and its immediate aftermath.

As in the metallurgy industry, there was a close fit between female labor and semiskilled labor. But the relationship between skill and gender was not posed the same way in the two industries. In the metallurgy industry, the reworking of the reality and conception of skilled labor through the industrial change of the period meant that skill was transformed from a principle of excluding women into one of integrating them. Female labor in that industry was nearly totally associated with the slowly growing semiskilled proletariat while skilled work remained nearly exclusively the preserve of some men. In the mechanical weaving, dyeing, and finishing sectors of the Lyonnais silk industry, however, virtually all work had become mechanized, semiskilled work. Women constituted a majority of the workforce but the male minority was semiskilled as well. In these sectors, therefore, women and men were not divided along skill lines even if men routinely enjoyed higher wages and most supervisory personnel were former skilled male workers. Segregation along gender lines was still found, however, in the rapidly disappearing pockets of traditional handicraft production.

The CGT on the one hand, and the CGTU with its PCF ally on the other, actively sought to appeal to silk workers. Throughout the 1920s, the CGT with its strategy of negotiation over striking had greater success in attracting silk worker support than the CGTU with its strategy of strikes and united front action. In the early 1930s, however, the CGTU began to attract increasing support among dyers and finishers. As we saw, until the 1930s the CGT and the SP benefited from the fact that they were the inheritors of the prewar political and trade union current that enjoyed hegemony among silk workers. The PCF and the CGTU lacked such roots, and the strategy favored by these organizations was poorly suited to the realities of the Lyonnais *fabrique*. The strikes they routinely called for were difficult to carry out and not very effective in this industry marked by low capital investment and high unemployment.

Around 1933, however, the PCF and CGTU began to reap the benefits of the sustained work they had done amongst silk workers. Their practice of factory cells and in-depth press coverage of the realities of the industry along with their steady denunciation of harsh working conditions and famine wages put them in closer contact with the workers and appeared to underscore their claims to be the best defenders of the working class. Eventually this began to strike a chord among silk workers at a time when it became clear that CGT negotiation failed to stop wage cuts. The changes in the structure of the industry also worked to their benefit. The move towards increasing amounts of fixed capital in many silk plants at the end of the 1920s also rendered those employers more vulnerable to the type of strike tactics favored by the CGTU and the PCF.

Notes

1. Solange Garcin, "La fabrique lyonnaise des soieries, 1900–1930" (Master's thesis, University of Lyon II, 1969), 56.
2. Ibid., 217.
3. *Travail,* 11 January 1930.
4. Michel Laferrère, *Lyon, ville industrielle. Essai d'une géographie urbaine des techniques et des entreprises* (Paris, 1960), 88–89.
5. Yves Lequin, *Les ouvriers de la région lyonnaise, 1848–1914* (Lyon, 1971), 1:175.
6. Ibid., 179–80.
7. *Travail,* 12 May 1923.
8. ADR 10/Mp/C120.
9. See Bernard Bensoussan and Henriette Pommier, *Soierie: Artisans et métiers* (Paris, 1991), 64.
10. Laferrère, *Lyon, ville industrielle,* 123.
11. Françoise Bayard and Pierre Cayez, eds., *Histoire de Lyon des origines* à *nos jours* (Lyon, 1991), 328.
12. Garcin, "La fabrique lyonnaise," 71.
13. Christiane Gloria, "La fabrique lyonnaise des soieries et la grande dépression, 1929–1939," (Master's thesis, University of Lyon, II, 1970), 32.
14. Laferrère, *Lyon, ville industrielle,* 219.
15. Ibid.
16. ADR 10/Mp/C61, C64, C66, C67, C69, C70.
17. *Travail,* 31 March 1928.
18. *Travail,* 1 November 1930.
19. Ibid.
20. ADR 10/Mp/C75.
21. *Travail,* 6 September 1930.
22. *Travail,* 22 March 1930.
23. Garcin, "La fabrique lyonnaise," 70.
24. Emanuelle Bonnet, "Des femmes à l'usine: La Société lyonnaise de textiles artificiels, 1924–1939" (Master's thesis, University of Lyon, 1990), 34–35.

25. Ibid.
26. Garcin, "La fabrique lyonnaise," 63.
27. Annie Fourcaut, *Les femmes à l'usine en France pendant l'entre-deux-guerres* (Paris, 1982), 82.
28. *Travail,* 16 September 1931.
29. Fourcaut, *Femmes à l'usine,* 74.
30. ADR 10/Mp/C56, 57.
31. ADR 10/Mp/C61.
32. ADR 10/Mp/C67.
33. ADR 10/Mp/C70.
34. ADR 10/Mp/C79.
35. ADR 10/Mp/C145.
36. *Travail,* 4 October 1930.
37. ADR 10/Mp/C61.
38. ADR 10/Mp/C70.
39. ADR 10/Mp/C81.
40. Henri Olivieri, "Un aspect de la Bolchevisation du Parti communiste: L'implantation d'usines à Lyon. 1924–1929" (Master's thesis, University of Lyon II, 1995), 34.
41. *Travail,* 16 March 1929.
42. ADR 10/Mp/C145.
43. *Travail,* 1 November 1930.
44. See for example, March, April, and May 1928 and October and November 1931.
45. See *Travail,* 6 April 1932 in particular.
46. ADR 10/Mp/C78
47. *Travail,* 16 April 1932.
48. *Travail,* 1 November 1930.
49. George Lefranc, *Le mouvement syndical sous la Troisième République* (Paris, 1967), 410.
50. ADR 10/Mp/C70, 73.
51. ADR 10/Mp/C79.
52. Lefranc, *Le mouvement syndical,* 214.

CHAPTER 8

METAL WORKERS IN LYON, 1921–1935

Postwar political and economic developments continued to shape the political identities of France's metal workers. The class independence, antinationalist political identity that so many metal workers had acquired during the decades before the war had developed on the basis of a fit between the ideology and program of anarchists, revolutionary syndicalists, and some socialists; the shop floor strength of skilled workers; and the reigning political opportunity structure. This chapter focuses on the ways that industrial and political changes of the postwar years until the Popular Front worked to reinforce this identity. The harsh Taylorist campaigns of French employers coupled with the (temporary) success of skilled workers in slowing down the deskilling process generated shop floor struggles that meshed with the strategies traditionally advocated by political independence, antinational forces, now represented by the French Communist Party. A political opportunity structure characterized by both repression of labor and political radicals and a parliamentary alliance of the Socialist Party and middle-class parties also favored this identity. We will see how by 1936 the net effects of industrial change had greatly altered the composition of the metal-working proletariat in favor of a semiskilled workforce with greatly reduced shop floor strength. Those changes coupled with a sharply altered political opportunity structure worked profound changes on metal worker political identity.

Here we begin with an overview of the structure of the metallurgy industry followed by a discussion of how industrial change altered the composition of the workforce in terms of skill and the struggles it generated. Then we will see how POS and ISR favored class independence, antinationalist political identity for metal workers.

Notes for this chapter begin on page 214.

Structure of Metallurgy Industry

We have seen how metal working as well as machine tool manufacturing and electrical component manufacturing occupied an increasingly important role on the local industrial scene from its beginnings in the nineteenth century through the World War I, when it surpassed the silk industry. Industries involving metal working continued to expand in the interwar period.

While the most striking and visible development in the local metallurgy industry was the expansion of large metal-working firms, small and often extremely small metal-working shops continued to exist. A set of file cards drawn up by the prefect of the Rhône in 1936 listing industrial enterprises in Lyon and Villeurbanne reveals the wide extent of small metal-working shops in the area. The cards list the name, address, industrial specialty, and number of workers in over 180 metal-working establishments. Despite the fact that the inventory does not include all bordering suburbs such as Vénissieux, site of the Berliet factories, it is a reasonably accurate record of the breakdown of the various branches of the local metal-working industry as well as industrial plant size from the point of view of numbers of workers employed.

The inventory reports that 36 metal-working establishments employed less than 5 employees and 33 less than 10. Another 36 employed between 10 and 20 workers. Twenty-seven establishments employed between 20 and 50 workers, and 23 factories employed between 50 and 259 workers. In other words, 99 or well over half the reported establishments employed less than 10 workers. The survival of artisanal metal-working establishments in mid-1930s Lyon is underscored by the fact that of the 61 shops employing 5 or less workers, a full 13 were run by independent artisans working alone without employees or helpers.[1] This persistence of small-scale production was not due merely to the dualist nature of French industry or its supposed "slowness." Rather, small shops often played the role of subcontractors and/or providers of general mechanical and unfinished metallurgy products to the large metal constructors. Berliet and other large metallurgy constructors often subcontracted to small artisanal shops to produce the initial stages of certain parts and then completed the finishing and mounting in their own factories.[2]

In his industrial geography of Lyon, Michel Lafferrère identified three characteristics of the Lyonnais metal-working industry. Though caution is necessary since Lafferrère's book was published in 1960, it is reasonably safe to consider this schema as at least an approximation of the nature of the local metal-working industry for the interwar period as well.

The first characteristic identified by Laferèrre was the predominance of manufacturers (that is, of firms assembling complete machines and metallic mounters, boilermakers, etc.) over manufacturers of unfinished products and hardware. The second characteristic was the coexistence of heavy and light production. Third was the development of a local industrial complex in which the manufacturers of unfinished products produced for other manufacturers. There were three types of manufacturers: mechanical builders, electrical assemblers, and boilermakers. Mechanical manufacturers were those firms that produced motors, vehicles, and public works material. Berliet was the largest firm in this sector. Electrical manufacturers specialized in cables, transformers, lamps, and the like. Boilermaking also included the building of tubing, bridges, and hangars.[3]

The industrial sectors that fell outside of the manufacturers included general mechanics, unfinished parts, and hardware. General mechanics can be divided into several subgroups: tool design and tool and die making, and auto and gear box manufacturing. Manufacturers of unfinished products and hardware consisted of foundry work, metal plating, wiredrawing, tube building, stamping and metal cutting, and metal packing.

These industrial subgroups of metallurgy were "very often the furnishers, and subcontractors for the local constructors." Thirty-two of the industrial establishments listed on the industrial register fell into this category (six general mechanical construction shops; fourteen tool and die shops, capstan lathe works, and packing houses; seven foundries; two mechanical electrical shops; one wiredrawing factory; and two electrical apparatus specialists). Modeling shops also often worked as subcontractors for large constructors as well.[4] Five modeling shops were present on the prefect's 1936 list. Though not all of these shops were necessarily subcontractors, it is very likely that a good proportion were.

Government reports published during ten strikes in Lyon between 1919 and 1924 noted that there were between 30,000 and 35,000 metal workers in Lyon and the surrounding area in this period.[5] Within the metallurgy industry, the automobile industry occupied an especially important place. The 36,000 workers employed in French automobile plants in 1913 increased to 75,000 in 1919 and 109,000 in 1929.[6] In Lyon, Berliet consolidated its place in French automobile manufacturing in general and its central importance to the local economy in particular. In May 1935, Berliet alone employed 4,576 workers.[7]

In chapter 5 we saw that women were recruited into metal-working establishments in large numbers during the First World War after having only the most ephemeral presence in this industry beforehand, and how they were forced out afterward to accommodate returning male military personnel.[8] Women gradually returned to metallurgy plants in the 1920s and 1930s. In Lyon, the evidence suggests that women's employment in metal working was highly uneven throughout the industry. For example, though they seemed to have been completely or totally absent from production jobs in many local shops and factories, they constituted 40 percent of the workforce of eight hundred at the Zenith carburetor manufacturing plant in 1930.[9] By the mid-1930s unskilled and semiskilled female workers were commonly employed in metal-working plants.

Employers' Organizations

The industrial changes associated with the war motivated employers in the metallurgy industry to modify the structure of their professional organization. In 1919, the organization changed its name from the Association métallurgique to the Chambre syndicale des industries métallurgique et connexe du département du Rhône et de la région, with the equally wordy subtitle Syndicat des industries mécaniques, métalliques, de chaudronnerie, d'automobiles, d'aviation, d'electricité, fonderie, scierie et de toutes les industries se rattachant a la métallurgie. The Chambre syndicale or CSIMR doubled in size at this time. To accommodate this, the CSIMR acquired new premises in the rue Molière on Lyon's left bank.[10]

The Chambre syndicale worked closely with the Lyonnais Association of Industry, Commerce, and Agriculture (AICA). Local metallurgy industrialist Edmond Weitz was a leading member of both organizations. These two organizations were important components of the Civic Union, a sort of vigilante organization created in 1919 to assure public and private services in the event of a general strike or other civil disturbances. The Chambre syndicale represented mostly the large metal-working employers. Most medium and small companies working with metal remained outside of the CSIMR. In 1935 many of them created their own organization, the Chambre syndicale patronale lyonnaise des industries or CSPLIM.

The CSPLIM consciously sought to establish relations with labor representatives on the basis of collaboration in the pursuit of a supposed harmony of interests between capital and labor. Its pursuit of this strategy involved a hard line against class-struggle labor activists in its industries. This took the form of a policy of refusal to engage in any discussions or negotiations with the CGTU while privileging relations with the Christian unions.[11] As we have seen, the CSPLIM also established relations with the unions affiliated to the CGT.

Industrial Change and Skill

In order to grasp the significance of industrial change for relations between metal workers across skill and occupational lines and ultimately its ramifications for workers' politics, it is first necessary to arrive at an understanding of the nature of the industrial change in this industry in general, and its effects on workers in terms of skill. As we do so, it must be kept in mind that what is meant here by industrial change involves far more than what occurs at the point of production or on the shop floor. It means the totality of relations between wage earners and capitalists including labor markets, and the intervening effects of labor and employer organizations and occasionally local and national governments. An overall picture of these changes can be drawn by looking at the following areas: (1) technological change in the strict sense; (2) reorganization of the labor process with existing machinery, mechanized or not, including systems of surveillance and control; (3) payment systems; and (4) hiring practices including the evolution of subcontracting and apprenticeship systems and labor supply networks. Though for analytical purposes each will be initially viewed separately, an accurate view of industrial change emerges only out of an understanding of these elements in their totality. It must also be remembered that while all of these changes were employer-inspired attempts to deepen the process of eliminating the remaining pockets of workers' control over the labor process that was begun before the First World War, we will see how many were bitterly opposed by workers with various degrees of success.

We begin with technological change in the strict sense. We have seen how the mechanization of French industry was greatly accelerated during World War I, particularly in the metal-working plants producing for the war effort. In an overview treating the period 1913–1983 in the French auto industry, Patrick Fridenson identified the period 1936–1938 as one in which the mechanization of work considerably increased in the auto factories.[12] But widespread automation in French automobile plants only occurred according to Fridenson in the 1970s.[13] This would imply that the pace of mechanization was rather modest for the period 1919–1935. But what technological changes did occur? Unfortunately, information on the advance of mechanization is rare for this period. Nevertheless, available evidence indicates that significant amounts of mechanization did nonetheless develop during this period. At the Citroën plants, new machinery led to big increases in productivity. Fifteen chassis instead of four (an increase of 37.5 percent) and 150 engine blocks instead of 90 were produced per worker per day at the end of the 1920s.[14] In Lyon, mechanization increased in Berliet's principal shops in the 1920s. In the pig iron and steel foundries, seven rolling electrical bridges were at the center of operations. In the forges, a twenty-ton rolling bridge spanned the entire length of the 200-by-58-meter building.[15]

But Taylorist and Fordist methods did not always involve dramatic developments in terms of mechanization and automation. In the article mentioned above, Patrick Fridenson published two revealing photographs from Peugeot's Sochaux auto plant taken in 1931. In the first, workers are pictured working on rear axles with an obviously mechanized assembly-line conveyor belt. In the second, however, workers operate mechanical boring machines to work on engine blocks transported to their work posts with nonmechanical conveyors on rollers.[16]

We have seen how French auto makers inspired by the writings of Frederick Winslow Taylor, especially Renault and Berliet, experimented with the stopwatch before the First World War. In the 1920s and 1930s this practice was generalized. From 1920 on, and especially from 1926, industrial rationalization radically transformed factory structure. In the space of a few years assembly lines multiplied in the mechanical industry.[17] At Citroën, auto mounting was systematically subjected to the stopwatch in 1926. An employee stationed next to the assembly line recorded the succession of movements and the time they took in a large notebook.[18] In 1928, the Lyon metallurgy employers' organization released a report that called for generalizing American systems of labor control, including the establishment of a new post of "demonstrator" who would be charged with overseeing work and assuring that work tasks would be carried out in the fastest time possible.[19] At the Rochet Schneider auto works, the local communist press reported workers' complaints about a speed-up drive in the chassis department in July 1929. Workers there were henceforth responsible for fitting out chassis in four and a half hours rather than the five or six hours they claimed necessary.[20]

Forge and foundry work was a prime example of industrial production in the metallurgy field in which employers in the 1920s and 1930s consistently sought to increase output although possibilities for technological change were extremely limited.[21] The local newspaper of the metal workers union in Lyon wrote in 1937 that workers in some plants worked with "tools in use when molders wore swords and silk stockings."[22]

Rationalization also involved new forms of surveillance and control. This can be seen by looking at a variety of control methods including spying, paid informers, the maintenance of files of union militants, and the changing role of foremen and other supervisors.

A method favored by employers for imposing work discipline involved fines for lateness, supposed poor quality work, or violation of other regulations. At Berliet, workers taking a two- or three-minute break were fined five francs.[23] Bitter complaints were raised against these fines. The worker-writer George Navel, who worked at Berliet at this time, remembered the "excessive number of uniformed guards who continually patrolled the factory."[24]

The changing role of foremen in the Second Industrial Revolution has only recently begun to attract scholarly attention and much needs to be done before a complete picture can be drawn with confidence. But evidence suggests that their prewar role as shop floor enforcers of labor discipline changed considerably. In the 1920s and 1930s the role of the foreman in French automobile plants seems to have shifted towards administrative tasks, which according to Sylvie Schweitzer, came to take 70–80 percent of their time.[25] These administrative tasks involved accounting for stocks, the state of tools and equipment, etc. Foremen often helped workers in circumventing company rules including tolerating tricks by workers to increase their wages under the bonus system.[26] At Berliet, foremen with solid technical competence were respected by workers while part of the antipathy workers showed to the guards reflected the guards' lack of technical knowledge.[27]

In interviews conducted with retired metal workers from the PLM railroad shop at the Lyonnais suburb Oullins, just south of the city, Christian Chevandier repeatedly encountered favorable impressions of foremen by workers speaking of this period. "Generally, they left us alone," said one; "I never had any problems," said another.[28] Indeed, the firing of foremen was raised in only one strike (6–9 May 1930) during this period.[29] This is in stark contrast to the prewar period where, as we have seen in chapter 5 demands to fire foremen were frequently raised in metal strikes in Lyon. The responsibility for enforcing work discipline seems to have shifted towards the *chef d'équipe* or floor boss as well as *demonstrators* or timers whose job consisted of conducting the time motion studies upon which pay rates under piece work systems were determined.[30] But as we will see, the various pay systems instituted at this time were designed to force workers into a sort of self-discipline.

One of the favored methods of metal-working employers for increasing production and control was through the institution of various payment systems. The most widespread among these was piece work. As we have seen, piecework was resented by workers before the war as well. The spread of this form of payment in this period was reflected in frequent demands for its abolition during strikes against the big local auto manufacturers Berliet and Rochet Schneider. It was also seen at the big Zenith plant that manufactured carburetors, as well as other metal-working plants like La Gallia, L'Aluminium du Rhône and the Sclave foundries where molders too were subject to this practice. All told, demands for the suppression of piece work were raised in five strikes, and bitter complaints were aired in the communist press on three other occasions during this period.[31]

One of the key ways in which metallurgy employers in the Second Industrial Revolution sought to alter the balance of power between themselves and their workers was through seizing control of hiring practices and apprenticeship programs. This aspect of industrial change in Lyonnais metal-working establishments is best illustrated in the changing structure of external and internal labor markets, subcontracting, and apprenticeship arrangements.

Metal-working employers relied on a combination of external and internal labor markets. In the interwar period metal-working employers in Lyon benefited from an abundant supply of skilled labor. In fact, the area surrounding Lyon was, after the Parisian region, the second-largest French market for skilled automobile labor.[32] When unskilled workers were needed, Berliet sent labor recruiters to distant rural areas in the Dauphinais and Lyonnais countrysides in search of docile peasant workers without traditions of labor union experience.[33] Whenever possible, Berliet hired only those workers who had been recommended by a trusted employee or preferably a local priest.[34]

At the same time, local metallurgy employers carefully constructed extensive internal labor markets through elaborate employee apprenticeship programs. These internal labor markets were significant in at least two respects: on the one hand they assured a labor supply whose skills were custom tailored to the specific needs of local firms (which made it more difficult for workers to leave). At the same time they took apprenticeship programs out of the hands of the unions, a further blow to workers' control over labor markets and, ultimately, the labor process.

In chapter 5 we saw how worker-controlled apprenticeship began to decline for certain occupations in metal working. After the war, that stream became a torrent. The Astier law of 25 July 1919 put municipal governments in charge of technical schooling. A conference on apprenticeship held in Lyon in October 1921 decided to establish a parity craft council called the Chambre des métiers directed by a board made up one third by employers, one third foremen and one third workers. Though the Lyon Chamber of Commerce approved this scheme, the metallurgy employers' association, the CSIMR, rejected it as giving it insufficient control and autonomy.[35] In general, the CSIMR felt that existing technical schools did not sufficiently train apprentices for its particular needs.[36] As a result, the CSIMR took the decision in June 1922 to establish its own school, a move considered by one historian as "its most important work in the interwar period."[37] The CSIMR invested considerable resources in the school and insisted on complete control and autonomy. For example, an offer by the local industrial professional school, La Martinière, to lend its premises was rejected when La Martinière insisted on controlling the administrative aspects of the school.[38]

The directors of the school, mainly leading local metallurgy employers, were anxious that the curriculum reflect as closely as possible the needs of Lyon's metal industrialists. At the opening ceremony of the school on 13 October 1923, leading metal industrialist and member of the CSIMR Edmond Weitz, president of both the CSIMR and the school, articulated his and his colleagues' preoccupations. Speaking of existing technical schools, Weitz declared that these often produced "young apprentices occupied with work that only had a very vague and distant relationship with their future profession."[39] The school was created to correct this.

The length of the apprenticeship was three years. Work was split between the shops and theoretical courses: twenty-eight of the forty hours of weekly courses were spent in the school's workshops. The remaining time was spent in courses dealing with design, technology, arithmetic, physical sciences, mechanics, geometry, French, hygiene, and labor laws. During the three-year period, the students received hourly payment for work performed for local industrialists according to formulas established between the school and the apprentice's parents at the beginning of the apprenticeship. The school itself was free.[40] At the beginning the courses were designed to train mechanical fitters and millers. In 1925, curriculums designed to train mechanical modelers were introduced. Foundry and boilermaking courses were added in 1926 and electrical specialties in 1932.[41]

The financing of the school reflected the close ties between the CSIMR and the local municipal government. A full third of the budget was provided by the city government, another third by the chamber of commerce, and the remaining third by the CSIMR. When the school expanded and acquired new premises in 1936, the state paid one third of the expenses.[42] The beneficiaries of the school, the local members of the CSIMR, donated machine tools, soldering equipment, vices, and light material. Other material was donated by the National School of Arts and Crafts.[43]

Though the school was designed and run by and for the larger metallurgy firms in Lyon, the largest metallurgy industrialist in the region, Marius Berliet, remained outside both the CSIMR and the school. Berliet set up his own school to respond to his labor needs and short circuit local labor organizations. Berliet's school accepted students from the age of fourteen who had completed the equivalent of a certificate of primary studies. The apprenticeship lasted three years. Instruction involved two hours of theoretical classroom instruction and eight hours of work in the shops per day. At the end of their apprenticeship the young worker was considered a skilled worker.[44] The one hundred apprentices present in Berliet's 1938–1939 class accounted for a total of 5.26 percent of the French automobile industry students for that year.[45]

The school founded by the CSIMR and Berliet's own apprenticeship program were further steps in the direction of the constitution of a capitalist labor market where control of hiring was increasingly in the hands of employers. This represented a further erosion of workers' control over the labor process and a significant advance in the direction of the construction of a capitalist labor market.

Nevertheless, subcontracting and older forms of hiring seem to have survived. We have seen how the very structure of Lyon's metallurgy industry included an entire subsector devoted to producing semifinished parts and subcontracting for the manufacturers. The employer solidarity represented by its powerful organization, the CSIMR, occasionally took the form of filling orders for one another in the event that a work stoppage paralyzed production in a given enterprise. This is exactly what happened during a strike at the Brondel Company in early 1929. Brondel was able to minimize the damage of the strike by contracting with other enterprises to fill its orders. Likewise, central hiring departments and the CSIMR and Berliet schools for training highly qualified workers do not seem to have completely eliminated hiring by foremen free of central administrative control. There were complaints about a foreman at Zenith who was in the habit of hiring outside of the factory and demanding compensation in the form of drinks in return for jobs.[46]

Before attempting to draw conclusions about the net effects of all these changes on skill, relations between workers across skill and occupational lines, and their effects on workers' politics, it is important to look at their ramifications on workers of all categories in terms of health and safety in their daily work routines. A variety of sources converge to indicate that, overall, the heavy machinery and Taylorist production methods including pay systems and quotas made work hazardous and stressful for workers in most occupations and skill categories; "sickness, death, amputation were part of daily life" for workers in the mechanized and mechanizing metalworking plants.[47]

At Berliet, there were ten to twelve accidents *a day*.[48] The local communist press was full of reports from its *rabcors* about industrial accidents, most of which occurred in the largest, most mechanized factories. *Travail* attributed these accidents to "rationalization" and employer negligence. A few examples give a flavor of the daily danger encountered on the shop floor. The 30 November 1929 issue of *Travail* carried an article reporting on an accident that befell a female worker at Berliet. A stray metal bar attached to a piece of moving machinery caught the woman's scarf as she passed through a narrow pathway between two machines. As she grabbed her scarf to prevent herself from being strangled, several of her fingers were pulled off of her hand. *Travail* blamed management for failing to place a protective screen around the metal bars. In September 1930, a young worker was partially scalped by a machine tool as he raced to produce enough for a bonus. The rolling electrical bridges installed at Berliet in the 1920s were widely used throughout France in the large metal-working factories of the day. Between 1920 and 1927 they were responsible for eighty-one accidents which left thirty-two dead and sixteen crippled in metal-working factories in the eastern *département* of Meurthe-et-Moselle alone.[49] The giant presses used at Berliet were particularly dangerous. A retired Berliet worker recalled how "it was rare for day to pass without a woman suffering cuts on her fingers or arm."[50]

Many of the chemicals that some workers used were quite dangerous. At Zenith, bronze workers were slowly poisoned by bronze dust. In the thermal treatment department at Berliet, the high levels of lead that workers constantly breathed had similar effects. The worker played by Jean Gabin in Marcel Carné's 1939 film classic *Le Jour se lève* consumed large quantities of milk to offset the noxious effects of the lead. *Travail* demanded that Berliet provide workers in this department with milk. In addition, suffocating heat meant that these workers were constantly covered with sweat. In the sanding department, conditions were reputedly worse. Teams of two or three poorly paid immigrant workers had only defective masks to protect themselves from inhaling dangerous metallic dust.[51] Years later a retired Berliet worker recalled the dangerous conditions in this department. These workers "were given two liters a day to draw out the sand lodged in their lungs. That extended their lives a bit but that's all. They were basically condemned to death."[52] At Zenith there were no ventilators to reduce the heat in the enameling department where the temperature often reached 55 degrees Celsius.[53] Workers at Berliet's Montplaisir plants complained that the temperature of the radiators were not high enough to keep them warm in the winter. In some shops worker pressure forced management to install heaters, but these were cheap and dangerous coke-fueled *braseros* that caused headaches.[54]

A woman who worked in metal-working factories in the years following the First World War described an aspect of labor in a large metal-working factory in the Paris region. This involved "dipping small pieces of steel into melted lead. We had to do it quickly because others were waiting for the pieces. The work was difficult. The sound of the blowtorch that melted the lead was deafening. The heat of the blowtorch and the ovens next to us where another worker removed the red-hot pieces of steel that he passed to us with a large pincer burned our throat and eyes."[55]

French industrial sociologist Michel Collinet considered cadence and monotony as the two defining characteristics of the work of the semi-skilled *ouvriers spécialisés* or o.s.[56] Workers in the mechanized factories of the interwar period were confronted with noise, stress, and boredom, all of which compounded the risk of bodily harm from heavy machinery and moving parts. A French metal worker explained this in 1930: "Listening to the continuing sound of the motors puts you to sleep and this must be resisted. But you're alone on the machine, the minutes are like hours and the slightest weakening means an accident."[57] At the same time, the constantly lowered piece rates in this industry and the use of stop watches and production norms meant that workers were driven to exhaustion. The pace they were forced to adopt in order to produce enough to keep up with these ever-increasing norms often bordered on the absurd. For example, the molders at the Sclave foundry in Lyon were forced to adopt such a furious pace that in order to earn a livable salary, they dared not leave their work posts. Some did not even have time to go to the rest-rooms, preferring to relieve themselves near their work stations.[58]

The hygienic conditions in these factories were abominable. In the late 1920s the number of washrooms at Zenith and Berliet were inadequate. Those that did exist were often filthy and lacked running water. In some departments at Berliet, workers had only buckets of usually dirty water with which to wash themselves following their shifts.[59] There were no showers in most of Lyon's metal-working establishments at that time. Even where they did exist, as in the locomotive shops at PLM Oullins, workers were required to have written authorization from foremen to use them.[60]

What were the net effects of these developments on metal workers in terms of skill in this period? We have seen how the rise of semiskilled work-ers and the decline of skilled workers was far slower than often assumed in France during the Second Industrial Revolution as a whole. But what did this mean for metal workers in Lyon during this period? An overall picture of the evolution of labor in this industry can be drawn through a two-tiered approach. At the first level we will examine the evolution of individual occupations and job titles. At the second, we will attempt to determine how these changes altered the composition of the metal-working workforce by looking at several industrial establishments to see how industrial change altered the percentages of skilled, semiskilled, and unskilled labor in several local metal-working enterprises.

This task is complicated by the fact that the various occupational lists assembled by different parties were designed with different purposes (and interests) in mind. Even serious attempts at cataloguing different occupa-tions like the 1909 industrial dictionary were not updated periodically, which limits their value in charting changes over time. Another serious problem is the confusion between job title, occupation, and craft. Different jobs often bore the same occupational title. Widely different types of work often lurked behind the facile classifications established by officials. In fact, employers and workers often contested these classifications. What did it mean to be a skilled or semiskilled worker in metal-working shops and factories between 1919 and 1935? And how did various occupations change under the effects of employer-inspired changes modified by worker resistance? Nevertheless, it is possible to arrive at least an approximation of the evolution of job and occupation titles by carefully comparing the list of occupations mentioned in prefects' reports of industrial strikes discussed in chapter 5 with a similar list assembled for this chapter.

One reasonably safe manner of determining this is to look at the definitions agreed upon by trade unions and employers and codified in collective bargaining agreements. In the wake of the Matignon accords in June 1936, regional prefects throughout France brought employers and trade unions together to reach local accords. In Lyon, an elaborate series of agreements focusing on wage rates was reached on 25 June 1936 between the two metallurgy employer associations, the CSIMR and the CSPLIM, on the one hand, and the Lyon metal-worker union and the Rhône CGT departmental union, on the other.[61] Besides setting wage rates and other issues such as shop floor delegates, these accords specified what constituted skilled and semiskilled labor and what work tasks were included in different occupational titles. Article 19 of those accords defined skilled and unskilled workers. The following is a translation of that article:

> A skilled or professional worker (*ouvrier qualifié* or *ouvrier professionnel*) is a worker possessing a craft (*métier*) for which apprenticeship can be demonstrated by a professional aptitude certificate (or a worker who practices a craft equivalent to an apprenticeship) and who has passed a professional test.

> A semiskilled worker is a worker working on machine tools, mounting, assembly line, furnaces, etc., which are tasks that do not require a craft knowledge for which apprenticeship can be certified by a certificate of professional aptitude.

These definitions set the dividing line between skilled and semiskilled work around the question of formal and informal apprenticeship, though the question of job tasks, particularly industrial labor involving parcelized work tasks, was also considered a dividing line. While these definitions give a broad picture of the differences between skilled and semiskilled labor, they are nonetheless rather vague. Fortunately, far more precise definitions emerge from the portions of the agreements that actually deal with specific occupations within metallurgy industries.

In the section dealing with automobile workers, men, women, and young production workers were divided into various categories, each with distinctive pay scales. Four broad categories of male workers were identified, each with a distinct wage rate. For men, this involved two categories of "skilled workers": "highly qualified professionals" (*professionels hautement qualifiés*) and "professionals on fabricating machines" (*professionnels sur machines de fabrication*). The other two categories were "semiskilled male workers" (*ouvriers spécialisés*), the famous o.s., and "unskilled workers" (*manoeuvres*).

The highly skilled workers were to be paid 6.50 francs an hour. These workers included professional tool makers. Listed under this category were various types of tool and die makers and mechanical crane operators, smiths, smelters, precision tool makers, gear box builders, and millers. The other category of skilled auto worker, skilled workers on fabrication machines, was to be paid 6 francs an hour. They were machinists and fitters. The semiskilled workers, the o.s., were to receive 5.50 francs an hour. They were workers on automatic and semiautomatic self-acting power lathes and drillers, sand blasters, and industrial waste removal workers. Finally, the unskilled workers had two pay levels. Those working on furnaces and power hammer operators and other unskilled workers were to be paid 4.50 francs. Workers paid 4.15 francs included cleaners, stock workers, and the like.

Women's work was not divided in quite the same way. Four different pay rates running from 3.40–4.50 francs were tied to job classifications that, unlike those for men, were not categorized into groups according to broad skill definitions. Female workers paid 4.50 francs an hour were those working on large presses (*grosses presses*) and hard machine labor (*travaux pénibles sur machines*). Workers paid 4.15 francs an hour included those working on small presses, cutting off lathes, drillers, screw cutters, and assorted machines. Mounters and controllers were paid 3.75 francs. The lowest paid category was unskilled workers (*femmes manoeuvres*), sweepers, stock room workers, and sorters who were paid 3.40 francs. Though the authors of these accords did not categorize the jobs of these female workers in terms of skill, a comparison with their male colleagues makes it reasonable to consider the first three pay categories as semiskilled work and the fourth as unskilled labor. For their part, the jobs of "young workers" (presumably male) were not defined in terms of skill or job title or description, but rather in terms of age. Workers fourteen to fifteen years of age were to be paid 2.50 francs an hour, those fifteen to sixteen 3.00, and those sixteen to eighteen, 4.10. Table 8.1 lists skilled occupations assembled from information recorded by the prefect of the

Rhône during strikes between 1919 and 1936. Table 8.2 lists semiskilled occupations for the same period.

Keeping this information in mind, we now turn to a comparison of these lists of occupations with the one assembled in chapter 5 for the prewar period. As we compare the two periods, it must remembered that the employers routinely used the favorable balance of forces that evolved in the interwar period to violate established norms of production, job titles, and pay rates. For example, in late 1938 complaints were raised in the trade union press that Berliet was forcing skilled workers to relinquish their status as skilled workers and accept the title and pay rates of semi-skilled workers.[62]

The terms employed by the prefect, especially for the latter period, indiscriminately mix occupations with job titles. For example, we find millers and turners listed alongside workers designated as *métallurgistes-professionels* and *métallurgistes spécialistes*. We have seen how the term *spécialistes* was often synonymous with what were regarded as semiskilled workers while *professionel* was another term for skilled. Wage rates also indicate that it is safe to consider the former as skilled workers and the latter as semiskilled. For example, in 1924, the *professionels* were paid between 3.25 and 3.50 francs an hour, while *spécialistes* were paid between 2.50 and 3.00 francs an hour. In addition, the pay scale of the *professionels* was closer to that paid adjusters in 1923 than to the *specialists*—between two francs seventy five and three francs ten an hour.[63]

Table 8.1 *Skilled occupations in metallurgy present in Lyon, 1919–1936*

Auto Mechanics (*Mécaniciens-constructeurs*)
Adjusters (*Ajusteurs*)
Blacksmiths (*Ferblantiers*)
Coppersmiths (*Chaudronniers*)
Coremakers (*Noyauteurs*)
Electricians (*Electriciens*)
Forgers (*Forgerons*)
Millers (*Fraiseurs*)
Smelters (*Fondeurs*)

Table 8.2 *Semiskilled occupations in metallurgy present in Lyon, 1919–1936*

Automatic Capstan Lathe Workers (*Décolleteuses:* Female)
Machine Trimmers (*Ebarbeurs*)
Semiskilled Workers (*Metallurgistes Spécialistes*)
Stokers (*Chauffeurs*)

Unlike the first period, the second is rich in additional job titles suggesting semiskilled work, such as *spécialistes, spécialistes femmes, ouvriers sur machines,* and *conducteur de machines.* In addition, there also appeared a category called *manoeuvres spécialisés.* This seems to be an intermediate post between unskilled and skilled. In 1920, *manoeuvres spécialisés* were receiving daily wages of between 17.20 and 18.80 francs while simple *manoeuvres* were paid 13.60.[64]

The most striking aspect of a comparison of the two periods is the large number of job titles listed in the first period but not the second. Over forty titles seem to have disappeared from one period to the next. However, this does not necessarily mean that industrial change had eliminated all of these occupations. For example, three types of *chaudronniers* were listed in the first period: *chaudronniers, chaudronniers en fer,* and *chaudronniers en cuivre,* while in the second, only *chaudronniers* appear. As we have seen, *chaudronniers en cuivre* (copper) was a more prestigious occupation or occupational title than *chaudronnier en fer* (iron). On the other hand, since these lists were assembled by government agents rather than census takers who would have asked the worker to describe him- or herself, it is very possible that the boiled down definition of *chaudronnier* actually reflected real changes in work and skill. The absence of boiler scalers (*piqueurs de chaudriers*) in the second period buttresses this hypothesis.

These lists also suggest that industrial change transformed some skilled work into semiskilled work. Workers listed as *décolleteurs* or capstan lathe workers in the earlier period were replaced by female *décolleteuses* in the later period. The 1909 industrial dictionary gave two definitions for this work. One involved fabricating custom-made parts from design patterns. This was most likely highly qualified labor. The other consisted of monitoring machines (*tours décolleter*), which was most likely semiskilled labor. This double definition probably reflected the fact that technological change had by that time begun to transform this type of work without, however, completely eliminating the older craft type techniques. Since *décolleteurs* in Lyon during the earlier period had their own union and were paid at rates similar to the adjusters, it is reasonable to conclude that in Lyon, at least, this was still well-paid, skilled male labor. In the second period, the job of the *décolleteuses* was specifically described in the collective bargaining agreements discussed above in terms consistent with the other definition from 1909, and was placed in the third of the four women's pay scales; this would make it semiskilled work. Therefore, it is safe to conclude that the combined effects of the various facets of industrial change discussed above resulted in the transformation of capstan lathe work from a highly paid, skilled, male occupation before the First World War, into a semiskilled, female, and poorly paid one in the interwar period.

Another striking aspect of the two lists is that only two occupations appear in the list for the second period that were not listed for the first. These were fettlers and coremakers. Pay rates suggest that the fettlers were semiskilled workers and that the core makers were skilled workers.

Many skilled occupations were spared—at least temporarily—by the movement towards rationalization. Chief among these were tool and die makers. George Navel remembers how work in this sector at Berliet in the early 1920s was not Taylorized. "It was varied, challenging. Workers were sensitive to the quality of their work."[65]

Even allowing for imprecision, different classification schemes, and other shortcomings of these sources, it is reasonable to conclude that industrial change during the extended period of the Second Industrial Revolution vastly simplified what had been an extremely rich industrial landscape in terms of specialization and job titles, either through outright elimination or combination of some occupations due to technical advances and/or elimination of job titles as the result of the decline of a craft labor market in favor of a capitalist one.

How did these changes in individual jobs and occupations alter the composition of the workforce as a whole in metal-working establishments in this period? Information gathered by the local prefect during strikes in individual firms included an occupational classification of the workforce. Data drawn from these prefects' reports preserved in the Rhône departmental archives in Lyon for nine local medium-sized factories employing between 50 and 250 workers between 1919 and 1924 gives an idea of the evolution of skilled, semiskilled, and unskilled labor in the metallurgy industry.[66]

As seen in Table 8.3, skilled workers in six of these factories constituted the largest group. Their presence and the lack of semiskilled workers (those who were not skilled were considered unskilled) reflect the continuing importance of craft production. The other three industrial establishments, however, give a somewhat different picture. In each of them the skilled worker element did not constitute the largest group. At the Faugier Company, 50 skilled workers—35 turners and 15 forgers—worked alongside 90 laborers in 1922. But in the remaining three establishments skilled workers were not only a minority, there were also semiskilled workers present. While there were only 14 semiskilled workers for 54 skilled stokers, molders, polishers, and hammermen and 175 unskilled laborers building industrial furnaces in a local factory in 1919, there were 50 semiskilled machine tenders for 50 skilled workers (20 turners, 20 adjusters, and 10 millers) and 10 laborers at the General Magnet Company in 1920. In addition, at the electrical manufacturing company where 50 skilled workers were the largest single group in skill terms, there were also 25 semiskilled workers and 22 laborers.

Table 8.3 *Occupational structure in metallurgy, 1919–1926*

COMPANY	SKILLED	SEMISKILLED	UNSKILLED	TOTAL
Luchaire 1919	60		10	70
Jurine 1923	59		9	68
Thibaud 1926	50		30	80
Steurs 1924	30		10	40
Electrical factory 1924	50			50
Galva 1919	200			
Faugier 1922	50			90
Industrial Furnace Company 1919	54	14	175	
General Magnet 1920	50	50	10	
Electrical Manufacturing 1920	50	25	22	97

Semiskilled workers then were present in three of the nine medium-sized establishments in Lyon for which detailed information is available. In two cases their numbers were greater than the unskilled element and in one case there were as many semiskilled as skilled.[67]

What does this tell us about the rhythm of industrial development in the Lyonnais metallurgy industry and its effects on the workforce in terms of skill in the years following the First World War? It will be recalled that industrial work during the First Industrial Revolution was largely the preserve of artisans and skilled laborers. Unskilled laborers were often employed in the same shops as aides and helpers charged with transporting material throughout the enterprise, heating ovens, and the like. Semiskilled workers were largely associated with the Second Industrial Revolution. They were differentiated from laborers by higher pay and specialized work tasks. Rare before the twentieth century, they became the emblematic workers of the Second Industrial Revolution. The modest but real place they occupied in the classification of workers in terms of skill in interwar Lyon metal-working plants indicates the importance of a nuanced view of the progress of industrial change in this period: industrial change had clearly made serious inroads on the dominance of skilled labor, but the skilled worker element was far from eliminated.

These degraded working conditions were the result of the attempts by metallurgy employers to increase production, reduce labor costs, and above all to seize control of as much of the labor process as possible. But workers did not accept all or even most of them passively. A variety of forms of organized and individual resistance slowed, and even on occasion prevented the implementation of many of them. In many cases, the actual forms of various aspects of metal-working factory production in interwar France represented a compromise between capitalists and workers.

Worker Resistance

While management hoped that the institution of machinery would strip workers of the specialized knowledge over the labor process that was the source of much of the shop floor power of nineteenth- and early twentieth-century skilled workers, employers were often disappointed to find that maximum output from these machines was only attained by those who knew them most intimately, and nobody knew them as well as the workers who spent all day working on them. Workers used this knowledge in a variety of ways, including limiting output. At Berliet, the assembly line was introduced at the end of the war before other aspects of unmechanized production were transformed. As a result, poorly standardized parts had to be disassembled, filed down, and reassembled. In this way deskilled assemblers became skilled fitters again, thus recovering the know-how against which the assembly line had been directed.[68]

Workers resisted the ever-increasing pace of production that piece rate and other systems were designed to bring about with both individual and collective strategies. Semiskilled machine operators often discovered shortcuts unknown to demonstrators, technicians, industrial specialists, and other agents of management. On an individual basis, workers forced to meet production norms often subjected themselves to short bursts of rapid production in order to be able to rest, read, talk with their colleagues, and even sleep. Workers also found ways to slow down the trend towards speed-up that occurred as piece rates were lowered. For example, American sociologist Donald Roy found during his year-long employment in a piece work machine shop shortly after World War II that while their work was timed, workers "deemed it essential to embellish the timing performance with movements only apparently functional to the production of goods: little reachings, liftings, adjustings, dustings, and other special attentions to conscientious machine operation and good housekeeping that could be dropped instantly with the departure of the time-study man."[69]

Resistance also took the form of an unwritten collusion among workers around acceptable production rates. Workers whose excessive pace threatened to increase production norms and lower piece rates were often rebuked, sometimes physically by their colleagues. Similarly, workers who agreed to work overtime during periods of unemployment were often ostracized. The communist press, always interested in recording the daily situation in the factories, often ran *rabcor* articles protesting against those who accepted overtime. A 1928 article in *Travail* identified three workers by names from the chassis mounting shop at Berliet's Montplaisir factory. These "boot lickers" not only worked sixty hours a week, but Sunday mornings as well.[70] Of course most of the collective struggles waged by workers against the debilitating effects of rationalization took the form of strikes. We will see below in greater detail how industrial change generated this form of protest.

Organized collective resistance to the constantly degraded conditions of labor in the factories involved, of course, unionization. Before 1936 unions were banned by management at Berliet. Union membership was a risky affair and union business was conducted clandestinely. Workers hid behind machines during lunch breaks to pay their union dues and receive their union stamps. Union meetings were held outside behind trees or in trains.[71]

Industrial Change and Metal Worker Militancy and Solidarity

Having examined the nature of industrial change in this period and how it altered the composition of the labor force in terms of skill in Lyonnais metal-working plants, we now look at ways in which industrial change shaped the types of demands workers raised as well as the effect of these changes on relations between workers and their ramifications for the ability of workers to engage in collective action.

In chapter 5 it was seen how the beginnings of the employer offensive against skilled worker control over the labor process provoked strikes against these practices. In that period resistance often took the form of demands for the firing of foremen—the most visible agents of the employer offensive. This demand was raised in twenty metal worker strikes between 1900 and 1914. As we have seen in this chapter, employers continued to aggressively rationalize production in this period. But curiously, strikers demanded the firing of foremen in only one case and the dismissal of a technical director in only one other. And the sole demand for the firing of a foreman was in a strike that took place at the Berger and Caslani foundry in May 1930 (foundry work was one of the few areas where the possibilities of technical improvement and rationalization were quite limited, suggesting that this sector still bore many of the marks of earlier industrial production, thus making it less representative of metal working as a whole in this period).[72]

How can the virtual disappearance of this demand that was so wide-spread in the first period be explained? We have seen how the role of foremen as enforcers of labor discipline seems to have declined in the postwar period. Work discipline took other forms, particularly through pay systems. The most common demand by far was for wage hikes. The virtual disappearance of demands aimed against the direct agents of rationalization, accompanied by frequent demands around piece work and wages, meant that metal workers in the postwar period were obliged to shift their struggle from the terrain of resisting change, to that of the struggle against its most visible and pernicious effects: lowered wages, speed-up drives, and the health and safety dangers they involved. In other words, industrial change had proceeded to the point that worker control over the labor process was so undermined that metal workers in most sectors were reduced to fighting for the best deal possible under these new conditions, rather than struggling to defend traditional prerogatives as they did in the prewar period.

A close look at the question of piece work supports this analysis. It was seen above how the imposition of piece work payment systems angered metal workers and provoked strikes both before and after the war. But an examination of strike demands around piece work reveals an interesting difference. In the prewar period, workers demanded its simple abolition in seventeen strikes. In the second period, piece work figured in the strike demands of metal workers on ten different occasions. On five of these occasions the workers demanded it be abolished. But in the other five cases they demanded that the pay rates for piece work be raised.[73] This suggests that metal workers may have begun to consider that the fight against the simple existence of this practice was lost, and thus shifted to struggle for the best deal possible out of a system they resented, but considered difficult or impossible to remove.

The question of subcontracting points in a similar direction. We have seen that subcontracting did not disappear after the war. But while thousands of workers in hundreds of metal-working shops and factories in Lyon struck against subcontracting between 1906 and 1911, this demand was totally absent from strike demands in the second period. This too could signify that craft labor markets had been eclipsed by capitalist ones to the point that demands for the suppression of subcontracting were viewed as hopelessly ineffective rearguard actions.

As we have seen, employers were motivated to implement rationalization with or without the introduction of machinery, as a way of stripping skilled workers from as much of the control over the productive process as possible. The results, however, were not always those intended. The automobile industry provides an example of this. The traditional manner of organizing production in metal-working plants, including in pre-Fordist auto factories, was by grouping workers and machines together on the basis of the given item under construction. Part of the idea behind continuous process production was to eliminate the time lost transporting individual components and matching them to each other. In Lyon, Marius Berliet consciously sought to organize production in his auto plants in this manner. He attached considerable importance to the disposition of his machinery. In his B factory, the shop floor was organized in this fashion.[74] By organizing the work process and positioning machinery along the lines of the productive process rather than by the component or worker specialty, the system pioneered by Ford grouped workers of different specialties and skills together physically. The effects of this on worker solidarity were predictable; lathe operators, adjusters, molders etc., spent virtually all of their time working in close physical proximity to one another and tended to form on-the-job solidarities. This created at least the possibility that exclusive craft or specialty solidarity created through close physical proximity during the production process would decline in favor of increased sociability and eventually result in solidarity among workers of different grades, specialties, and skills.

The study of the American machine shop mentioned above highlighted the remarkable collusion of workers both across task and skill divides. Machine operators working under the piece rate system often had to frequently change the fittings on their machine tools. These items were kept in storage areas where they were dispensed by stockmen who were supposed to demand work-order slips before locating and distributing the material. This was a management attempt to control timed piece work. The machine tool workers' intimate knowledge of these items was often far superior to that of the unskilled stockmen and tool-crib workers whose job was to locate and dispense these items as needed. As the machine tool workers laboring under the piece work system had an interest in being able to rapidly locate tools, blueprints, gauges, and other equipment, and the stockmen and crib workers had an interest in alleviating their overcharged workload, the latter often allowed the former to enter the storage rooms against company rules. This allowed the machine workers to both reduce idle moments and get a head start on production norms.[75] In this way, the structure of the piece work system brought about collaboration between skilled and unskilled workers, which helped create bonds of solidarity that could in turn facilitate collective action.

There were other features of the nature and pace of industrial change in French metallurgy that favored unity among metal workers and promoted displays of united collective action across skill and occupation lines. In chapter 5 we saw how metal workers before the war conducted impressive displays of collective action across skill and occupational lines. It was also seen, however, that skilled and unskilled workers occupied different worlds and how this was reflected in the fact that unskilled workers did not have the same culture, commitment to trade organizations, or militant working-class consciousness as skilled workers. For their part, the deeds and actions of skilled workers did not always measure up to the revolutionary syndicalist and socialist principles of working-class solidarity that many espoused.

As we have seen, semiskilled workers in this period began to slowly form an important part of industrial workforces without, however, eliminating the skilled (or unskilled) worker element. It can be hypothesized that this had several positive effects on efforts of united collective action and overall relations across the skill divide. As an intermediate grade between skilled and unskilled workers, the slowly growing ranks of the semiskilled workers could bridge the gap between the skilled and unskilled by his or her relatively close position to both in terms of wages and work. At the same time, the preservation of significant amounts of skilled labor continued to provide the labor movement with the seasoned and highly organized labor militants traditionally furnished by the ranks of the skilled.

The revolutionary metal worker trade union leaders who led the long strike wave running from the end of the war to the spring of 1920 were aware of the importance of the skilled worker element. During the mass meetings held during the strikes in the spring of 1920, leading militants such as Antoine Garin, Fombonne, and the Bolshevik Berthet all looked to skilled workers to provide leadership in the strikes. At a mass meeting of strikers held on 12 March, 2,500 metal workers were told that "victory was possible as long as the skilled workers hold on." A week and a half later Garin believed victory possible since seasoned militants and skilled workers continued to make up most of the ranks of those still on strike.[76] The esteem that the young George Navel and other workers had for his older friend Vacheron was due to his high competence as a skilled worker in the tool and die department as well the role he played in the strikes at the end of the war.[77]

Metal Workers and Labor Strategy

By the mid-1930s it had become clear that metal worker labor activists proposing the class independence, antipatriotic current embodied by the CGTU and CGTSR unions and the Communist Party enjoyed greater success in attracting metal workers than those proposing the program of reformism and class collaboration. This success was, however, relative;

metal worker unions belonging to all currents did not organize more than a fraction of the workers in this industry before 1936 and the Communist Party did not become a truly mass party before the Popular Front. Yet, as will be seen, a significant number of workers followed its lead in industrial disputes and in parliamentary and extraparliamentary politics. In this section we will examine the basis of this success.

The Communist Party, the main political organization committed to the class independence, antipatriotic current, was closely identified from an early date with metal workers. French historian Jacques Girault refers to the PCF as a "party of metal workers." At the party congress held in Clichy in January 1925, 24 percent of the delegates were metal workers. Fully 42.4 percent of the delegates were metal workers at the congress of the Young Communists held several weeks before, as well as 39.3 percent at its 1929 congress.[78]

The PCF was quite successful in recruiting metal workers in the department of the Loire that bordered the Rhône. The Loire department had extensive steel and other metal-working establishments. This was quite striking given the strength of revolutionary syndicalist hostility to the PCF in that department. From the founding of the CGTU in 1922, the communists under the leadership of Benoît Frachon and Petrus Faure won the metal worker unions in the industrial towns of Firminy and Chambon-Feugerolles to their current.[79] By 1923, the PCF had won control of the Saint-Etienne metal workers' union. In November 1924, four of the eight factory party cells in Saint-Etienne were in metal-working establishments.[80]

No complete record of PCF strength in Lyon exists. However, fragmentary evidence indicates that there too, the PCF enjoyed substantial success among metal workers. Most of the prominent wartime revolutionary syndicalist metal union leaders joined the CGTU and/or the PCF in the early 1920s. While many revolutionary syndicalists left the PCF and later the CGT in the dispute over party–trade union relations, most joined the CGTSR, which, as we have seen, shared the class struggle/political independence orientation with the PCF and the CGTU. Two prominent metal workers—Edmond Chambon, secretary of the CGTU metal worker union and Doron, secretary of the Rhône PCF in the late 1920s—figured on a list of thirty-seven prominent Communist Party and CGTU militants in Lyon and its suburbs drawn up by the police.[81]

An approximation of PCF influence among metal workers can be established by looking at how metal workers responded to the extraparliamentary activity called by the PCF and supported by the CGTU. In chapter 6 we saw how twelve thousand workers in the Lyon agglomeration participated in the political strike called by the Communist Party in solidarity with the general strike in Le Havre in 1922. While no precise figures are available, the police reported that the strike was virtually general among building and shoe workers and partial among metal workers.[82] Given the large numbers of metal workers in Lyon, it is likely that thousands responded to this call. It is also significant in comparison to weavers, dyers, and finishers who did not strike at all, a fact that will be recalled and analyzed in the next chapter.

The political strike that the PCF called on 12 October 1925 to protest against the threat of French military action in Syria and Morocco enjoyed a modest, but real success. Four thousand to five thousand workers participated despite the divisions in the workers' movement. Citing its "political" nature, the Bourse du travail, the CGT, and the "autonomous" unions all refused to endorse the strike. However, a look at those who did strike indicates relative success of the PCF among metal workers. Police reports to the Ministry of the Interior, which are usually remarkably consistent, gave slightly different accounts on this occasion. Two police reports dated 12 October, the day of the strike, varied slightly in their estimation of the numbers involved. One reported "no more than four thousand" while the other "no more than five thousand." A telegram sent that day indicated that 50 percent of the city's construction workers and 20 percent of the metal workers struck, while one of the police reports declared that only 8 percent of the city's metal workers responded to the strike call.[83] If there were no more than five thousand strikers, the lower percentage figure is probably correct. If there were still 30,000 metal workers in Lyon at that time and we accept the lower figure of 4,000 total strikers, 8 percent would mean that 3,500 metal workers were a large part of the 4,000 or 5,000 strikers—a quite significant fact given the sharp divisions in the labor movement at that time and the repressive atmosphere in general. Further, if accurate, this estimate means that metal worker strikers outnumbered the usually militant and organized construction workers whose participation according to the police themselves was expected to be bolstered by the fact that the masons had already been on strike for a month preceding this action.[84]

What accounts for the increasing success among metal workers of the class struggle/political independence current embodied by the Communist Party, the CGTU, and the remaining elements of revolutionary syndicalism and anarchism in Lyon? We have seen in previous chapters how a repressive government, the discrediting of the reformist orientation of the wartime Socialist Party and CGT, and the presence of a new coherent revolutionary force epitomized by the Russian Revolution and the Third International created a political opening for a French Communist Party in the aftermath of the war. In addition, the evolution of the class

structure of French society in this period, particularly the growing proletarianization of workers and the narrowing possibilities for social mobility, increased the potential appeal of a working-class political current that
pitched its appeal to wage earners as such, rather than as the "citizens"
or "republicans" of the 1848 ideal of a multiclass, democratic social republic. But the success of both currents varied tremendously between
different groups of workers. For metal workers, the following four sets of
factors explain the success of this current.

The first is continuity. The Communist Party and the CGTU were
in many ways the heirs of the prewar revolutionary syndicalist tradition
of class struggle/independent politics. Since this current enjoyed much
influence amongst prewar metal workers, it is not surprising that its postwar successor in the guise in the PCF and the CGTU would inherit metal
worker support. The revolutionary class struggle profile that it adopted
from the beginning helped it claim continuity with the class struggle/
political independence current represented by prewar revolutionary syndicalism and some strands of French socialism. Tradition and the effects
of long-term implantation are therefore part of the explanation of why
many metal workers were drawn to early French communism, just as silk
worker attachment to SFIO reformist/class collaborationist politics is
partly explained by the earlier Guesdist interest and success in recruiting
textile workers.

Second, PCF propaganda was well geared to the social and political climate of the day. Communist propaganda presented the state and the employers as two sides of the same antiworker monster. This struck a chord
with metal workers because they, more than any other group of workers,
had first-hand experience with the depressed wages, long hours, and harsh
working conditions in the metal plants working for the war effort where
the collusion between the state and private industry was unmistakable. At
the same time, progressive social legislation could not really be expected
in the conservative and repressive climate of the 1920s and 1930s. This
reality made the strategies based on class collaborationism favored by the
socialists and the CGT difficult to sell to workers.

Third, the propaganda campaigns of the Rhône communists and their
CGTU allies were also well adapted to local industrial conditions. For
example, the manner in which the Rhône communist press frequently
denounced capitalist rationalization was particularly well calibrated to the
way that industrial change was reshaping the composition of the metallurgy labor force in terms of skill distribution. In the communist press,
rationalization was synonymous with aggressive drives for reduced labor costs through speed-up, forced overtime, wage cuts, and dangerous
working conditions. The very imprecision with which the phrase *capital-*

ist rationalization was employed allowed it to appeal to both skilled and semiskilled workers. By adopting such a sweeping view of rationalization rather than a more narrow and precise one centering on the specific despoiling effects felt by skilled workers, the communists and the CGTU were able to appeal to metal workers at all skill levels.

Fourth, PCF organizational methods were designed in a way that maximized their efforts to reach metal workers. The factory cell structure that the party adopted in 1924 helped it establish close relations with workers on the job. Likewise, the *rabcor* reports provided the party with first-hand information about the concerns and working conditions of metal workers. These workers could read how the PCF alone articulated their immediate material concerns and publicized their harsh working conditions.

Finally, PCF and CGTU strategy in industrial disputes was well matched to the realities of the local metallurgy industry. Foremost among these was the CGTU policy of agitating for strikes. Metal-working plants tended to be highly capitalized, which made strikes a potentially powerful (and therefore attractive) weapon in the hands of workers in such industries, and the PCF and the CGTU, unlike the Socialist Party and the CGT, preferred the strike to simple negotiation and bargaining. In a booming industrial sector like metals (especially automobile manufacturing) where there was much competition between firms who did not have the option of easily picking up and moving their operations, strikes could be a very effective weapon.

Conclusion

In chapter 5 it was seen how metallurgy employers in Lyon in the years before 1914 conducted an assault on skilled worker control over the labor process. The source of skilled workers' strength lay not only in their superior knowledge of the work process but also with the manner in which that knowledge was diffused. Control over labor supply and access to the profession were essential ingredients of the totality of relations that were craft labor markets. And the employers attacked at all of these points. Rationalization and mechanization were only the most visible expressions of this. The results of the employer offensive to reduce skilled worker control over access to the trade and the diffusion of technical knowledge were seen in the decline of worker-controlled apprenticeship programs.

By 1914, however, the balance sheet was a mixed one. Rationalization and mechanization made a much publicized, but in fact quite limited, impact. Though craft labor markets in a number of trades were eliminated and capitalist labor markets were beginning, large pockets of skilled worker control, and therefore craft market conditions, remained. The demands raised by the strike-prone French workers reflected this. The strikes concerning foremen were part of the struggle over control over the shop floor in the most literal sense. This struggle was also seen in demands against subcontracting and piece work.

During the war, French employers—with metallurgy industrialists at the forefront—received unprecedented help from the state to step up their offensive. The war mobilization temporarily removed much of the seasoned skilled worker element, while the militarization of labor neutralized that which remained. After the war, industrial change resumed its uneven course. The information available suggests that skilled labor control gradually declined, matched by a slow but steady increase in semiskilled labor. An analysis of the demands raised in strikes suggests that the advance of capitalist labor markets had reached the point that the very nature of worker demands had begun to change. This is apparent in the near disappearance of the type of demands aimed at preserving the shop floor strength of skilled workers that were so frequent before the war.

The reconstituted practices and notions of skill that emerged from the tug of war between metallurgy employers and workers had profound ramifications for female labor. During the war the drive of the state and the arms industry to assure adequate supplies of labor, boost production, and eliminate skilled worker control over the labor process involved radically new policies toward female labor. While women had been effectively shut out of the metal-working industry before the war, they were now recruited into the semiskilled positions that occupied increasingly significant portions of the labor force. This trend continued in the interwar period.

The 1936 collective bargaining agreements carefully codified what was meant by skilled, semiskilled, and unskilled labor. Implicit in this development was a recast notion of the place of female labor. While men's work was sharply divided into these three categories, the identification of women with semiskilled and unskilled work was so imbedded by that time that the agreements did not even bother to categorize the four groups of women's jobs in terms of skill. Job tasks and wage rates indicate, however, that three of these categories represented semiskilled jobs and the fourth, unskilled. Most women workers were semiskilled.

In Lyon as elsewhere, the Communist Party had its greatest success in attracting workers from the metallurgy industry. We have identified several factors that contributed to the success of the class struggle/political independence current represented largely by the Communist Party and the CGTU. They were: (1) Continuity: the revolutionary class struggle profile that it adopted from the beginning helped it claim continuity with the class struggle political/independence current represented by prewar revolutionary syndicalism and some strands of French socialism. Tradition and the effects of long-term implantation are certainly part of the explanation of why many metal workers were drawn to early French communism, just as silk worker attachment to SFIO reformist/class collaborationist politics is partly explained by the early Guesdist interest in and success at recruiting textile workers. (2) The ways in which PCF and CGTU political and industrial propaganda concerning the links between the French state and private capital on one level and the phenomenon of rationalization on another clearly reflected the realities of the time. PCF propaganda denouncing "rationalization" was cast imprecisely, so that it could appeal to both the skilled workers facing deskilling and the semi-skilled workers facing dangerous shop floor conditions and low wages in a way that united them rather than dividing them along skill lines. (3) The organizational methods adapted by the PCF, particularly its institution of factory cells, worker correspondents, and frequent reports of shop floor conditions, put it in a position to influence metal workers and underscore its claims to represent workers in ways that the Socialist Party and the CGT could not. (4) Finally, CGTU industrial strategy favoring strikes was a plausible one in an industry marked by heavy capital investment in its industrial plant.

In terms of the larger theoretical model concerning the links between class positions, political opportunity structure, and worker politics employed in this book, the four factors contributing to PCF strength enumerated above coincided with much larger processes that have been discussed throughout. Communist Party and CGTU strategy was particularly well suited to the ways in which Lyon's metallurgy employers shaped the labor force during this period. We have examined the commitment of Lyon's highly organized metal industrialists to a radical restructuring of industrial production. The net effects of this included the destruction of craft labor markets and the rise of a capitalist labor market, which did not, however, completely eliminate the skilled worker element. Under such conditions, the strategy of bargaining or isolated industrial action was ineffective in defending worker interests. This chapter's analysis of strike demands indeed shows how metal workers largely relinquished the fight to retain the control over the labor process in favor of demands for the best possible deal under the new industrial conditions. By calling for mass united front tactics and aggressive strike action, communist and CGTU strategy was particularly well geared to workers laboring under capitalist labor market conditions. The fact that the skilled worker element was far from totally eliminated also favored this type of strategy. The threat that industrial change posed to skilled workers gave them reason to resist.

The significant numbers of older skilled workers with militant political experience who remained in the plants were well placed to influence their younger, less-skilled colleagues who were confronted by a far more aggressively antiworker state than they had faced at the turn of the century. And indeed, as we have seen, skilled workers continued to play leadership roles in strikes and militant political action. For many, adherence to the Communist Party and CGTU was consistent with their prewar revolutionary commitments.

The class collaboration, nationalist current represented by the Socialist Party and the CGT adopted quite different tactics in applying its policies of class collaboration and reformism. On the national level, Léon Jouhaux offered CGT support for some aspects of shop floor rationalization, such as the employer campaign against *flanerie* (taking frequent breaks from work stations). In Lyon, the CGT metal unions took advantage of the CSIMR's refusal to negotiate with the militant CGTU and corresponding willingness to negotiate with the accommodating CGT. The CGT was a frequent negotiating partner with the CSIMR or individual metallurgy employers, often with the participation of Herriot himself and/or the prefect. The results of these privileged bargaining relations with the employers were quite meager. The frequency with which workers struck against wage cuts and piece work suggests that only strike action forced metal employers to come to terms with their workers. The absence of socialist factory cells prevented the SP from collecting detailed knowledge of metal workers' conditions and articulating demands tailored to their daily problems on the job and their aspirations.

The class independence, antinationalist political identity forged in the nineteenth century therefore continued into the postwar period. But the advent of the Popular Front in 1936 was accompanied by profound shifts in political identity for metal workers. Those developments are explored in the next and final chapter.

Notes

1. ADR 10/Mp/C77.
2. Michel Laferrère, *Lyon, ville industrielle. Essai d'une géographie urbaine des techniques et des entreprises* (Paris, 1960), 255.
3. Ibid., 253.
4. Ibid., 255.
5. ADR 10/Mp/C63–C72.
6. Patrick Fridenson, "Automobile Workers in France and Their Work, 1914–1983," in *Work in France,* ed. Steven Kaplan and Cynthia Kopp (New York, 1987), 515.
7. ADR 10/Mp/C71.

8. Jean-Louis Robert, "1914–1920," in *La France ouvrière,* ed. Claude Willard (Paris, 1995), 1:438.
9. ADR 10/Mp/C76.
10. Sheri Satwell Brun, "L'association métallurgique du Rhône, 1919–1939" (Master's thesis, University of Lyon, 1992), 17.
11. Ibid., 34.
12. Fridenson, "Automobile Workers," 529.
13. Ibid., 539.
14. Sylvie Schweitzer, *Des engrenages à la chaine, les usines Citroën, 1915–1935* (Lyon, 1982), 145.
15. Gérard Déclas, "Recherches sur les usines Berliet, 1914–1949" (Master's thesis, University of Lyon II, 1977), 85.
16. Fridenson, "Automobile Workers," 20.
17. Michel Collinet, *L'ouvrier français: Essai sur la condition ouvrière, 1900–1950* (Paris, 1951), 69.
18. Schweitzer, *Des engrenages,* 73.
19. Ibid., 75.
20. *Travail,* 16 July 1929.
21. Schweitzer, *Des engrenages,* 82.
22. *Le métallurgiste,* March 1937.
23. *Travail,* July 1931.
24. George Navel, *Travaux* (Paris, 1969), 63.
25. Schweitzer, *Des engrenages,* 75.
26. For an extended discussion of how this worked in an American machine shop, see Donald Roy, "Efficiency and 'The Fix': Informal Intergroup Relations in a Piecework Machine Shop," in *American Journal of Sociology* 60, no. 3 (November 1954): 255–66.
27. Alain Pinol, "Travail, travailleurs et production aux usines Berliet, 1912–1947" (Unpublished master's thesis, University of Lyon II, 1980), 175.
28. Christian Chevandier, *Cheminots en usine, les ouvriers des ateliers d'Oullins au temps de la vapeur* (Lyon, 1993), 101.
29. ADR 10/Mp/C/76.
30. Schweitzer, *Des engrenages,* 73.
31. *Travail,* October 1923; March, October, November 1924; April, May 1925.
32. Déclas, "Recherches," 92.
33. Ibid., 124–25.
34. Elisabeth Chaninian, Sylvie Murgia, and Marie-Noëlle Pichon, "La vie quotidienne de vingt cinq ouvriers chez Berliet entre 1919–1939" (Master's thesis, University of Lyon, 1979), 76–77.
35. Brun, "L'association," 49.
36. Ibid., 51.
37. Ibid., 48.
38. Ibid., 53.
39. Quoted in ibid., 57.
40. Brun, "L'association," 64.
41. Ibid., 58.
42. Ibid., 58–59.
43. Ibid., 54–55.
44. Chaninian et al. "La vie quotidienne," 107.
45. Déclas, "Recherches," 94.
46. *Travail,* April 1928.
47. Chevandier, *Cheminots,* 35.
48. Chaninian et al., "La vie quotidienne," 88.

49. Gérard Noiriel, *Longwy: Immigrés et prolétaires* (Paris, 1984), 151.
50. Chaninian et al., "La vie quotidienne," 88.
51. *Travail*, 19 October 1929.
52. Chaninian et al., "La vie quotidienne," 84.
53. *Travail*, 12 June 1930.
54. *Travail*, December 1930. A retired Berliet worker recalled how some workers became "sick, asphyxiated by the gasses" that these heaters emitted. Chanian et al., "La vie quotidienne," 82.
55. Quoted in Annie Fourcaut, *Les femmes à l'usine en France pendant l'entre-deux-guerres* (Paris, 1982), 95.
56. Collinet, *L'ouvrier français*, 117.
57. Noiriel, *Longwy*, 48.
58. *Travail*, 28 October 1928.
59. Ibid.
60. Chevandier, *Cheminots*, 36.
61. ADR 10/Mp/C120.
62. *Le Métallurgiste*, December 1938.
63. ADR 10/Mp/C37.
64. ADR 10/Mp/C35.
65. Navel, *Travaux*, 64.
66. ADR 10/Mp/63-72.
67. French sociologist Michel Collinet adopted a similar strategy for determining the evolution of skilled labor in French metal-working plants. In the work discussed above, he examined two different metal-working plants. The first, "factory A," was a large mass-production automobile factory. The second, "factory B," produced custom-made vehicles in small batches. According to Collinet, this factory did not differ much from a medium-sized factory thirty years before. He found that there was one semiskilled worker in factory B for four skilled workers, as opposed to eight skilled workers per semiskilled worker in factory A. (73).
68. Fridenson, "Automobile Workers," 522.
69. Roy, "Efficiency and the Fix," 160.
70. *Travail*, March 1928.
71. Chaninian et al., "La vie quotidienne," 119–20.
72. ADR 10/Mp/C80.
73. November 1919, ADR 10Mp/C/64; April 1923, ADR 10Mp/C/67; July 1923, ADR 10Mp/C/67; 11 May 1926, ADR 10Mp/C/69; *Travail*, 24 April 1929; *Travail*, 26 July 1929; *Travail*, 5 October 1929; 25 October 1930, ADR 10Mp/C/70.
74. Déclas, "Recherches," 79–82.
75. Roy, "Efficiency and The Fix," 56.
76. ADR 10/Mp/C63.
77. Navel, *Travaux*, 65, 71.
78. Stephane Courtois and Marc Lazar, *Histoire du Parti communiste français* (Paris, 1995), 155.
79. Daniel Colson, *Anarcho-syndicalisme et communisme: Saint-Etienne, 1920–1925* (Lyon, 1986), 114.
80. Ibid., 144.
81. ADR 10/Mp/C69.
82. ADR 10/Mp/C65.
83. Ibid.
84. ADR 10/Mp/C73.

CHAPTER 9

THE FRENCH POPULAR FRONT AND POLITICAL IDENTITY

In the mid-1930s France's political opportunity structure radically changed. In the context of a sharply polarized national and international political environment, a broad-based coalition known as the Popular Front united previously divided working-class organizations with the Radical Party. A wave of popular support brought a resounding victory to the coalition in the May 1936 elections and Leon Blum, the SFIO party leader, became France's first socialist prime minister. The next month the largest general strike France had ever experienced to that point forced employers to make dramatic concessions including union recognition, agreement to engage in collective bargaining, the forty-hour work week, paid vacations, and wage hikes from 7 to 15 percent. Massive street demonstrations were one of the most ubiquitous features of the Popular Front. Danielle Tartakowsky has calculated that there was at least one street demonstration every day in France between 13 February 1934 and 5 May 1936.[1] As we will see below, the tenor of those demonstrations was particularly significant for the forging of new political identities.

The Popular Front generated an enormous amount of hope and enthusiasm at the time. The experience continues to loom large in the popular imagination, its memory kept alive by journalists, historians, unions, and left-wing political parties, and the powerful images of those emotions left to us by the leading photographers of the day.

The very formation of the coalition, the political basis upon which it was built, the mass mobilizations, and the imagery employed to promote it all had a powerful impact on working-class political identities, particularly those relating to class and national identity. Popular Front leaders, including those representing working-class organizations, presented the *Rassemblement populaire,* as it was originally called, as above all a vast patriotic movement in defense of the Republic and the nation itself.

Notes for this chapter begin on page 243.

The left-wing political entrepreneurs who promoted nationalism in 1930s France drew on a rich cultural heritage that was familiar in one variety or another to French men and women across class, ideological, and regional lines. As we will see in greater detail below, the leaders of the Popular Front organizations resurrected aspects of a popular national identity reaching back to the French Revolution and artfully connected it to the specific conditions of the mid-1930s in a way that made popular aspirations and national identity compatible. This was represented particularly clearly in the writings, speeches, and political iconography of the most enthusiastic Popular Front organizations, the Communist Party and the CGT trade union confederation. More significantly, mass public demonstrations like May Day and Bastille Day marches and rallies involved masses of working people embracing symbols of class *and* nation.

This question had important implications for the main political formation of the class independence, antinationalist current, the PCF. The party broke with previous theory and practice by urging workers to think of themselves as both workers *and* citizens. The political dimension of this turn was represented in the alliance itself as working-class organizations allied with the middle-class layers that were the base of the Radical Party. Occupational groups like the metal workers enthusiastically took up the banner of the Popular Front with all its implications for their political identities.

It was in this period that workers from occupational groups that had possessed autonomous class-based political identities embraced a combined class and national political identity. Silk weavers and dyers had been traditionally associated with the class collaboration, nationalist current. We saw in chapter 7, however, how silk workers began to shift their allegiance from the CGT and the SFIO to the CGTU and PCF around 1933. This reflected deep changes that completely transformed weaving and dyeing in Lyon's silk industry from male-dominated artisanal trades to mostly semiskilled factory work with male and female work forces. For workers new to this sector, the new political identity generated by the PCF did not represent a break with past political identity as much as the acquisition of a new one. On the other hand, the PCF's new attitude toward nation and multiclass alliances would have been familiar for those workers who *did* inherit the class collaboration, nationalist identity that had been traditionally associated with silk weaving and dyeing. For metal workers, however, the acquisition of nationalist identity and by extension political collaboration with middle-class forces represented an important change in political identity. This chapter focuses on how the political opportunity structure of the Popular Front combined with the industrial social relations in the silk- and metal-working industries to shape the political identities of these two occupational groups.

The Popular Front opened up a new political opportunity structure in France. For much of the postwar period, popular protest had been repressed. The early days of the Popular Front government were characterized by an expanded room of margin for popular protest and the presence of elite allies. The popular masses considered the Blum government to be of their own making and expected it to defend their interests. The huge explosion of strikes and demonstrations and significant social reforms reflected this. However, as the government began to tone down its program and backtrack on some of its promises in response to pressure from the right wing of the coalition, the atmosphere became increasingly repressive.

We saw in chapter 8 how the overall growth of semiskilled labor meant that the shop floor strength of metal workers in France and Lyon in the years preceding the Popular Front had been greatly weakened in relationship to that enjoyed by workers of an earlier generation. This was reflected in the decline of the skilled worker and the rise of a semiskilled proletariat. It was during the Popular Front years that these processes came to mark significant changes in industrial social relations. French labor historian Patrick Fridenson has argued that Taylorized semiskilled labor became the norm in the French auto industry, a major employer of metal workers, precisely in the years 1936–1938.[2]

Semiskilled workers were often relatively new to the industrial work scene, having arrived within a generation from small towns and farms. Their political identities were not formed by the long traditions that skilled metal workers incarnated including antipatriotism and hostility to the Republic. For many of them the strikes and demonstrations of the Popular Front were their first experiences with politics.

The new political opportunity structure reflected gender relations in France in new ways. The institutional framework of politics continued to marginalize women. It was only in 1945 that women gained the right to vote or hold elected office. Even the extrainstitutional political scene reflected gender inequality in the sense that demonstrations were organized by male-dominated organizations. Nevertheless, women took advantage of the expanded POS to carve out larger spheres of influence within French society. On 12 July 1935, two days before the historic Bastille Day unity demonstrations, a group of women organized by veteran women's rights activist Louise Weiss demonstrated at the Bastille in chains to highlight the parallels between women's oppression and slavery.[3] This little-known protest foreshadowed sustained mass participation of women in the great mass mobilizations and strikes of the Popular Front. The Blum government named three women as undersecretaries. Scores of women were elected to municipal government positions, usually on the PCF ticket, but prohibited from assuming their posts. As we will see below, the collective bargaining agreements themselves, one of the great gains of the Popular Front, reflected and perpetuated gender occupational inequality.

Origin of the Popular Front

The Popular Front arose in the tense international political scene of the early 1930s. In Europe, fascist regimes had come to power in Italy in 1923 and Germany in 1933. To the east, Japan had invaded Manchuria in 1931 setting the stage for a full-scale invasion of China in 1937. The French political scene was highly polarized. In the 1930s monarchist groups like Action française, right-wing veteran's groups like the Croix de feu of Colonel de la Roque, the more directly fascist Parti populaire français, and the Parti social français of renegade communist leader Jacques Doriot organized noisy and sometimes violent street demonstrations against republican institutions, officials, and left-wing political groups. For years, these reactionary groups attacked the Republic as a corrupt institution responsible for France's social problems and loss of status internationally.

In January 1934, a well-known professional swindler named Alexander Stavisky came to the center of attention as a widespread fraudulent scheme publicly unraveled. When Stavisky was found dead by police, supposedly by suicide after several days on the run as a fugitive, the right-wing press seized on the large number of government officials who had either protected, collaborated with, or had been somehow involved with Stavisky to whip up antirepublican sentiment.

On 6 February a right-wing demonstration organized and attended by several of the leagues clashed with the police at the Place de la Concorde, leaving fifteen dead and 1,435 wounded.[4] At one point the crowd headed toward the bridge leading over the Seine to the Chamber of Deputies, France's lower house of parliament. Although evidence is contradictory as whether the demonstrators actually planned to storm the chamber and overthrow the Republic at that moment, the events galvanized center and left-wing political opinion.

Most historians consider the response to the violent far-right demonstrations of 6 February and in the days following as the beginning of the Popular Front. The PCF and the CGTU participated in the antifascist demonstration on 12 February called by the CGT and supported by the SFIO, which was notable in that all the main working organizations participated.

The events of the capital found an echo in Lyon. In the late afternoon of 6 February, five hundred to six hundred far-right demonstrators rallied in the center of the city. By early evening small groups of these demonstrators began attacking the police and bringing automobile and tramway circulation to a halt. The police arrested twenty demonstrators who were later released. Later in the evening a column of left-wing working-class demonstrators arrived to counterdemonstrate. The next day more demonstrations took place as four thousand demonstrators from the left and right clashed. Local trade union leader Marius Vivier-Merle led a column of two thousand workers who demonstrated in front of the *Progrès* headquarters calling for the arrest of the "fascist leaders." Revolver shots were heard at the Place Bellecour and according to the communist press, the far-right Camelots du Roi set several cars on fire. The police arrested thirty-five demonstrators. On 9 February, the PCF organized a meeting at the Unitaire meeting hall. Afterwards four hundred to five hundred demonstrators clashed with police in the cours Lafayette. On 11 February, four thousand marchers according to the *Progrès* and twenty-five thousand according to the communist newspaper *La Voix du Peuple* demonstrated, crying "Down with fascism," "Liberty," and, prefiguring the dynamics of the Popular Front, "Unity."

In the meantime left-wing political parties and trade unions called for a massive strike and demonstration on 12 February to protest the events of the 6th. A million left-wing marchers responded to this call in Paris. The CGT estimated that 75 percent of the labor force in the Parisian area participated in the strike.[5] In Lyon, fifteen thousand to twenty thousand marchers according to the *Progrès* and twenty-five thousand according to the *Voix du Peuple* demonstrated that day against fascism and the "bloody events of the capital" but also for the forty-hour work week. CGT leader Marius Vivier-Merle spoke again. In the adjoining working-class suburb of Villeurbanne, the *Voix du Peuple* claimed that police fired on a crowd during a communist meeting injuring seventy, including ten seriously.

The PCF and the Nation

A particularly significant aspect of this first round of Popular Front elections was the participation (after an initial hesitation) of the PCF and the procommunist CGTU labor confederation, which called on its supporters to attend the demonstration. This was quite novel for the party because since 1929 the PCF had embraced the "Third Period" line of the

Stalinist-dominated Third International. This line, which had its origin in struggles within Soviet society and the Soviet Communist Party, analyzed the period as one of imminent revolution (the period opened up by the 1917 Bolshevik Revolution constituted the first period, and the defeat of the Polish revolution in 1923 inaugurated the second period). According to this analysis the socialist parties of the Second International were in fact reactionary "social fascist" enemies of the working class and socialism, and thus barriers to revolution. Pro-Moscow communist parties throughout the world bitterly attacked socialist parties during the period and refused united action. In Germany the Communist Party actually blocked with Nazis against the socialists in some state elections. Blocking with the socialists as well as the radicals in defense of the Republic was therefore a sharp political turn for the PCF. At its conference at Ivry held between 23 and 27 June, the PCF formally proposed an antifascist alliance with the SFIO, and on 27 July the two parties signed a pact promising to end "attacks, insults, and criticisms" in view of the fascist danger facing the world.[6] In October of that year, the PCF began orienting towards the left wing of the Radical Party as part of a strategy to build a broad antifascist alliance including workers and sections of the middle classes. The party now promoted a sort of class-infused patriotism. It henceforth claimed to speak not only for the working class but for the nation. The party combined class and nation in its everyday work. The PCF press in Lyon explained that metallurgy employers were making profits "at the expense of the entire nation and of national security while workers suffered from the *décrets-lois* of 1938."[7]

While the PCF explained the Popular Front in terms of the exigencies of the French and international political official scene, particularly the fight against fascism, it was carrying out a policy that became Comintern policy at the seventh congress of the Comintern in 1935. The first manifestation of the Popular Front in France was the 14 July 1935 Bastille Day parade, which saw the leaders of the radical, communist, and socialist parties march together. The legislative elections of the spring of 1936 that saw the stunning victories of the Popular Front coalition, the massive sit-down strikes, and the formation of the SFIO-led government and the Matignon accords that followed are all among the most important events in twentieth-century France. The reunification of the CGT was also part of the establishment of the Popular Front.

The about-face of the PCF has always been explained in the context of the international political situation. The Comintern decided on this course for reasons connected to internal Soviet politics and the Stalinist bureaucracy's own national and international interests. National communist parties were obliged to follow suit in their own countries. While this certainly explains why the PCF entered into a Popular Front alliance and altered its program in key areas, it is not a satisfactory explanation of why entire groups of workers embraced a new identity. On the eve of the Popular Front, the PCF had a well-established place in French political life and within the labor movement, but only a small percentage of French workers were actually members. It was only during the Popular Front that the PCF became a mass party. So the masses of workers who embraced the Popular Front and the political identity associated with it were not following party discipline in doing so. It is argued here that this shift in identity was largely the result of shifts in political opportunity structure (of which Comintern and PCF politics were a part, but only a part), and industrial social relations.

The rest of this chapter will explore how the political opportunity structure of the time contributed to an important shift in political identity for many French workers. We will look at how the electoral political campaigns of the period, mass demonstrations, and other political struggles on the one hand, and industrial conflict on the other hand combined to fuse social and patriotic issues in ways that left an indelible mark on the political identity of workers in France.

Alliances and Elections

The unfolding of the Popular Front in Lyon reveals much about the particular characteristics of politics in that city. The nonaggression pact between the SFIO and the PCF signed in the summer of 1934 was first applied on the electoral level in the Rhône at the time of the October 1934 elections to the regional council. The SFIO candidate stepped aside in favor of longtime PCF militant Jules Grandclément, who easily won those elections.[8] The PCF made greater gains in Lyon starting in 1934 than it did on the national level. At the same time, the Radical Party, which was the big loser in the context of the overall Popular Front victory, suffered a more serious defeat in Lyon than it did on the national level, registering a decline of 44.5 percent to 26.5 percent during that period. By late 1934, it was becoming clear that the Radical Party in Lyon was seeking to make alliances with the moderate right rather than the SFIO. For its part, the SFIO was divided between carrying out the electoral alliance with the PCF and continuing collaboration with the radicals. For example, in September 1934 the socialists and the communists were collaborating against the radicals for the upcoming cantonal elections, although in nearby Villeurbanne sections of the party leadership still favored an alliance of the SFIO with the radicals against the communists. The loosening of the bonds between the radicals and the socialists in the 1935 municipal elections contributed to the victory of the right in the Croix-Rousse.

The inconsistency of the radicals was a reflection of the political orientation of its leader Edward Herriot on the national and local level. Nationally, Herriot had become the leader of the current favoring alliances with the moderate right against the current led by Daladier, which leaned left. Herriot initially opposed the Popular Front alliance. For example, he was against Radical Party participation in the 14 July 1935 parade in Lyon organized by the PCF and the SFIO. But the momentum in favor of the Popular Front in Lyon, a city where republican sentiment was traditionally strong, was such that many in the Radical Party went along with the alliance in spite of the opposition of Herriot. By October the radicals agreed to participate in an antifascist committee with the PCF and the SFIO. Nevertheless, the radicals did not consistently apply "republican discipline" in the second round of the 1936 legislative elections. This helps explain their stinging defeat in these elections. On the one hand, by appearing to favor alliances with the right over the Popular Front candidates, the Lyon radicals benefited less from the left-wing tidal wave than radicals did nationally. On the other hand, they were sufficiently identified with left-of-center politics in the minds of right-wing voters that they were not a natural choice for that part of the electorate which preferred established right-wing parties.

The 1936 Elections

The May 1936 legislative elections led to a resounding victory for the three parties of the Popular Front coalition. They also involved a major shift in the balance of forces between the radicals, socialists, and communists. The socialists saw their parliamentary delegation increase from 131 to 147, outdistancing for the first time the radicals who saw their delegation drop from 157 to 106. The PCF emerged as the biggest winner, increasing its number of deputies from 11 to 72.

In Lyon there was little advance indication that the May elections would be as dramatics as they proved to be. A front-page article in the 24 April 1936 issue of the largest local daily newspaper, the center-left *Le Progrès,* said, "A foreigner traveling in France would be surprised to learn that he has arrived during an electoral political campaign. There are no tumultuous meetings, no great speeches either." Although, foreshadowing the coming events, the article also held that "there is nevertheless an instinctive desire in mass meetings to defend republican institutions."

France's two-round electoral system allows voters to display their preferences in the first round and support the best-placed candidate of the left or right in the second round. In the first round of the 1936 legislative elections, each of the three parties campaigned for its own candidate. Out of step with the pro-unity mood within the city and country as a whole, Mayor Edward Herriot, also a national leader of the Radical Party, found himself in second place in the first district, beaten by a right-wing candidate, Dr. Francillon. This uncharacteristic defeat was also due to his deflationary policies that were harmful to the small business owners who dominated his electoral and party constituency. Radical losses in both rounds accrued in part to other left parties but also to Lyon's relatively weak right-wing Republicans. This helped to give a sharper tone to political and social conflict in the city during the period.

Jean-Luc Pinol's careful study of voting patterns in Lyon during the Popular Front demonstrates the close connection between work and residential space. Local voting patterns are therefore a strong indication of occupational voting patterns.[9] In the first round of the elections in the twelfth district, which was located in an industrial quarter where many metalworkers lived and worked, the PCF registered a stunning victory, receiving 42.6 percent of the vote for its local leader George Lévy, one of only five of fifteen candidates in the department of the Rhône elected to parliament in the first round. In Vénissieux alone, home of the huge Berliet auto plant, Lévy received over 54 percent of the vote.[10] In the industrial ninth district, home to chemical and metal-working plants and workers' residences, PCF candidate Félix Brun was victorious in the first round, receiving 37.86 percent of the vote—a large improvement over the 13.41 percent he received in the 1932 elections.

In the second round the parties largely respected the Popular Front alliance, withdrawing in support of the best-placed Popular Front candidate. Herriot, who had initially balked at unity with the left, finally accepted the Popular Front. He was elected deputy in the second round thanks to the withdrawal of the SFIO candidate and SFIO and PCF support. In the industrial 9th district home to chemical and metal working plants and worker's residences, Communist candidate Félix Brun was victorious receiving 37.86% of the vote (as opposed to the 13.41% he received in 1932).

Although Lyon's June strikes did not involve mass street demonstrations (except a downtown demonstration by striking waiters) a sharply polarized political climate descended on the city.[11] The dissolution of the leagues following a physical attack on Leon Blum in Paris on 13 February 1936 by Action française members led to violent fights between left and far-right political activists. Downtown storeowners, even those not directly affected by the strikes, felt it prudent to close their doors, and buses and tramways were halted for several days. Around 6:00 pm on 23 June, fifty young far right-wing demonstrators marched down the rue de la République behind the tricolor flag, singing the "Marseillaise" and chanting anti-Blum government slogans. A communist counterdemonstration soon appeared singing the "Internationale." The police were able to keep to the two groups apart for a while, but running fights broke out all evening as supporters of both sides arrived on the scene. While the intensity of emotion was to be repeated many times over the next two to three years, none of the other sources I have consulted through 1939 show the right-wing enemies of the Popular Front using republican symbols like the tricolor and the "Marseillaise." These symbols became the possession of the left. Communist and CGT demonstrations still sung the working-class anthem the "Internationale," but always coupled with the patriotic "Marseillaise."

Following the elections, Lyon's communists held meetings to explain their position to both their own followers and their middle-class radical partners. One such meeting was held on 15 May in the adjacent working-class suburb of Villeurbanne, attended by 1,500 people. The newly elected communist deputy George Lévy commented on the Radical Party losses. "I am not happy about this at all," he explained. "It is not desirable that in France the middle classes see their political party, the radicals, disappear. We should remember that it is in countries where the middle-class parties have disappeared that fascism has been able to take root." National PCF leader Rochet Waldeck, also recently elected to parliament, developed this line of reasoning: "As far as wanting to eat the radicals (a reference to right-wing anti–Popular Front propaganda), it would not only have been not loyal, it would run the risk of throwing them into the hands of the right. We appeal to the Radical-Socialist Party to struggle against fascism." And explaining PCF strategy he explained, "We communists will help the government but not participate ourselves. This is a decision we made before the elections and we will keep our word. We think that the presence of two or three PCF ministers in the future cabinet, far from helping, would compromise the government by inspiring fear of a premature social revolt." PCF leader Jacques Duclos went out of his way to assure the radicals and their electorate of the nonrevolutionary intentions of his party and the Popular Front. Writing in the 27 June issue of *l'Humanité*, Duclos stated that the "radicals are right when they say that they will accept no threats to private property … in fact they are right when they point out that the agreement of the parties of the Popular Front is basically a copy of the old Radical-Socialist program."[12]

The Imagery of Class and Nation

The symbols and slogans of the period reflected the political and social ethos of the Popular Front. As masses of working people embraced them, they became significant dimensions of the working-class political identity that emerged at this time. Socialist and communist parties and their allied trade unions used every occasion to promote the Popular Front alliance and build support for patriotic sentiment among their followers. Bastille Day in France had been traditionally a national holiday with heavy patriotic tones, rejected as we have seen by the radical labor organizations that represented the antipatriotic current. But with the advent of the Popular Front alliance and government, the PCF encouraged workers to celebrate the holiday as both citizens *and* workers. In the words of French labor historian Antoine Prost, the huge popular street demonstrations that took place during this period "combined the Republican heritage with class struggle just as it combined tricolor flags and red banners."[13]

The 1936 Bastille Day parade in Lyon was, in the words of *Le Progrès,* an "imposing demonstration of the Popular Front." Workers marched in the work clothes of their occupations and industries under the banners of unions and working-class political parties. It took two hours for the various contingents to assemble. The radical, socialist, and communist parties marched together joined by the unions, veterans' groups, and the league of human rights. The *Progrès* described how "employees, in vests, symbol of the middle classes, marched alongside their brothers in (worker) overalls." A young woman dressed as the republican symbol Marianne wore the Phrygian bonnet escorted by two marchers dressed as sans-culottes. At the end of the progression demonstrators found the statue representing Equality draped with the tricolor and the red flag. The "Internationale" was sung followed by the "Marseillaise." All in all these types of parades represented a stunning combination of working-class and patriotic imagery and sentiment.

The messages conveyed from the speaker's platform at these demonstrations were often well-crafted presentations of key Popular Front themes. Speaking on behalf of the affiliated organizations at the Bastille Day celebrations in Paris on 14 July 1935, the Nobel Prize–winning physicist Jean Perrin spoke the following words in a speech that recast French national history as the heritage of its popular masses:

> They have taken Joan Arc from us, this daughter of the people, abandoned by the king and rendered victorious by the élan of the people, then burnt by the priests who have since canonized her. They have tried to take from you the flag of '89, this noble tricolor flag of the republican victories of Valmy and Jemappes. ... They

have tried to take from us the "Marseillaise," the revolutionary song which caused the thrones of Europe to tremble.[14]

Over the next two to three years May Day and Bastille Day celebrations continued to be great displays of patriotic and working-class identity. The 1937 May Day demonstrations were also celebrations of the first anniversary of the elections that brought the Popular Front to power. The traditional workers' holiday reflected the new combined class and national identity emerging among many French workers. A contingent of fifteen locals of the metal workers' union marched at the head of a demonstration of 120,000 workers. The *Lyon Républicain* wrote, "Citizens celebrated the triumph of republican freedom and popular demands with enthusiasm and dignity." Edmond Chambon, the secretary of the metal workers' federation, was one of the speakers at the rally held when the march arrived in front of the Perrache train station. His speech deftly combined republican and national themes. The "liberation of the working class has not yet arrived," he told the crowd. "Let us take an oath to remain united. The examples of Austria, Germany, and Spain teach us to avoid proletarian division. Let us stay united and fascism will be defeated."[15] By couching his appeal to unity in terms of a solemn sermon or oath, Chambon was connecting contemporary threats to industrial workers to the patriotic, republican tradition of the French Revolution. One of the key moments of the beginning of the great revolution was the tennis court oath when the locked-out third estate delegation swore to stay united until they were recognized as the national convention, an event memorialized by Jacques-Louis David's famous painting. Local trade union leader Marius Vivier-Merle told the crowd that "the era of privilege is over. ... All proletarians must unite to overcome capitalism."[16] Referring to capitalism as an era of privilege also connected contemporary labor struggles to patriotic language drawn from the Revolution. During the old regime, the social position of the aristocracy was regularly referred to as one of privilege, and subsequent generations were familiar with that term.

As workers fought defensive battles to preserve the gains of June 1936, the Popular Front remained a main reference point. On 12 February 1938 the Popular Front coalition held demonstrations. In Lyon the trade union movement and the official Rassemblement populaire committee held a demonstration attended by thousands of "workers of all ages and professions" according to the *Progrès,* which published a photo of a large crowd filling the Wilson bridge, many carrying umbrellas to protect them from a light snow as they marched to the local republican monument at Place Carnot. The "Internationale" and the "Marseillaise" were both sung. Marius Vivier-Merle, sharing the platform with local communist, socialist, and other union leaders, told the crowd that the "mystique" of the Popular Front had not disappeared. He linked the protection of reforms and the winning of new ones to the defense of the Republic. The "Cagoulards" (a far-right paramilitary group) will see that the people will protect the "democratic regime"[17]

One of the enduring symbols of the period was the raised, clenched fist. Begun as an antifascist salute, the fist became associated with the Popular Front. Numerous photographs of the time depict demonstrators raising their fists in demonstrations or during the singing of the "Marseillaise" or the "Internationale."

The posters issued at the time by Popular Front organizations combined national and class imagery. One such poster issued by the CGT for a national labor festival coinciding with the 150th anniversary of the French Revolution combined class and national themes from the past and present in a particularly rich and colorful manner. At the top of the poster a profile of the Jacobin leader Maxime Robespierre, who combined antimonarchism with defense of private property, is depicted facing the protocommunist Gracchus Babeuf. Between the two is a tablet bearing the inscription "Rights of Man and Citizen" in reference to a key democratic document of the early phase of the revolution. Below, a sans-culotte—that amorphous social actor, part protoworker, part artisan—shakes hands with a miner and a farmer from the 1930s. The poster is also highly gendered. All five figures are male. The miner is portrayed bare-chested and muscular.

A particularly powerful visual image of the Popular Front and its combined class and national character was Jean Renoir's film *La Marseillaise*, produced in 1935 with CGT funding. An advisory committee was established that included leaders of Popular Front organizations such as Léon Jouhaux of the CGT, Jacques Duclos and Maurice Thorez of the PCF, Victor Basch of the Ligue des droits de l'homme, and Edward Herriot of the Radical Party.[18]

The film is constructed in a manner consistent with Popular Front sensibilities. "The nation," it proclaims at the beginning, is "composed of the fraternal union of French citizens," a definition that accorded perfectly with the Popular Front.[19] The phases of the Revolution covered in the film also reflect Popular Front politics. The film ends with the bloody pitched battle in the Tuileries gardens on 10 August 1792 between Parisian sans-culottes and the monarchy's Swiss guards. That event led to the end of the monarchy and the beginning of the Republic. By ending

Figure 9.1 *Postcard reproduction of the 1939 CGT poster in celebration of the 150th anniversary of the French Revolution. From author's private collection.*

at that point, the film suggests a parallel between the broad social alliance of the early phase of the Revolution and the working class–middle class alliance of the Popular Front. Had the film covered the radical phase of the Revolution in 1793–1794, it would have suggested a more distinctly plebian and radical message at odds with the broad social and political alliance of the Popular Front.

The rise and spread of this Popular Front imagery took place within the particular political opportunity structure in France at that time. The sharply polarized national and international political environment gave support for the Third Republic a decidedly patriotic twinge, reinforced by the availability of a coherent propatriotic political program and strategy on the part of authoritative working-class trade union and political organizations. But the development of a combined national and class identity among French metal workers was also due to the tenor of shop floor labor struggles. It is to this arena we now turn.

Industrial Conflict

Scholars of labor protest in France are presented with novel problems during the Popular Front. The traditional police reports collected by local prefects and deposited in departmental archives with copies sent to the minister of the interior are a rich source of information from the nineteenth century on. However, these documents are lacking for the period opened up by the June 1936 strikes. Scholars have speculated that the sheer volume of industrial strife overwhelmed the capacities of officials to keep track of them. It is also possible that Vichy officials, the German occupiers, or labor militants removed these documents after 1940. In any event few police reports chronicling the strikes of the period exist in the departmental archives of the Rhône. One important exception is the 30 November 1938 strike and its aftermath, for which extensive government documents exist. I have collected information on this and other strikes and labor conflict during this period largely from reports in the center-left daily newspaper *Le Progrès*, and the trade union and communist press.

Labor historians and other students of industrial strife have often debated the connection between labor struggles and politics. Were strikes motivated by "bread and butter" or political issues? Scholars have made a convincing case for the political nature of the 1936 strikes. Edward Shorter and Charles Tilly see the influence of "informal political groups and single militants coming from areas of political rather than union action"[20] and conclude, "The strike wave was an explicitly political act."[21] Strikes and labor conflict in general throughout the period also had a distinct political flavor to them. As we will see, shop floor struggles did assume a political character because of the presence of promanagement guards and foremen often recruited from far-right and fascist political groupings. The strikes were often provoked by employer refusal to respect tripartite agreements brokered by the government. Furthermore, the trade unions and PCF protested lay-offs and reduced production in patriotic terms and these demands struck a large chord among rank-and-file workers. In addition, the PCF practices of factory party cells as well as its tight control over many unions constituted a strong relay between its political strategy and rank and file workers on the shop floor. We will focus on periods of sharp labor struggles such as the strikes of June 1936 and 30 November 1938.

Few participants or observers were prepared for the huge strike wave that followed the victory of the Popular Front coalition in the May elections. Sensing that they finally had a government sympathetic to their interests, French workers embarked on strikes that frightened not only employers, but the government and trade union organizations as well. For the year 1936 as a whole, 2.5 million workers participated in 17,000 strikes, with three quarters of them taking place in June alone.[22] This was the largest strike wave France had ever seen. It was not surpassed until the massive May–June strike wave of 1968 that involved as many as 10 million strikers.

A first wave of strikes broke out in Parisian metal-working plants. Already May Day, which fell between the first and second rounds of the legislative elections, saw 120,000 of the region's 250,000 metal workers strike and demonstrate.[23] On 26 May sit-down strikes began in metal-working plants in the region. By the 28th Renault's 35,000 metal workers joined the movement. These sit-down strikes took place during this period in the United States and elsewhere as well. Seventy-four percent of the strikes that took place in June 1936 were sit-downs.[24] Although most occurred in the Paris, Lyon, and Marseille regions, they happened throughout the country, not only in manufacturing establishments but in retail stores and offices as well.

French worker-intellectual Simone Weil found the occupation strike profoundly liberating. "Of course we knew that the hard (factory) regime would return in a few days, but we didn't dwell on that. We were like soldiers on leave during war. Whatever happened afterwards, we'd still have that experience. At least, for once and for all, memories besides silence, constraint, and submission would float around these heavy machines. This put some pride in the heart and left some human warmth on all that metal."[25] The sit-down strikes were a novel form of industrial protest whose implicit challenge to capitalist private property generated tremendous concern among employers, and as we shall see, the Popular Front government and coalition as well. The CGT scrambled to the calm the situation. On 29 May it called for the end of the strike on the basis of what one recent historian of the period has called a "mediocre compromise" involving pay hikes of only 3.25 to 3.5 percent.[26] By the first of June only ten metal-working plants in the Parisian regions were still occupied. But virtually overnight a second wave of strikes, often involving factory occupations, broke out. By the next morning sixty-six plants were on strike. By that evening the number had climbed to 150. Once again the situation seemed out of control. A meeting of 900 of the region's 1,200 metal-working employers discussed how the unions seemed to be unable to control the workers. Leon Blum's close associate and future interior minister SFIO leader Roger Salengro demanded an immediate end to this "unjustified agitation" declaring, "For my part, my choice is made: between order and anarchy, I would maintain order against anyone." The PCF daily *Humanité* ran the headline, "Order will assure success," in its 6 June edition. But by 8 June the strike in metallurgy was general throughout the country, except curiously in Lyon.[27]

As was the case in Paris, it was metal workers who kicked off the June strikes in Lyon. On 3 June, fifty workers in the Rivollier bronze-aluminum foundry went on strike. The strike was ostensibly begun to protest the firing of two workers, a father and son.[28] But given the general social and political atmosphere in the city and country as a whole, we can consider the strike as an offensive action stimulated by workers anxious to benefit from the new balance of forces represented by the Popular Front government. In order to prevent the hiring of scabs, the workers followed the lead of their Parisian comrades and refused to leave the plant. They organized guards at the factory gates, elected a strike committee, and spent the night with the help of their families who brought food and blankets. In the following days, the strike spread to other metal-working plants like the Brondel foundry, the Thiebault iron foundry, the Roux Foundry, Sclave, Bocuze, the Usines du Rhône, the Acières de Longwy, the Compteurs Garnier, the Moulaire and Son aluminum foundry, and especially the Berliet auto works and SOUMA metal-working factory. The union demanded wage raises and collective bargaining agreements.[29] These strikes, including the occupations that lasted several days, involved male and female workers.[30]

Lyon's silk workers from all occupations played an important role in the June 1936 strikes. Gillet's Villeurbanne, Gerland, and Serin shops were among eight different factories occupied by strikers as of 10 June. By that date, the strike was general among dyers and finishers, not only in Lyon and its suburbs, but throughout the region.[31] By the 17th the occupation strikes had spread to all the nearly two hundred factories employing 25,000 workers.[32] Strikers detained two directors in their offices at Gillet.[33] The strikes finally ended with the signing of an accord between the weavers and the employers on 19 June.

This was the social and political context in which a previously arrogant and powerful employing class met on 7 June at the prime minister's office, the Hotel Matignon, with representatives of the government and CGT including Marcel Sembat of the national metal workers' union. The negotiations, which continued well after midnight, resulted in the famous Matignon accords. These included reforms such as paid vacations, wage hikes between 7 to 15 percent, and the forty-hour workweek. The accords also stipulated recognition of unions as bargaining agents on behalf of their members, which represented a sea change in industrial relations in France. A collective bargaining agreement was signed on 20 August 1936 and made compulsory by ministerial order on 18 November of that year.

The first article of the agreements left a profound impact on shop floor relations. It bound employers to enter into collective bargaining agreements. Although a law guaranteeing collective bargaining agreements had been passed in 1919, few employers respected it. Article 3 bound employers to respect "freedom of opinion" and the rights of workers to join unions, which would not affect hiring, firing, or the assignment of work tasks. Article 5 stipulated the naming of shop floor union delegates.

On 12 June, more detailed accords were signed concerning the metallurgy industry. These involved the procedures for electing shop floor delegates and the actual pay raise accorded to each metal-working occupational group. In Lyon, the prefect Emile Bollaert presided over local accords. These had the effect of ending some strikes, but other shops continued to strike. It was only around 20 June that work had resumed its normal rhythms.

But workers did not seem satisfied and many strikes continued. On 11 June, PCF leader Maurice Thorez made his well-known speech in which he declared "one must know how to end a strike [Il faut savoir terminer une grève] once satisfaction is obtained." The socialists were no more sympathetic to the sit-down strikes with their implicit threat to private property. In September, Blum himself declared, "I believe that I can, and that I must affirm that forms of worker struggle like factory occupation must not become a habit. I say that they must not continue, that they will not continue."[34] Not surprisingly, the radicals also joined the chorus condemning the sit-down strikes. At its Biarritz congress in October, future prime minister Camille Chautemps authored a unanimously approved resolution pledging continued support for the Popular Front and condemning "the occupation of factories, stores, and farms, which amount to a blow against liberty."[35]

French unions had traditionally organized only small percentages of the workers in most industries and workplaces. June 1936 saw the advent of mass unionization. Between 1936 and 1938 union membership in metallurgy grew by 1,800 percent and 800 percent in textiles.[36] This was not just a result of the massive wave of enthusiasm resulting from the electoral victory of the Popular Front and the strike wave; it was also a function of the collective bargaining agreements themselves. As veteran trade unionist and former revolutionary syndicalist leader Pierre Monatte explained in the pages of *La Révolution prolétarienne,* the officially recognized shop floor delegates guaranteed by the collective bargaining agreements in industrial enterprises employing at least ten workers were an important element in the growth and maintenance of mass unionism.[37]

Metal worker unionization exploded during this period. In Lyon, there were between 2,000 and 3,000 members of the metal union on the eve of the strikes. By that fall there were 26,000.[38] By January 1938, the metal workers' union claimed to have 30,000 members, the "quasi totality" of metal workers in Lyon, organized into 302 local units.[39] The PCF experienced growth as well in French working-class sectors. The party reported new sections at Berliet and elsewhere in the working-class suburbs of St. Fons and Vénissieux.[40]

Gender Inequality and Collective Bargaining

The collective bargaining agreements signed throughout the period recorded large wage increases for male and female workers of all skill levels. They also reflected and perpetuated gendered wage and skill inequality. In an agreement signed between union leader Marius Vivier-Merle and M. van de Putte of the national textile federation, a series of trades exercised by women including silk weavers would receive 3.75 francs an hour. Skilled male workers having completed an apprenticeship would be paid 6 francs an hour at hiring, 6.25 the second year, and 6.50 the first year. Unskilled male "*hommes de peines*" charged with hauling heavy material and other low-skill jobs were to be paid 4.40 francs an hour.[41] In addition to reflecting gendered wage inequality, these accords also reflected the ways that skill itself in France's capitalist labor market excluded women from the ranks of the skilled. While it *might* be argued that the wage differentials between skilled males who had completed apprenticeships and female weavers might have reflected real skill differences, the fact that unskilled male workers earned more than female weavers, a trade that could only be thoroughly learned after an extended period, underscores how gender inequality structured the social relations surrounding skill.

The same process was at work in the metallurgy industry. The local collective bargaining agreement in metallurgy stipulated skilled male wages from 5.95 francs an hour to 6.40. Female line workers would receive 3.75 francs while the most unskilled men would be paid 4.15.[42]

The collective bargaining agreements were greatly resented by the employers. Employers, particularly those in smaller and medium shops where paternalistic relations were traditionally widespread, found the new atmosphere unbearable. By the fall of 1936 workers were beginning to notice that while collective bargaining agreements might look good on paper, seeing them actually put into effect was another matter. One delegate after another at a congress of the 26,000-strong metal workers' union of the Lyon region complained of the reinstitution of piece work and the failure of many employers to respect their engagements concerning the payment of social insurance funds.[43]

Employers used a number of maneuvers against the shop delegates. One was to claim that it wasn't shop floor delegates who were being laid off, but simply workers and this due to insufficient demand or other reasons, not their union activity. One example of such a case occurred at the Genoud metal-working factory in early 1938.[44] In fall of 1938 Berliet took advantage of declining orders to lay off workers, many of whom were shop floor delegates, including several who had worked there for as much as twenty years.[45] The employers also challenged the competence of the arbitration board. When the Genoud case came before the board, the company claimed that the board had no jurisdiction. It also claimed that the law on conciliation and arbitration was no longer valid, having expired on 23 February 1938. The union noted that union delegates could be fired on any pretext or even without any pretext at all.[46]

Metal-working employers consistently harassed and fired worker delegates and union activists, especially those who insisted that collective bargaining agreements be respected. The *Voix du Peuple* wrote that in spite of management's claims that a lack of orders forced the layoffs of twenty-two workers at the Berliet auto works on 12 November 1937, the action "seems to be a punishment against them for wanting the collective bargaining agreements to be respected."[47] Mass firings at Berliet in the summer of 1938 also targeted union activists.[48] The local metal workers' union newspaper, the *Métallurgiste,* commented on worker discontent in the fall of 1937: "Over the last year, Lyon's metal workers have accumulated an enormous amount of discontent at employer resistance to applying the new social laws. They must constantly fight to make the employers respect the contracts. Worker delegates have been harassed."[49] These issues provoked strikes like the one of 110 male and female workers against the Genoud Company, which fired "a duly elected union delegate for union activity."[50] Significantly, the metal workers' union also appealed to the local representative of the state, the prefect, for help in ending these practices.[51]

As soon as they believed that the time was ripe, metallurgy employers began to refuse to respect the collective bargaining agreements they had signed. One of the ways they did this was to claim that strikes nullified the contracts. This was the tack taken by Madame Bailly-Comte at her metal-working factory in Lyon against workers who struck on 3 June 1937 to protest the firing of an unskilled worker.[52] In addition to openly refus-ing to respect collective bargaining agreements, employers resorted to a number of subterfuges. One of these was to deny that some enterprises actually belonged to the industries covered in the contracts. At the time of talks held in March 1938 to renew the collective bargaining contracts in metallurgy, the employers sought to divide the workers to avoid hav-ing to deal with them as a block. The chassis workers were told that even though they have been long part of the automobile industry; they were in fact wood workers and had no business in metal contract negotiations. The *mécanographes* learned that they were in fact employees, not workers. Other skilled metal workers like those who built silk looms (*graveurs sur cylinders* and *petite trefilerie*) were not metal workers but textile workers because they produced products destined for the textile industry. The *Voix du Peuple* countered that this would be like saying that glassmakers who make medicine bottles are pharmacists and workers who build meat-slicing machines are delicatessen workers.[53] Another feature of the em-ployer offensive was the recrudescence of piece work, long resented and resisted by workers. Berliet in particular used this practice.[54]

Apprenticeship had long been part of the terrain of struggle over control over the labor process. Unions attempted to use the collective bargaining agreements to protect union control over apprenticeship. In Lyon, the local metal worker newspaper, the *Métallurgiste*, explained how, "besides several rare exceptions like the Electro-Mécanique company",

> the majority of firms have never really done anything in favor of apprenticeship. Most apprentices leave after two or three years, incapable of professional work and find themselves as unskilled machine tenders. ... In other shops, there is complete exploitation. Since the contract allows for a minimal salary for apprentices, one or several are hired and in spite of the terms of the contract work in production, which in turn allows management to lay off other workers. Some employers don't train their apprentices because they are put to work doing work that does not involve learning. There are many complimentary courses but contrary to all prec-edent, some employers don't hesitate to have the parents pay. ... There exists at the prefecture a shadowy commission on apprenticeship but it is plunged into a deep sleep. In our new collective bargaining agreement we must absolutely demand the right of our organization to control the apprentices in our shops.[55]

The *Métallurgiste* continued to agitate around the theme of apprenticeship and its connection to unemployment. In the summer of 1938 it wrote:

> There is lots of unemployment in metallurgy but those who are unemployed are mostly the unskilled who are expendable as the reserve army of capital. The unskilled worker is the poor cousin; poorly paid, looked down at by the boss and sometimes the other *compagnons,* he is the first fired. … How many young workers have worked for years on a *tour* executing batches of work [piece work] under the surveillance of a foreman [*chef d'équipe*] without knowing anything more than the day they were hired, while other [skilled] workers do not have to work on piecework and are more protected from unemployment? [56]

The union believed that training workers as skilled workers would be a form of protection. "Every conscious worker without skill or having not enough must try to get more. … It is these workers who the union has in mind and would like to help complete their apprenticeship in order acquire professional knowledge and become skilled workers." The vulnerable position of apprentices in such a context made them unreliable allies in strikes and potential strikebreakers. At the time of the strikes of late November 1938, only apprentices and "Christians" failed to join their nine hundred colleagues on strike at Berliet's Monplaisir factories.[57]

The handling of skill and apprenticeship issues by the metal workers' union reflected an amalgam of very different forms of worker struggle and is indirectly connected to different types of class and national identities. By urging workers to acquire skills, the skilled metal worker veterans who still controlled the union were hoping to strengthen the skilled worker–based shop floor power of workers at a time when that power had been seriously eroded, in many cases, irrevocably. This reflected an older mentality that relied on the independent shop floor strength of the workers themselves, itself an aspect of the class independent, antipatriotic metal worker identity. At the same time, the use of state-sponsored collective bargaining agreements to enforce apprenticeship and calls for state officials like prefects to enforce those agreements reflected a new willingness to use the formal machinery of the state for which workers now believed they had a stake in defending.

Employers were comforted and encouraged by the government itself. On 13 February 1937 Blum announced his "pause" in terms of pro-work social and labor reforms. In order to maintain the Popular Front coalition intact, the PCF voted for or abstained on governmental measures it clearly disagreed with, such as that limiting aid to the Spanish Republic. Caught in the vice of the contradictions of a government attempting to serve both capital and labor, the Blum government began taking half measures designed to please all. In June 1937 Blum announced measures designed to control the flow of capital, which were vigorously opposed by the right, while also raising indirect taxes on consumer items like tobacco, which fell inordinately on the working class.

Fascist and far-right groups began to once again hold public meetings and demonstrations while the government was increasingly using force against left-wing demonstrators. On 14 March, De la Roque's PSF held a meeting in Lyon that led to violent counterdemonstrations. The PCF sent a protest letter to the government protesting its failure to ban the "fascist demonstration" and police indulgence towards the PSF.[58] Two days later on 16 March, the PSF scheduled a meeting in the Parisian suburb of Clichy. When the government refused to ban the meeting, local socialist and communist leaders called for a counterdemonstration. The police intervened against the counterdemonstrators, killing six and wounding two hundred.

Increasingly isolated on his right and left, Blum resigned as prime minister on 21 June 1937 and was succeeded by radical leader Camille Chautemps. By this time French employers had recovered from the shock of May–June 1936 and had embarked on a full-scale campaign to roll back the concessions it had been forced to make. As early as 26 November, the main employers' organization, the CGPF, had refused to recognize the binding arbitration machinery established by the government. Likewise, the *commissions paritaires* established on 31 December 1936 remained a dead letter. But workers clearly still felt that they had the wind in their sails and vigorously opposed the employer offensive. The 1937 May Day demonstrations reflected this. May Day that year fell on a Saturday, which due to the forty-hour workweek was now a day off for workers. In Lyon the police expected 120,000 demonstrators,[59] which is exactly the figure that the republican press reported the day after the demonstration. The *Lyon Républicain* wrote, "Never in the memory of the Lyonnais has there been such a march in the streets of Lyon." The *Progrès* also marveled at the "scope and character" of the demonstration. In recognition of the important role played by metal workers and their union, metal union secretary Edmond Chambon gave one of the main speeches.[60]

The close connection between political and labor conflict was underscored by the use of fascist political groups and company unions to oppose the worker gains of June 1936. In November 1938 workers at the Renault auto plant near Paris once again struck and occupied the factory. Workers used metal bars to defend themselves against the 3,000 *gardes mobiles* and 1,500 policemen who stormed the factory gates. At 9:30 pm the police forced open the main doors as the workers retreated from one shop to another. At 10:00 pm the police fired nerve gas canisters into the plant. When the workers finally emerged at 11:30, the police forced them to file out in groups of four shouting "Vive la Police" and giving the fascist salute. A local police commissar stood by tapping an iron bar as he loudly shouted "One for Blum! One for Thorez! One for Jouhaux!"[61] In Lyon, Berliet set up a special office headed by a member of Doriot's PPF who worked with PSF members to root out worker and union activists.[62]

Employers used company unions run by fascist activists as a counterweight to the CGT. Workers were pressured on the job and even at home to join these yellow unions.[63] Silk fabricants even tried to divide the few remaining *canuts* of the Croix-Rousse by trying to give orders only to those holding PSF cards.[64] Fascist thugs tracked left-wing militants outside the factory gates as well. In August 1938 six members of Doriot's group physically attacked the communist leader Félix Brun, a parliamentary deputy elected from a metal-working quarter of Lyon on the Popular Front ticket.[65]

The scope of the employer offensive intensified after the fall of the second Blum government and the constitution of the government of the right-wing radical Edward Daladier. The *décrets-lois* of 1938 promulgated by Daladier's finance minister Paul Reynaud signaled a frontal assault on the gains of June 1936. At the top of the list was the forty-hour workweek.

The Forty-Hour Workweek

One of the great gains of the Matignon accords was the long-standing worker demand for the forty-hour week. But although this figured in the 7–8 June 1936 agreements French workers found that they had to struggle industry by industry and often plant by plant for its actual implementation. Workers then found that employers used this issue to cut or slow down production, claiming that its costs led to higher production costs and eventually unemployment. Workers used the new state labor machinery to force the employers to respect the law. The local labor inspector fined M. Morin, the owner of a factory in the rue Flachet in Villeurbanne, for violating the law. Workers at Berliet sent a delegation to the minister of the interior, André Février, who promised to convoke Berliet.[66] But this issue remained a hotly contested one. Daladier's decree laws finally put the state clearly on the side of anti–forty-hour-week position of the employers. By May 1939, the forty-hour workweek was over even where it had existed. Under the guise of augmenting production in war industries, Lyon's metal workers were working forty-eight, fifty-four, and sixty hours a week even though large numbers of skilled workers were unemployed, many having been laid off after the 30 November strike.[67] Silk workers complained that management did not respect the ministerial decree of 17 November 1936 limiting textile work to eight hours a day.[68] Throughout the period employers did not increase production and instead sought to reduce labor costs through speed-up and further rationalization of their productive processes.

Metal workers were at the forefront of the struggle for the forty-hour week. Metal workers discussed ways to force their employers to respect the forty-hour workweek at their congress in October 1936. On 3 November, a national accord on the forty-hour week was signed between the metal workers' union and the employer organizations. Nevertheless, employers continued to drag their feet. While large employers like Berliet bitterly resisted the forty-hour week, it was especially in Lyon's small enterprises where workers worked over forty hours.[69] Berliet complained that the social laws drove up labor costs leading to fewer orders, which in turn forced him to lay off workers. But union militants pointed out that Berliet sold trucks for 145,000 francs while Renault sold the same truck made in Paris where wages were much higher for 110,000.[70] In the summer of 1938 Berliet laid off one thousand workers claiming a lack of orders. But the metal workers' union pointed out that at the same time Berliet was sending out orders to foundry factories in the departments of the Allier and Isère and was subcontracting chassis and mechanical work to Peugeot.[71]

The 30 November 1938 Strike

The second Blum government proved to be short lived, lasting only around a month in the spring of 1937. The Daladier government that succeeded it was far less interested than its predecessors in maintaining the Popular Front alliance and the social reforms upon which it was based. Daladier represented the right wing of the Radical Party and several of his ministers were clearly hostile to the entire course of events since May 1936. In mid-November 1938 his finance minister Paul Reynaud issued thirty-two decree laws. These included a 2 percent tax increases on wages, abolition of the "5x8" workweek (the forty-hour, five-day week), and roll-backs in the areas of shop floor steward representation and collective bargaining machinery. Although the government presented the decrees as necessary for the augmentation of armament production for national defense, they were widely viewed in labor circles as a wholesale attack on the gains of June 1936. This provoked an angry response from rank-and-file workers, particularly metal workers. Spontaneous strikes, including factory occupations, broke out daily.[72] The CGT vacillated between trying to calm rank-and-file passions and canalize the movement into a symbolic one-day strike, in spite of broad sentiment in favor of a more vigorous response. The CGT finally chose 30 November as a one-day general strike without occupations and street demonstrations. Between 150,000–200,000 workers took part in the strike nationwide. Metal workers had one of the highest strike rates of all occupations with 72.48 percent participating nationwide.[73]

In Paris between 75 and 90 percent of the metal working proletariat struck.[74] Jacques Kergoat has divided strike participation by city into three categories. Lyon is among the cities with the weakest participation.[75] The metal employers' *chambre syndicale* estimated strike participation at 20–30 percent overall although shops dominated by skilled workers walked out at a rate of 60–70 percent. Berliet reported that only 20 percent of its workforce struck. Violent clashes occurred, such as that at the Grammont factory where between 150 and 200 strikers tried to block nonstrikers from reentering the factory after the noon.[76] But the strike seems to have spread in the days following the 30th and in several cases involved factory occupations. A state of siege was declared. Strike participation for silk weavers and dyers was also uneven. *Le Progrès* estimated that 15 percent of the workers in this sector struck, although in some shops strike participation reached 80 percent.

Encouraged by the government's strong show of force and resolve, French employers went on the offensive with mass layoffs and lockouts. The minister of labor estimated the numbers of firings nationwide at 800,000.[77] In Lyon 20,000 metal workers were fired or laid off in the days following the strike.[78] Nearly 2,000 workers from the textile and chemical industry that employed silk workers were fired. By the end of December employers had begun hiring back workers on a large scale. But it soon became apparent that the employers did not intend to rehire union activists, especially shop floor delegates and union officials. The union continuously raised this question in its press and in communications with the prefect.[79] According to the local labor inspector, as of 13 June 1939, only 927 of the 1,848 workers laid off in this sector following the strike had been rehired.[80] A new round of layoffs hitting mostly shop stewards began in the summer of 1938. Women and older workers were hit extra hard by these firings.[81] As of April 1939, 1,203 of the 4,318 workers in Lyon who had been fired in the aftermath of 30 November had still not been rehired.[82]

The employers were clearly attempting to not only roll back the gains of June 1936 but break the unions as well. Employers aggressively promoted their company unions. Here they had little success. In shop steward elections in the summer of 1938 the procompany Syndicat professionel français (SPF) failed to win a single post as CGT candidates were elected to all positions. Metal workers continued to resist the employer and government offensive with strikes and protest meetings. But they did so with a government hostile to labor and social reform and determined to roll back the gains of June 1936. The Popular Front was over.

Conclusion

One of the great novelties of the Popular Front was the transformation of central elements of a current in the French labor movement with which whole occupational groups had identified. The shift in political identity for these workers was stimulated by several interrelated forces. For decades workers in many industries had experienced a slow loss of skill and control over the labor processes as craft labor markets gave way to capitalist ones. This had an overall effect of weakening the shop floor power of such workers. By 1936 semiskilled workers, lacking the shop floor strength and political culture of a previous generation of skilled workers, had come onto the industrial scene in big numbers. This was significant for political identity formation because the class independence, antinational current had long promoted shop floor struggle. Such a strategy was less effective, and therefore less attractive, given the new industrial social relations prevailing in that industry. At the same time a political opportunity structure characterized by openness, elite allies, and the possibility of real social reform arose in France. This, coupled with two mass working-class political parties promoting class collaboration and nationalism, combined to create a favorable climate for a new political identity for workers in a number of occupations. The mass strikes, mobilizations, and cultural imagery used by pro–Popular Front labor leaders served as catalysts for the formation of this new identity.

Notes

1. Danielle Tartakowsky, "Stratégies de la rue, 1934–1936," *Le mouvement social,* no. 135 (1986), 32.
2. Patrick Fridenson, "Automobile Workers in France and Their Work, 1914–1983," in *Work in France,* ed. Steven Kaplan and Cynthia Kopp (New York, 1987), 529.
3. Patricia Latour, *Le 36 des femmes* (Paris, 2006), 21.
4. Serge Berstein, *Le six février, 1934* (Paris, 1975), 168.
5. Morgan Poggiolo, *La CGT du Front populaire à Vichy: De la réunifaction à la dissolution, 1934–1940* (Paris, 2006), 34.

6. Henri Dubief, *Le déclin de la Troisième République, 1929–1936* (Paris, 1976), 166.

7. *La Voix du Peuple,* 12 May 1939.

8. Françoise Bayard and Pierre Cayez, eds. *Histoire de Lyon des origines à nos jours* (Lyon, 1991), 377.

9. Jean-Luc Pinol, *Les mobilités de la Grande Ville: Lyon fin XIXe–début XXe* (Paris, 1991), 104.

10. Joel Rosier, "Lés elections législatives a Lyon: 1932–1936" (Master's thesis, University of Lyon, 1976), 119.

11. *Le Progrès,* 24 June 1936

12. Quoted in Jacques Kergoat, *La France du Front populaire* (Paris, 1986), 202–3.

13. Antoine Prost, *Republican Identities in War and Peace* (Paris, 2002), 316.

14. Julian Jackson, *The Popular Front in France, 1934–1938* (Cambridge, 1988).

15. *Le Progrès,* 2 May 1937.

16. *Le Progrès,* 2 May 1938.

17. *Le Progrès,* 13 March 1938.

18. Poggioli, *La CGT,* 143.

19. Ibid.

20. Edward Shorter and Charles Tilly, *Strikes in France, 1830–1968* (Cambridge, 1974), 133.

21. Ibid., 136.

22. Ibid., 127.

23. Kergoat, *La France,* 98.

24. Poggioli, *La CGT,* 114.

25. *La Révolution prolétarienne,* 10 June 1936.

26. Kergoat, *La France,* Paris, 1986, 102.

27. Ibid., 120.

28. *Le Progrès,* 3 June 1936.

29. *Le Progrès,* 10 June 1936.

30. Ibid.

31. *Le Progrès,* 10 June 1936.

32. *Le Progrès,* 18 June 1936.

33. *Le Progrès,* 15 June 1936.

34. Kergoat, *La France,* 205.

35. Quoted in ibid., 206.

36. Prost, *La CGT,* 193–94.

37. *La Révolution prolétarienne,* 10 July 1936.

38. *Le Progrès,* 25 October 1937

39. *La Voix du Peuple,* 28 January 1938.

40. *La Voix du Peuple,* 19 November 1937.

41. *Le Progrès,* 14 June 1936.

42. *Le Progrès,* 15 June 1936.

43. *Le Progrès,* 25 October 1936.

44. *Le Progrès,* 3 March 1938.

45. *Le Progrès,* 18 October 1938.

46. Ibid.

47. *La Voix du Peuple,* 19 November 1937; see also 26 November.

48. *La Voix du Peuple,* 5 August 1938.

49. *Le Métallurgiste,* November 1937.

50. *La Voix du Peuple,* 4 March and 11 March 1938.

51. Letter from union to prefect of Rhône, 25 August 1937, ADR 10 M 359; See also *La Voix du Peuple,* 30 December 1938, which reported on a letter sent to the mayor and prefect protesting against layoffs in the metallurgy industry.

52. *Le Nouvelliste,* 21 July 1937.

53. *La Voix du Peuple,* 18 March 1938.
54. *Le Progrès,* 24 November 1937.
55. *Le Métallurgiste,* December 1937.
56. *Le Métallurgiste,* July 1938.
57. *La Voix du Peuple,* 2 December 1938.
58. *Le Progrès,* 14 March 1937.
59. ADR 10M 359.
60. *Le Progrès,* 2 May 1937.
61. Kergoat, *La France,* 278–79.
62. *La Voix du Peuple,* 8 July 1938.
63. See *Le Progrès,* 25 November 1937, and *La Voix du Peuple,* 11 March 1938.
64. *La Voix du Peuple,* November 1938.
65. *La Voix du Peuple,* 12 August 1938.
66. *La Voix du Peuple,* 19 November 1937.
67. *La Voix du Peuple,* 12 May 1939.
68. *La Voix du Peuple,* 7 January 1938.
69. *Le Métallurgiste,* December 1937.
70. *La Voix du Peuple,* 19 November 1937.
71. *Le Métallurgiste,* August 1938.
72. Michael Torigian, *Every Factory a Fortress: The French Labor Movement in the Age of Ford and Hitler* (Athens, OH, 1999), 285.
73.
74. Ibid., 170.
75. Kergoat, *La France,* 285.
76. *Le Progrès,* 1 December, 1938.
77. Kergoat, *La France,* 290.
78. *Le Progrès,* 3 December 1938.
79. ADR 10M 473.
80. Inspecteur du travail à M. le Prefet, ADR10 M/473.
81. *La Voix du Peuple,* 26 August 1938.
82. Letter from M. Baret, labor inspector to the prefect, 11 May 1939, ADR 10M 473.

CONCLUSION

This book has sought to explain the connection between occupational groups and political identities in France. We have seen both continuity and change in the formation, reproduction, and transformation of the political identities of silk and metal workers as we followed them over the first four decades of the twentieth century. A major premise about French labor here has been that for all of its nuanced differences of ideology and practice, two broad sets of political ideology and practice concerning central issues such as the proper terrain of struggle and attitudes toward the nation were on offer for workers in France. The reformist, nationalist current looked to the political arena for social change and claimed the heritage of a progressive French Republic where workers had their place as citizen-producers. The class struggle, antinationalist current promoted collective struggle at the point of production and an autonomous working-class culture that was hostile to cross-class alliances. It counterpoised proletarian solidarity to identification with the nation. Identities consisted not only of ideologies and forms of collective action but of historical symbols and images as well. Once embraced by workers, these sets of ideas, political practices, and symbols constituted class-based political identities.

The approach here has been unabashedly structuralist, materialist, and Marxist. I have argued that these political identities were formed by social and political structures, but not in the ways that an earlier labor history had suggested. Rather than "causing" a given identity, the social relations of production have been seen as helping, through their *interaction* with political structures, to constitute a given set of options for collective action. Various forms of collective action were generally part of the programs of the political currents. The act of being exposed to and engaging in those forms of collective action thereby helped establish and fortify the political identities to which they were attached. Changes in industrial social relations and political opportunity structures could, depending on the specific juncture, help solidify or change those identities.

The silk and metal workers studied here differed considerably in terms of their political identities and the industrial social relations of their industries. The beginning of our analysis of silk workers in 1900 in chapter 4 saw those workers solidly rooted in the reformist, nationalist current. Important changes in the organization of Lyon's silk industry were altering industrial social relations in this industry. The attacks on skilled labor weakened the shop floor strength of dyers and finishers. As this happened, shop floor–based collective action become less and less a viable arena of struggle. Since struggles at the point of production were at the heart of revolutionary syndicalist strategy, revolutionary syndicalism and its attendant political identity held little appeal for silk workers. At the same time, local conditions favored a working class–middle class alliance around a program of progressive social reform, and a local and national political climate that had actually produced real (if modest) reforms made this political current attractive to silk workers.

Metal workers entered the twentieth century as the most solid occupational component of revolutionary syndicalism. As a group, they bore the class struggle, antinational political identity. As skilled male workers exercising a large degree of control over the labor process, metal workers found shop floor–based forms of struggle particularly attractive. Taylorist attacks on skilled worker power and autonomy were designed to undercut that shop floor power, but the battle was a protracted one. Inroads on the relatively strong position of skilled male metal workers on the shop floor were gradual enough that shop floor–based forms of struggle retained much of their attractiveness until at least the First World War. The revolutionary syndicalism of the CGT advocated these forms of struggle. This helped expose metal workers to the broader ideas of revolutionary syndicalism including mistrust of political parties, class autonomy, and hostility to the nation as a bourgeois and therefore hostile force. World War I and its immediate aftermath began to upset these arrangements. Employers and the state used the emergency of the war to accelerate the implementation of Taylorist methods and a general reorganization of the labor market in order to undercut the shop floor strength of skilled labor. The drafting into the army of many skilled male workers, their replacement by semiskilled workers including many women, and the militarization of labor contributed to the shifting balance of power on the shop floor in favor of the employers.

Postwar developments altered both industrial and political structures. Taylorist attacks on remaining pockets of skilled worker autonomy and strength continued and began to register real inroads in most industrial settings. The advent of the French Communist Party altered the political opportunity structure and meshed in complex ways with not only politics but the party and trade union programs and strategies that constituted such an important part of working-class political identity. By advocating autonomous working-class culture and politics, unambiguous anticapitalism, shop floor–based forms of struggle (like the strike) and organization (the factory party cell), and proletarian internationalism opposed to nationalism, the PCF continued to embody the ideas and practice of the class struggle, antinational current previously represented by the prewar revolutionary syndicalist CGT. But the PCF also fought on the terrain of institutional politics, running candidates at all levels. As a Leninist party of a "new type," the early PCF could appeal to workers who still found the shop floor a useful terrain as well as those whose skills and therefore shop floor strength had been undermined by Taylorist attacks (or were semiskilled newcomers to industrial work) and were willing to consider struggles at different levels. The PCF also benefited from identification with the Soviet Union, which enjoyed tremendous prestige in working-class circles throughout the world at that time. The aggressive employer attacks in factories and plants and the actions of a repressive state seemed to confirm PCF analysis of capitalism.

During the interwar period metal working saw a steady increase in the intensity of Taylorist drives aimed at skilled labor and speed-ups aimed at the semiskilled workers that were taking their place. Skilled metal workers in a number of trades saw their skills rendered redundant. But remaining pockets of skilled workers served to transmit class struggle, antinational political identity to the newer semiskilled workforce that now included large numbers of women.

The industrial social relations of the silk industry including the actual composition of the labor force in terms of skill and gender underwent deep changes during the interwar period. In chapter 7 we saw how virtually all of the remaining pockets of male skilled worker control had been eliminated in dyeing and finishing. The longstanding structure of the silk industry and the protoindustrial social arrangements and relations surrounding it collapsed in favor of hierarchical factory relations. The advent of artificial silk and the ease with which it could be produced by machines operated by semiskilled workers was part and parcel of this process. The workforce became increasingly feminine and semiskilled. These changes in industrial social relations ultimately helped lessen the appeals of the nationalist, reformist current to female silk workers. The appeal of the nationalist, reformist current was also undermined by its electoral emphasis at a time when the right-wing governments and parliamentary majorities that succeeded the *Bloc des gauches* were more apt to mete out repression to labor militants than pass progressive social legislation. And finally, a political strategy and identity with electoralism as its focus had limited appeal to women who did not have the right to vote until 1945.

These developments in industrial social relations and political opportunity structure help explain why by the late 1920s the sustained efforts of the PCF and the CGTU to recruit workers in this industry were beginning to show signs of success.

The longstanding political currents and the political identities to which they were connected were profoundly altered by Popular Front–era developments. Although the Popular Front years did not signal a distinct moment in industrial change, long-brewing developments in industrial organization had begun to register effects on the composition of the working class in terms of skill and gender. The advent of mass unionism in France in 1936 reflected this. Large numbers—a majority in most cases—of industrial workers were now semiskilled, and important industrial sectors were made up of significant numbers of women. These workers had a tenuous connection at best to the older political identities that were common among their elders. Changes in political opportunity structure meshed with the new industrial sociology that was becoming increasingly apparent in ways that offered and promoted a reconfigured political identity. Historical symbols and imagery played a particularly important role in the transformed political identity that developed during that period. By calling for struggles in the political arena including street demonstrations as well as political campaigns, the PCF could appeal to variety of workers across the skill divide. The abandonment of antinationalism by the PCF meant that this older plank of antinationalism in the class struggle, antinational current was now borne only by small anarchist, revolutionary syndicalist, and Trotskyist formations with limited access to working-class audiences. In a certain sense the Popular Front politics of the PCF meant that for all their formal doctrinal differences, much of the differences between the two currents and the political identities of which they formed the basis had disappeared. At a high level of generality there was a certain fusion between the political currents and their respective political identities. Both currents promoted a form of national, and to different degrees class, identity. Those identities endured for decades after the end of the period treated here.

This book is part of the recent trend to bring politics back into labor history. It has tried to combine the best insights of the social history project with an improved structuralist and materialist theoretical approach. As a gendered labor history we have seen not only how industrial and political structures affected men and women differently but how those very structures were gendered. As a theory of the mid-range, the theoretical framework that has guided this study of early twentieth-century occupational groups in France should illuminate many other cases of worker political identity formation across time and space.

BIBLIOGRAPHY

Aminzade, Ronald. *Ballots and Barricades: Class Formation and Republican Politics in France, 1830–1871.* Princeton, NJ, 1993.

Auzias, Claire. *Mémoires libertaires: Lyon 1919–1939.* Paris, 1993.

Badie, Bertrand. "Les grèves du Front populaire aux usines Renault." *Le mouvement social* 81 (1972): 69–109.

Baron, Ava. "Gender and Labor History: Learning from the Past, Looking to the Future." In *Work Engendered,* edited by Ava Baron. Ithaca, NY, 1991.

———. "Masculinity, the Embodied Male Worker, and the Historian's Gaze." *International Labor and Working-Class History* 69 (Spring 2006): 143–60.

Bayard, Francoise, and Pierre Cayez, eds. *Histoire de Lyon des origines à nos jours.* Lyon, 1991.

Becker, Jean-Jacques, and Serge Bernstein. *Histoire de la France du vingtième siècle.* Paris, 1994.

Bensoussan, Bernard, and Henriette Pommier. *Soierie: Artisans et métiers.* Paris, 1991.

Berstein, Serge. *Le six février, 1934.* Paris, 1975.

Blauner, Robert. *Alienation and Freedom.* Chicago, 1964.

Bonnell, Victoria. *Roots of Rebellion: Workers' Politics and Organizations in St. Petersburg and Moscow, 1900–1914.* Berkeley, CA, 1983.

Bonnet, Emmanuelle. "Des femmes à l'usine: La société lyonnaise de textiles artificiels, 1924–1939." Master's thesis, University of Lyon, 1990.

Braverman, Harry. *Labor and Monopoly Capitalism: The Degradation of Work in the 21st Century.* New York, 1974.

Bron, Jean. *Histoire du mouvement ouvrier français.* Paris, 1970.

Brun, Sheri Satwell. "L'association métallurgique du Rhône, 1919–1939." Master's thesis, University of Lyon, 1992.

Cazzelles, Didier. *Apprenti à Berliet.* Lyon, 1999.

Chagny, Robert. "La presse socialiste à Lyon, 1896–1914." Master's thesis, University of Lyon, 1960.

Chaninian, Elisabeth, Sylvie Murgia, and Marie-Noëlle Pichon. "La vie quotidienne de vingt-cinq ouvriers chez Berliet entre 1919–1939." Master's thesis, University of Lyon, 1979.

Chevailler, R., B. Girardon, V. T. Nguyen, and B. Rochaix. *Lyon: Les traboules du mouvement ouvrièr.* Paris, 1980.

Chevandier, Christian. *Cheminots en usine, les ouvriers des ateliers d'Oullins au temps de la vapeur.* Lyon, 1993.

Colley, Linda. "Whose Nation? Class and National Consciousness in Britain 1750–1830." *Past and Present* 113 (1986): 97–117.

Collinet, Michel. *L'ouvrier français. Essai sur la condition ouvrière, 1900–1950.* Paris, 1951.

Colson, Daniel. *Anarcho-syndicalisme et communisme: Saint-Etienne, 1920–1925.* Lyon, 1986.

Courtois, Stéphane, and Marc Lazar. *Histoire du Parti communiste français.* Paris, 1995.

Déclas, Gérard. "Recherches sur les usines Berliet, 1914–1949." Master's thesis, University of Lyon II, 1977.

Dewerpe, Alain. *Le monde du travail en France, 1800–1950.* Paris, 1989.

———. *Industrie et travail en France, 1800–1968.* Paris, 1993.

Dolléans, Edouard. *Histoire du mouvement ouvrier.* Paris, 1967.

Downs, Laura Lee. *Manufacturing Inequality: Gender Division in the French and British Metalworking Industries, 1914–1939.* Ithaca, NY, 1995.

Dubief, Henri. *Le déclin de la Troisième République, 1929–1936.* Paris, 1976.

Eley, Geoff, and Keith Nield. *The Future of Class in History: What's Left of the Social?* Ann Arbor, MI, 2007.

Fourcaut, Annie. *Les femmes à l'usine en France pendant l'entre-deux-guerres.* Paris, 1982.

Fridenson, Patrick. "Automobile Workers in France and Their Work, 1914–1983." In *Work in France,* edited by Steven Kaplan and Cynthia Kopp. Ithaca, NY, 1987.

Gallo, Max. "Quelques aspects de la mentalité et du comportement ouvrier dans les usines de guerre, 1914–1918." *Le mouvement sociale,* no. 56 (1966): 3–33.

Garcin, Solange. "La fabrique lyonnaise des soieries, 1900–1930." Master's thesis, University of Lyon II, 1969.

Gardey, Delphine. *La dactylographe et l'expedionnaire: Histoire des employees de bureau, 1890–1930.* Paris, 2001.

Girault, Jacques. *Sur l'implantation du Parti communiste française dans l'entre-deux-guerres.* Paris, 1977.

Gloria, Christiane. "La Fabrique lyonnaise des soieries et la grande dépression, 1929–1939." Master's thesis, University of Lyon, II, 1970.

Gordon, David. *Segmented Work, Divided Workers: The Historical Transformation of Labor in the United States.* New York, 1974.

Gordon, Linda. "Moralizing Doesn't Help." *International Labor and Working Class History* 67 (2005): 26–32.

Granovetter, Mark, and Charles Tilly. "Inequality and the Labor Process." In *Handbook of Sociology,* edited by Neil J. Smelser. Newbury Park, CA, 1988.

Gras, Christian. "Presse syndicale et mentalités, l'ouvrier mouleur à travers le journal de sa fédération: La fonderie, 1906–1909." *Le mouvement sociale,* no. 53 (1965): 51–68.

Greene, Julie, Bruce Laurie, and Eric Arnesen, eds. *Labor Histories.* Urbana, IL, 1998.

Greenwood, Adriana Mata. "Gender Issues in Labour Statistics." In *Beyond Borders: Thinking Critically About Global Issues,* edited by Paula S. Rothenberg. New York, 2006.

Hanagan, Michael P. *The Logic of Solidarity: Artisans and Industrial Workers in Three French Towns, 1871–1914.* Urbana, IL, 1980.

Hunt, Scott, and Robert Bedford. "Identity Talk in the Peace and Justice Movement." *Journal of Contemporary Ethnography* 22, no. 4 (1994): 488–517.

Jackson, Julian. *The Popular Front in France, 1934–1938.* Cambridge, 1988.

Jones, Gareth Stedman. *Languages of Class.* Cambridge, 1983.

Joyce, Patrick. *Visions of the People: Industrial England and the Question of Class, 1840–1914.* Cambridge, 1991.

Julliard, Jacques, *Autonomie ouvrière.* Paris, 1988.

Kalb, Don. *Expanding Class: Power and Everyday Politics in Industrial Communities: The Netherlands, 1850–1950.* London, 1997.

Kemp, Tom. *Economic Forces in French History.* London, 1971.

Kergoat, Jacques. *La France du Front populaire.* Paris, 1986.

Klandermans, Bert and Marga de Weerd. "Group Identification and Political Protest." In *Self, Identity, and Social Movements,* edited by Sheldon Stryker, Timothy J. Owens, and Robert White. Minneapolis, 2000.

Koenker, Diane P. "Men against Women on the Shop Floor in Early Soviet Russia: Gender and Class in the Socialist Workplace." *American Historical Review* 100, no. 5 (December 1995): 1438–64.

Kriedte, Peter, Hans Medick, and Jürgen Schlumbohm. *Industrialization before Industrialization: Rural Industry in the Genesis of Capitalism.* Liverpool, 1976.

Kriegel, Annie. *Aux origines du communisme français.* Paris, 1969.

Laferrère, Michel. *Lyon, ville industrielle. Essai d'une géographie urbaine des techniques et des entreprises.* Paris, 1960.

Lapperière, Guy. *La séparation à Lyon, 1904–1908.* Lyon, 1973.

Latour, Patricia. *Le 36 des femmes.* Paris, 2006.

Laux, James M. *In First Gear: The French Automobile Industry to 1914.* Liverpool, 1976.

Lefranc, George. *Le mouvement socialiste sous la Troisième République.* Paris, 1963.

———. *Le mouvement syndical sous la Troisième République.* Paris, 1967.

Lequin, Yves. *Les ouvriers de la région lyonnaise, 1848–1914.* 2 volumes. Lyon, 1971.

Leschiera, Jacques. "Les débuts de la CGT à Lyon, 1890–1914." Master's thesis, University of Lyon, 1972.

Lorwin, Val. *The French Labor Movement.* Cambridge, MA, 1954.

Loubère, Leo. "The French Left-Wing Radicals: Their Views on Trade Unions, 1870–1898." *International Review of Social History* 7, no. 2 (1962): 203–4.

———. "The Left-Wing Radicals and the Military, 1880–1907." *French Historical Studies* 2 (1966): 93.

Mallet, Serge and Alain Tourain. *Evolution du travail aux usines Renault.* Paris, 1955.

Mann, Keith. "Political Identity and Worker Politics: Silk and Metal Workers in Lyon, 1900–1914." *International Review of Social History* 47 (2002): 375–405.

———. "Political Identity in Transition: Metalworkers in Lyon during the French Popular Front, 1935–39." *Labor History* 48, no. 3 (August 2007): 301–25.

Marigot, Michelle. "L'anarcho-syndicalisme à Lyon." Master's thesis, University of Lyon, 1966.

Marx, Karl. *The Economic and Philosophic Manuscripts of 1844.* Translated by Martin Milligan. Moscow: 1959 [1844].

McAdam, Doug. "Conceptual Origins, Current Problems, Future Directions." In *Comparative Perspectives on Social Movements,* edited by Doug McAdam, John D. McCarthy, and Mayer N. Zald. Cambridge, 1996.

Montgomery, David. *The Fall of the House of Labor.* Cambridge, 1987.

Mottez, Bernard. *Systèmes de salaire et politiques patronales. Essai sur l'évolution des pratiques et des idéologies patronales.* Paris, 1966.

Mouriaux, René. *La CGT, crise et alternatives.* Paris, 1982.

Moutet, Aimee. "Les origines du système de Taylor en France: Le point de vue patronal, (1907–1914)." *Le mouvement social* 58 (1965): 15–49.

Navel, George. *Travaux.* Paris, 1969.

Neufeld, Michael J. *The Skilled Metalworkers of Nuremberg: Craft and Class in the Industrial Revolution.* New Brunswick, NJ, 1989.

Noiriel, Gérard. *Longwy: Immigrés et prolétaires.* Paris, 1984.

———. *Les ouvriers dans la société française, XIXe–XXe siècle.* Paris, 1986.

O'Brien, Patrick, and Caglar Keyder. *Economic Growth in Britain and France, 1780–1914.* London, 1978.

Olivieri, Henri. "Un aspect de la Bolchevisation du Parti communiste: L'implantation d'usines à Lyon. 1924–1929." Master's thesis, University of Lyon II, 1995.

Omnès, Catherine. *Ouvrières parisiennes: Marchés du travail et trajectories profession-nelles au 20e siècle.* Paris, 1997.

Palmer, Bryan D. *Descent into Discourse.* Philadelphia, 1990.

Pèle, Edmond. "Le mouvement ouvrier lyonnais pendant la première guerre mondiale, 1914–1918." Master's thesis, University of Lyon, 1976.

Perrot, Michelle. "The Three Ages of Industrial Discipline in Nineteenth-Century France." In *Consciousness and Class Experience in Nineteenth Century Europe,* edited by John Merriman. New York, 1979.

———. "On the Formation of the French Working Class." In *Working Class Formation: Nineteenth-Century Patterns in Western Europe and the United States,* edited by Ira Katznelson and Aristide Zolberg. Princeton, NJ, 1986.

———. *Workers on Strike in France 1871–1890.* New Haven, CT, 1987.

Pinol, Alain. "Travail, travailleurs et production aux usines Berliet, 1912–1947." Unpublished master's thesis, University of Lyon II, 1980.

Pinol, Jean-Luc. "Les origines du communisme à Lyon." Master's thesis, University of Lyon, 1972.

———. *Espace social et espace politique: Lyon à l'époque du Front populaire.* Lyon, 1980.

———. *Les mobilités de la Grande Ville: Lyon fin XIXe–début XXe.* Paris, 1991.

Poggiolo, Morgan. *La CGT du Front populaire à Vichy: De la réunifaction à la dissolution, 1934–1940.* Paris, 2006.

Prévosto, Jacques. "Les élections municipales à Lyon de 1900 à 1908." *Revue histo-rique du sud-est* 14, no. 3 (1979): 52.

Prost, Antoine. *La CGT à l'époque du Front populaire, 1934–1939.* Paris, 1964.

———. *Republican Identities in War and Peace.* Paris, 2002.

Prothero, Iowerth. *Radical Artisans in England and France, 1830–1870.* Cambridge, 1997.

Rancière, Jacques. *La nuit des prolétaires.* Paris, 1991.

Rappe, David. *La Bourse du travail de Lyon.* Lyon, 2004.

Réberioux, Madeline. *La République radicale? 1898–1914.* Paris, 1975.

Reddy, William. *Money and Liberty in Europe: A Critique of Historical Understanding.* Cambridge, 1987.

Robert, Jean-Louis, "1914–1920." In *La France ouvrière,* edited by Claude Willard, vol. 1. Paris, 1995.

Robert, Vincent. 1995. *Les chemins de la manifestation, 1848–1914.* Lyon, 1995.

Rosier, Joel. "Lés elections législatives a Lyon: 1932–1936." Master's thesis, University of Lyon, 1976.

Rosmer, Alfred. *Le mouvement ouvrier pendant la premiere guerre mondial.* 2 vols. Paris, 1993.

Roux, Marie-Françoise. "L'ouvrière du textile à Lyon, 1880–1914." Master's thesis, University of Lyon, 1981.

Roy, Donald. "Efficiency and 'The Fix': Informal Intergroup Relations in a Piecework Machine Shop." *American Journal of Sociology* 60, no. 3 (November 1954): 255–66.

Schweitzer, Sylvie. *Des engrenages à la chaine, les usines Citroën, 1915–1935.* Lyon, 1982.

———. "Les hierarchies dans les usines de la deuxième industrialization." Thesis, University of Paris, 1994.

Scott, Joan. *The Miners of Carmaux: French Craftsmen and Political Action in a Nineteenth-Century City.* Cambridge, MA, 1974.

———. "Gender: A Useful Category of Social Analysis," *American Historical Review* 91, no. 5 (1986): 1053–75.

———. *Gender and the Politics of History.* New York, 1988.

———. "Gender and Labor History: Learning from the Past, Looking to the Future." In *Work Engendered,* edited by Ava Baron. Ithaca, NY, 1991.

Sewell, William. "Whatever Happened to the 'Social' in Social History?" In *Schools of Thought; Twenty-five Years of Interpretive Social Science,* edited by Joan W. Scott and Debra Keates. Princeton, NJ, 2001.

Shorter, Edward, and Charles Tilly. *Strikes in France, 1830–1968.* Cambridge, 1974.

Soboul, Albert. *The Parisian Sans-Culottes and the French Revolution, 1793–1794.* Oxford, 1964.

Stearns, Peter. *Revolutionary Syndicalism and French Labor: A Cause without Rebels.* New Brunswick, NJ, 1971.

Steinberg, Marc. W. "Talkin' Class: Discourse, Ideology, and Their Roles in Class Conflict." In *Bringing Class Back In,* edited by Scott McNall. Boulder, CO, 1991.

Tarrow, Sidney. *Power in Movement: Social Movements, Collective Action and Politics.* Cambridge, 1994.

Tartakowsky, Danielle. "Stratégies de la rue, 1934–1936." *Le mouvement social,* no. 135 (1986): 31–62.

Thévenet, Madeleine. "Le Guesdisme à Lyon, 1882–1905." Master's thesis, University of Lyon, 1971.

Tilly, Charles. *As Sociology Meets History.* New York, 1981.

———. "Inequality and Stratification." Working paper, New School for Social Research, Center for Studies of Social Change. New York, June 1992.

―――. *Stories, Identities, and Political Change*. Oxford, 2002.

Tilly, Charles and Chris Tilly. "Capitalist Work and Labor Markets." Working paper no. 139, New School for Social Research, Center for Study of Social Change. New York, 1992.

Torigian, Michael. *Every Factory a Fortress: The French Labor Movement in the Age of Ford and Hitler*. Athens, OH, 1999.

Van der Linden, Marcel. "Second Thoughts on Revolutionary Syndicalism." *Labor History Review* 63 (1998): 182–96.

Ville de Lyon, Office Municipal du Travail. *Statistiques et renseignements diverses questions ouvrières et sociales, 1913–1914.*

Voss, Kim. *The Making of American Exceptionalism: The Knights of Labor and Class Formation in the Nineteenth Century*. Ithaca, NY, 1993.

Willard, Claude. *Les Guesdists*. Paris, 1965.

―――. *La France ouvrière*, vol. 2. Paris, 1995.

Woronoff, Denis. *Histoire de l'industrie en France du XVIe siècle à nos jours*. Paris, 1994.

Zeitlin, Jonathan, and Charles Sabel. "Historic Alternatives to Mass Production: Politics, Markets and Technology in Nineteenth-Century Industrialization." *Past and Present* 108 (1985): 133–76.

INDEX